Mastering
Excel 2019

An All-in-One Tutorial Resource

Nathan George

Mastering Excel 2019: An All-in-One Tutorial Resource

Published 2020.

Published by GTech Publishing.

ISBN: 978-1-9162113-8-4

CONTENTS

Introduction

Welcome to *Mastering Excel 2019*, your all-in-one guide to the latest and most powerful version of Excel from Microsoft 365. This book contains everything you need to know to master the basics of Excel and a selection of advanced topics relevant to real-world productivity tasks. This guide has been designed to be a resource for you whether you're an Excel beginner, intermediate user, or a power user.

This book is concise and to the point, using clear and practical examples that you can adapt to your own needs. The aim is to show you how to perform tasks in Excel as quickly as possible without getting bogged down with unnecessary verbosity and filler text that you may find in some other Excel books. This book does not only show you how to use specific features but also in what context those features need to be used.

Mastering Excel 2019 is made up of three books that have been brought together and organized as an all-in-one guide.

How This Book Is Organized

Book 1: Excel Basics

This book starts with the very basics. You first get to familiarize yourself with the Excel user interface and Ribbon. You learn how to create, edit, format, organize and print your worksheets. You learn how to enter formulas and perform different types of calculations in Excel. You learn how to use named ranges, Excel tables, charts, and drop-down lists. You learn how to sort and filter your data in different ways. This book provides you with most of what you would need for everyday Excel tasks including all the fundamentals you need to progress to topics in Books 2 and 3 like functions and pivot tables.

Book 2: Excel Advanced Topics

This book covers a selection of topics that will enable you to take advantage of more powerful tools in Excel to perform tasks more geared for the power user. In this book you'll learn how to transform data with various data tools; import and use data from external sources like CSV files and Microsoft Access databases; troubleshoot and fix formula errors; deploy macros to automate repetitive tasks; create and analyze projections with What-If Analysis; analyze large sets of data with Pivot Tables and Pivot Charts; and protect workbooks, worksheets, or ranges.

Book 3: Excel Functions

This book is a deep dive into Excel functions and covers over 70 of the most useful functions in Excel from different categories. The functions covered include lookup and reference functions like XLOOKUP and VLOOKUP; math and statistical functions like SUM, SUMIF, COUNTIF, and COUNTA; logical functions like IF and IFS; date functions like DATEDIF, NETWORKDAYS, and TIME; text functions like MID, TEXTJOIN, and CONCAT; and financial functions like PV, FV, and NPV.

The functions covered in this book have been carefully selected based on how often they're used in common Excel tasks and specialized work. Each function is covered in detail including the syntax, description of arguments, and practical examples to demonstrate its use. You also learn how to combine different functions to solve more complex problems.

How to Use This Book

Mastering Excel 2019 can be used as a step-by-step training guide as well as a reference manual that you come back to from time to time. If you're a beginner, you ideally want to read all the chapters in Book 1 in sequential order. Book 1 provides all the fundamentals you need to proceed to selected topics of your choosing in Books 2 and 3. You also want to cover commonly used functions in Book 3 like SUM, IF, IFS, and XLOOKUP as these will come in handy for everyday Excel use.

If you're an intermediate or power user, you can read this book cover to cover or skip to specific chapters. Although the topics have been organized logically, as much as possible, each topic has been designed to enable you to read it as a standalone tutorial to learn how to perform a specific task. Book 3 in particular has been designed as a resource guide for Excel functions so the chapters are as self-contained as possible.

There are many ways to carry out the same task in Excel, so, for brevity, I have focused on the most efficient way of carrying out a task. On some occasions, however, I also provided alternative ways to carry out a task.

As much as possible, the menu items and commands mentioned are bolded to distinguish them from the other text. I have also included many images to illustrate the features and tasks being discussed.

Assumptions

The software and hardware assumptions made when writing this book is that you already have Excel 2019 installed on your computer and that you're working on the Windows 10 platform.

⚠️ **Important** Excel 2019 is the first version of Excel that is not compatible with previous versions of Windows. If you have an earlier version of Windows, for example, Windows 7 or 8, and you're subscribed to Microsoft 365 (previously Office 365), then the newest version of Excel you can run will be Excel 2016.

If you are running Excel 2016 you can still use this book (as long as you're aware that some of the dialog boxes shown may look slightly different). Many of the features covered are present in previous versions of Excel.

If you are using Excel 2019 on a Mac, then simply substitute any Windows keyboard commands mentioned in the book for the Mac equivalent. All the features within Excel remain the same for both platforms.

If you're using Excel on a tablet or touchscreen device, again, simply substitute any keyboard commands mentioned in the book with the equivalent on your touchscreen device.

Practice Files

Downloadable Excel files have been provided to save you time if you want to practice in Excel as you follow the examples in the book. All examples are fully detailed in the book, so these files have simply been provided to save you some time in recreating the sample data, so they're optional.

You can practice by changing the data to view different results. Please note that practice files have only been included for chapters where the examples use a sizable amount of sample data. You can download the files from the following link:

https://www.excelbytes.com/masteringexcel2019dl

Notes:

- The files have been zipped into one download. Windows 10 comes with the functionality to unzip files. If your OS does not have this functionality, you'll need to get a piece of software like WinZip or WinRAR to unzip the file.

- The files are Excel 2019 files so you will need to have Excel installed on your computer to open and use these files (preferably Excel 2013 and above).

- If you are having any problems downloading these files, please contact me at **support@excelbytes.com**. Include the title of this book in your email and the practice files will be emailed directly to you.

Book 1

Excel Basics

In Book 1

Excel Basics starts from the basics. This book provides you with most of what you will need for everyday Excel tasks including all the fundamentals to progress to topics in Books 2 and 3 within this guide like functions, pivot tables, What-If analysis, and macros.

Contents at a Glance

Chapter 1: Getting Started with Excel

C lick on the Windows start menu and scroll down to the group of applications starting with E. You'll see Excel as part of the list.

To be able to access Excel faster next time you can pin it to the **Start menu, Taskbar**, or place a shortcut on your **desktop**.

To pin Excel to your Start menu:

1. Click on the Windows **Start menu**.

2. Scroll down to the group of applications under **E**.

3. Right-click **Excel** and select **Pin to Start**.

To pin Excel to your Taskbar:

1. Click on the **Start menu**.

2. Scroll down to the group of applications under **E**.

3. Right-click **Excel** and select **More > Pin to taskbar**.

To place a copy of Excel's shortcut on your desktop:

1. Click on the **Start menu**.

2. Right-click on **Excel** and select **More** > **Open file location**. This will open the shortcut folder location of Excel.

3. In the folder, right-click on Excel and click on **Copy**.

4. On your desktop, right-click any area and select **Paste**.

1.1 Creating a New Excel Workbook

Launch Excel from the Start menu or the icon you have created on your taskbar or desktop.

Excel will launch to the **Home** screen. The Excel 2019 start screen enables you to create a new blank workbook or open one of your recently opened workbooks. You also have a selection of predefined templates that you can use as the basis of your workbook.

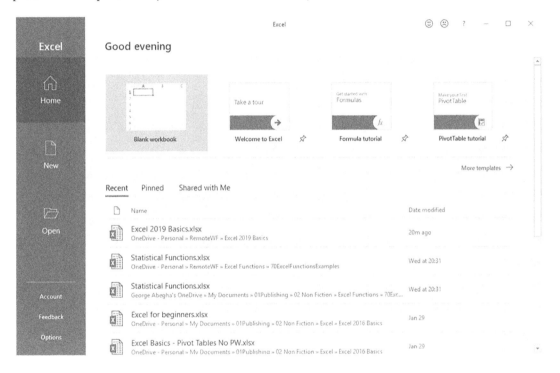

To create a new workbook, click on **Blank workbook**. This will create a new workbook with a worksheet named **Sheet1**.

Tip Another way to quickly create a new workbook when you already have a workbook open is to press **CTRL + N** on your keyboard. This will create a new workbook.

Create A Workbook Based on A Template

To create a new workbook based on one of Excel's predefined templates, click on the **New** button on the left navigation pane to go to the New screen. The categories of available templates are listed on the top of the screen next to **Suggested searches**.

You can narrow down the displayed templates by clicking on one of the categories - Business, Personal, Planners and Trackers, Lists, Budgets, Charts or Calendars.

Once you identify the template you'll like to use, double click on it to create a new worksheet based on it.

Saving Your Excel Workbook

To save your workbook for the first time:

1. Click the disk icon on Quick Access Toolbar (the top-left of the window) or click on the **File** tab and this will open the Backstage view.

2. Click **Save As** (you'll see **Save a Copy** if your file has been previously saved to OneDrive).

3. On the next screen, click on **OneDrive – Personal** (if you're using OneDrive) or **This PC** (if you're not saving it to OneDrive).

4. On the right side of the page, you get a text box to enter the file name. Enter the name of your worksheet here.

5. If you want to save it to a folder/sub-folder, navigate to the folder by double-clicking on the folder.

6. Click on the **Save** button to save the workbook.

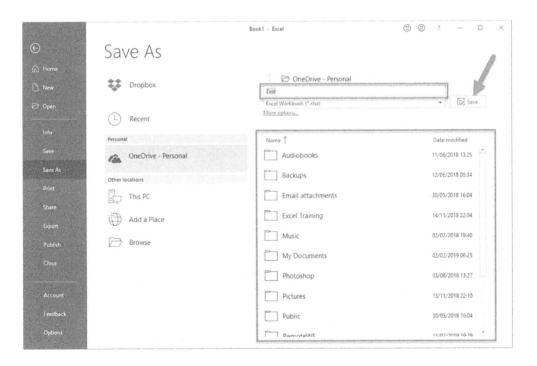

You'll be taken back to the **Home** tab after the file has been saved.

📝 Note   If your workbook has been previously saved to OneDrive or SharePoint and **AutoSave** is set to on, you'll have **Save a Copy** in place of **Save As**. You can use Save a Copy to save your workbook as a different file.

When you save a file, you overwrite the previous version of the file. If you want to keep an old version of the file while continuing to work on it, then you need to use **Save As** (or **Save a Copy**) as described above. This would save the workbook you're working on as a new file while the old version remains unchanged.

💡 Tip   For a quicker way to save your workbook, after the first save, you can use the **Ctrl + S** shortcut keys. For a list of the most frequently used shortcuts in Excel 2019, see the Appendix.

Open an Existing Workbook

Click on **File** to display the Backstage view, and then click **Open** or press **Ctrl+O**.

On the **Open** page of the Backstage view you'll see the following options:

- **Recent**: To open a recent workbook, select **Recent** and click on the workbook you want to open on the right.

- **OneDrive - Personal**: To open a workbook from OneDrive, click on OneDrive - Personal and select your file from the right.

  📝 Note   If you're not in the root folder of OneDrive you can use the blue up-arrow to navigate to the folder that contains your workbook.

- **This PC**: To open a workbook from the Documents local folder on your PC, click on **This PC** to display the Documents folder. Navigate to the folder containing your workbook. Click on the file to open it.

- **Browse**: To browse for a file on your computer, click the **Browse** button, and then use the Open dialog box to find the file you want to open, select the file, and click on the **Open** button.

Close a Workbook

Ensure you've saved the workbook (if you want to keep the changes).

Click on **File** to display the Backstage view, and then click **Close**.

Or

Press the **Ctrl+W** shortcut keys to close the workbook.

1.2 The Excel User Interface

This section provides an overview of the Excel 2019 user interface so that you're familiar with the names for various parts of the interface that will be mentioned throughout the book.

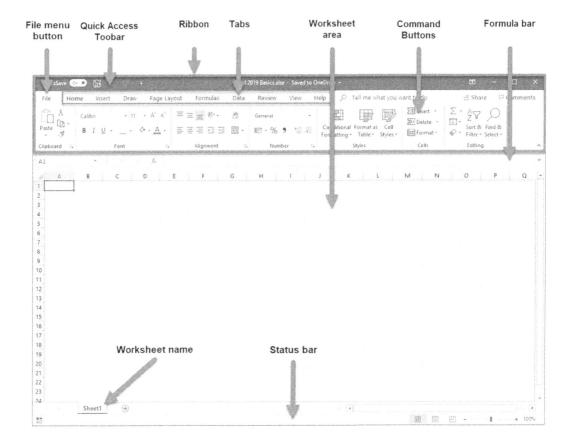

The **Ribbon** contains the bulk of the commands in Excel arranged into a series of tabs from Home to Help.

The **File** button/tab opens the Backstage view when clicked. The Backstage view has several menu options including Home, New, Open, Info, Save, Save As, Print, Share, Export, Publish, and Close. At the bottom of the list, you have the Account menu option where you view your user information. You also have Options where you can change many of Excel's default settings.

Note that if your Excel workbook is saved on OneDrive, and you have AutoSave set to On, you'll not see the **Save As** menu option, instead, you'll have **Save a Copy** in its place.

To exit the Backstage view, click on the back button (the left-pointing arrow at the top-left of the page).

The **Quick Access Toolbar** is an area where you can add commands that you can quickly access, hence the name. To add a command to the quick access bar, click on the drop-down arrow to get a pop-up list, then check the command you want to add.

The **Home** tab provides the most used set of commands. The other tabs provide command buttons for specific tasks like inserting objects into your spreadsheet, formatting the page layout, working with formulas, working with datasets, reviewing your spreadsheet etc.

The **Worksheet area** contains the cells that will hold your data. The row headings are numbered while the column headings have letters. Each cell is identified by the combination of the column letter and row number. So, for example, the first cell on the sheet is A1, the second cell in the first row is B1 and the second cell in the first column is A2. You use these references to identify the cells on the worksheet.

A **workbook** is the Excel document itself. A **worksheet** is a sheet inside a workbook. Each workbook can have several worksheets. You can use the tabs at the bottom of the screen to name, move, copy, and delete worksheets. The plus (+) button next to the name tab enables you to add a new worksheet.

The **Formula bar** displays the contents of the active cell including any formula.

The **Status bar** provides information on the current display mode and allows you to zoom in and out of your spreadsheet by clicking on the plus (+) and minus (-) signs at the bottom-right of the screen.

The **Dialog Box Launcher** is a diagonal arrow in the lower-right corner of some groups. When clicked, it opens a dialog box containing additional command options related to that group. So, if you cannot see a command on the Ribbon for a task you want to carry out, click on the small dialog box launcher to display more options for that group.

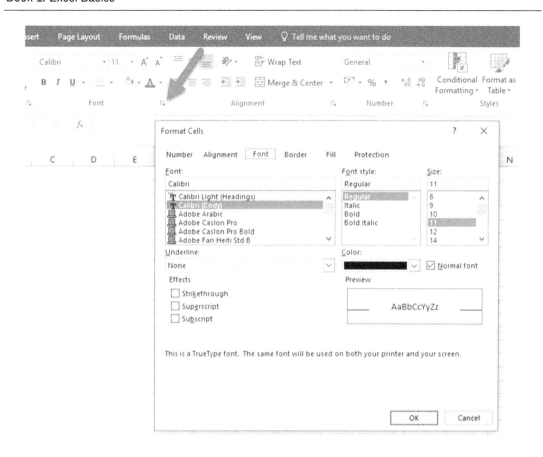

1.3 Using AutoSave

AutoSave is a feature in the Quick Access Toolbar that is enabled when a file is stored on OneDrive or SharePoint. It automatically saves your changes every few seconds as you are working. The main advantage of AutoSave is that if your PC were to crash for any reason, your changes right up to the point it crashed would have been saved to disk, hence you'll hardly lose any work.

With AutoSave on, the **Save As** menu option in the backstage view is replaced by **Save a Copy**. If you normally use **File** > **Save As** after amending your workbook, it is recommended that you use **File** > **Save a Copy** before making your changes. That way, AutoSave will not overwrite the original file with the changes but the copy.

If like me, you're in the habit of just closing the workbook without saving, if you do not want to keep the changes, then AutoSave becomes an issue. In that case, you can turn off AutoSave before you make any changes and then save your workbook manually if you want to keep the changes.

While **AutoSave** is on if you make a mistake that you want to undo, ensure you use the **Undo** button (on the Quick Access Toolbar) to undo the changes before closing the workbook.

Restoring a Previous Version

You can also restore a previous version of your workbook from the Version History.

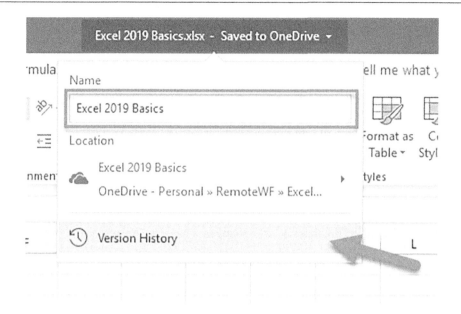

To restore an older version from the Version History list, do the following:

1. At the top of the window, click the file name.

2. Click on **Version History**.

   A **Version History** pane is displayed on the right of the screen that shows you the different versions of your document and the time they were saved. The versions are grouped under the day the file was saved. Look at the dates and times to find the version that you want to restore.

3. Double click the version that you want to restore, and this will open the workbook in a second window.

4. To revert to this version, click the **Restore** button that is displayed just under the Ribbon.

Renaming Your Workbook

You can rename a previously saved workbook from the popup screen that is displayed when you click the file name at the top of the screen. In the **Name** field, you can enter a name for the workbook and press enter to rename the workbook.

Switching off AutoSave

Switching off AutoSave is not recommended. However, if you want to be able to just close Excel and discard all changes, whenever you wish, then you could turn off AutoSave for that particular file and manually save your workbook.

The default setting for AutoSave is **On** for files that are on the cloud (OneDrive or SharePoint). However, if you turn AutoSave **Off** for a particular workbook, Excel will remember the setting and will keep it off every time you reopen that workbook. If you switch it back to On, it will remember to keep it on for that workbook.

1.4 Customizing the Ribbon

The area of the screen containing the tabs and command buttons is called the **Ribbon**. You can customize the Ribbon to your liking by adding or removing tabs and command buttons.

To customize the Ribbon, right-click anywhere on the Ribbon, below the tabs, and select **Customize the Ribbon…** from the pop-up menu.

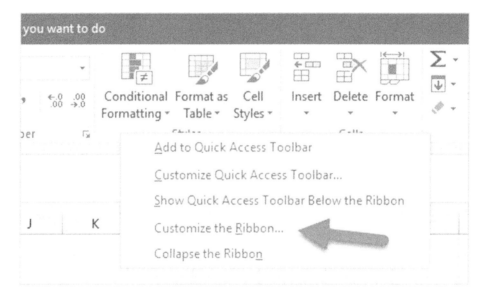

This will open the **Excel Options** window.

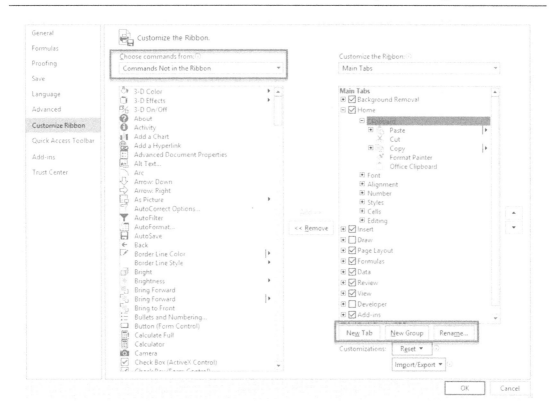

In the **Excel Options** window, the **Customize Ribbon** page will be selected, and on that page, you have two main boxes. On the right, you have the box that shows your current tabs - **Main Tabs**. On the left, you have the command buttons that you can add to the Ribbon.

To expand a group in the **Main Tabs** box, click on the plus sign (+) to the left of an item. To collapse a group, click on the minus sign (-).

To find commands that are not currently on your Ribbon, click the down arrow on the left box (named **Choose commands from)** and select **Commands Not in the Ribbon** from the drop-down list.

You will see a list of commands that are not on your Ribbon. This is useful as it filters out the commands that are already on your Ribbon.

Note   You cannot add or remove the default commands on the Ribbon, but you can uncheck them on the list to prevent them from being displayed. Also, you cannot add command buttons to the default groups. You must create a new group to add a new command button.

To create a new tab:

Click on the **New Tab** button to create a new tab. Within the tab, you must create at least one group before you can add a command button from the left side of the screen.

To create a custom group:

Select the tab in which you want to create the group. This could be one of the default tabs or the new one you've created. Click on the **New Group** button (located at the bottom of the screen, under the Main Tabs box). This will create a new group within the currently selected tab. Select the new group and click on **Rename** to give the group your preferred name. You now have a custom group in which you can add commands.

To add commands to your custom group:

1. Select your custom group in the list on the right side of the screen.

2. Select the new command button you want to add from the list on the left side of the screen.

3. Click on the **Add >>** button to add the command to the new custom group.

4. If you want to remove a command from your custom group, select the command on the right box and click **<< Remove**.

5. Click **OK** to confirm the change.

When you view the customised tab on the Ribbon, you'll see your new group and the command buttons you've added.

1.5 Getting Help in Excel

To access help in Excel, click on the **Help** command button on the Help tab on the Ribbon. This will display the Help pane on the right side of the screen. You can use this pane to search for the topic you want help on.

A quick way to access help is to press the **F1** key on your keyboard (while Excel is the active window). This will display the Help pane on the right side of the screen.

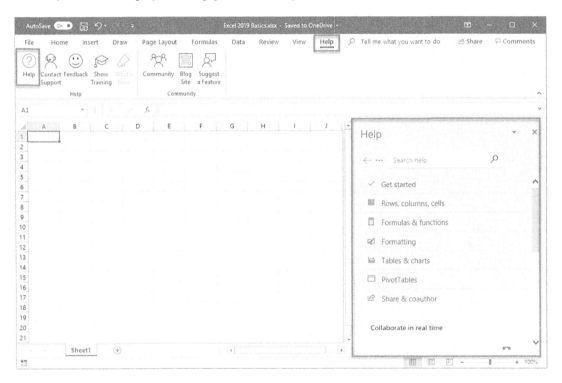

Microsoft Search

Another way to get help in Excel is to use the Microsoft Search box on the Ribbon, above the tabs. Click the Microsoft Search box or press ALT+Q to activate the search box.

Before you type anything, the search box will display a dropdown list of recently used actions and other suggestions based on what you appear to be doing. If any of the suggestions point to what you're seeking help for, select it from the list. Otherwise, you can enter words or phrases regarding actions you want to perform or a topic for which you want further information.

Depending on the topic or how direct your question is, Excel will either list the steps needed to complete the task, take you to the appropriate dialog box, or display information related to the topic in the Help pane.

Chapter 2: Entering and Editing Data

I n this chapter, we'll cover how to enter and edit data in your Excel worksheet including using automated features like AutoFill and Flash Fill.

2.1 Entering and Editing Data Manually

Entering data:

Click on a cell in the worksheet area and a rectangular box will appear around the cell. This is the **cell pointer** or the active cell. You can move the cell pointer with the left, right, up, or down arrow keys on your keyboard.

To enter data, simply type it directly into the cell or you can click in the formula bar and type the data in there. To enter a formula, you need to prefix your entry with the equal sign (=). We will cover this later in the chapter on formulas.

Editing data:

When typing in the worksheet area, if you want to make a correction, use the **BACKSPACE** key to go back and not the left arrow key. The arrow keys move the cell pointer from cell to cell. To use the arrow keys when editing data, select the cell then click in the formula bar to edit the data there.

To overwrite data, click in the cell to make it the active cell and just type in the new value. This will overwrite the previous value.

If you only want to edit parts of the data in a cell, for example, a piece of text, then select the cell and click in the formula bar to edit the contents there.

Deleting data:

To delete data from your worksheet, select the data and hit the **Delete** key.

Default content alignment:

In Excel, numbers and formulas are right-aligned in the cell by default. Everything else is left-aligned by default. So, you can tell if Excel recognises your entry as a number or text value.

2.2 Using AutoFill

The AutoFill feature in Excel enables you to fill cells with a series of sequential dates and numbers. It enables you to automate repetitive tasks as it is smart enough to figure out what data goes in a cell, based on another cell, when you drag the fill handle across cells.

Entering Dates with AutoFill

You may have a worksheet where you need to enter dates. You can enter *January* in one cell and use the AutoFill feature to automatically enter the rest of the months.

The **Fill Handle** is the small black square at the lower right of the cell pointer. When you move your mouse pointer over the lower right corner of the active cell, a black plus sign (+) appears. This change is an indication that when you drag the selection down (or to the right), Excel will either copy the contents of the first cell to the selected cells or use it as the first entry in a consecutive series.

So, you first need to click on the cell to select it and then move your mouse pointer over the bottom right corner to display the small plus sign (+).

To AutoFill dates, enter *January* or any other starting month in one cell then grab the small fill handle and drag it across the other cells.

AutoFill also works with abbreviations, but they must be 3 letters. For example, if you enter Jan and then drag down, it will be filled with Feb, Mar, Apr, May etc.

Let's say you want to enter the 7 days of the week as your row headings. In the first cell of your range, enter *Monday* or *Mon*. Then drag the autofill handle down over the remaining 6 cells. This will AutoFill the remaining cells with Tuesday to Sunday.

Excel keeps the filled days selected, giving you a chance to drag the handle back if you went too far, or to drag it further if you didn't go far enough.

You can also use the **AutoFill Options** drop-down menu to further refine your fill options. To access the AutoFill options, with the cells still selected, you will see a drop-down button that appears on the last cell. When you click on it, you will get a list of options that enable you to select whether you want to copy the data across the cells, fill the series, copy formatting only, ignore the formatting, flash fill etc.

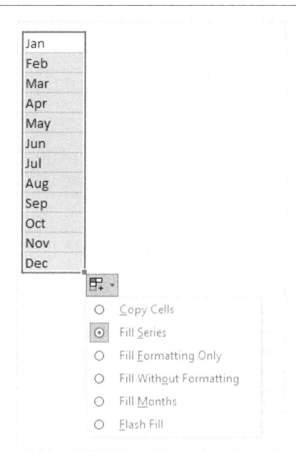

Note If you don't see a button that enables you to access the AutoFill Options drop-down menu (shown above) after an autofill, it is most likely because the option hasn't been set in Excel Options.

To enable AutoFill Options (if it isn't available), navigate to:

1. **File** > **Options** > **Advanced**.

2. Under the **Cut, copy, and paste** section, select the checkbox for **Show Paste Options button when content is pasted**.

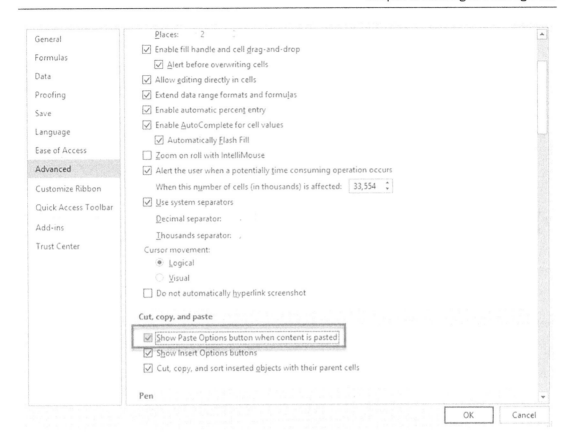

AutoFill Incremental Values

To AutoFill other incremental values, you need to first let Excel know what the difference is. So, you would need to enter values in at least two cells before dragging the fill handle across the other cells.

Let's say you want to enter dates that increment by seven days i.e. a weekly interval. You would need to enter two dates (for example, 01/10/19 and 01/17/19). Then you select <u>both</u> cells and drag across the empty cells to autofill the other cells with dates having an interval of 7 days.

You can do the same with other numbers. If you enter 1 and then drag down, the number 1 will just be copied to the other cells. However, if you enter numbers 1 and 2 in two cells, and then select both cells and drag down, you will get 3, 4, 5, 6 etc.

AutoFill Formulas

To AutoFill a formula across several cells enter the formula in the first cell and then drag the fill handle over the other cells in the range. If the cell references are relative, then the references will also change to match the position of the active cell.

For example, if the first cell of your formula is $= A1 + B1$, when you drag this formula down to the other cells, the formula in the other cells will be, $=A2+B2$, $=A3+B3$, $=A4+B4$ and so on.

Another way to use AutoFill is to click on the **Fill** button in the **Editing** group on the **Home** tab.

Note   If the cell references in your formula are absolute, then the cell references will not change when you use AutoFill to copy it to other cells. See the difference between relative and absolute cell references in chapter 6 in this book.

AutoFill the Same Values

To AutoFill the same value across a series of cells, enter the value in the first cell then hold down the **CTRL** key while dragging the fill handle across the other cells.

For example, if you want to fill a range of cells with $6.99:

1. Enter **$6.99** in the first cell.
2. Hold down the **CTRL** key.
3. Move your mouse pointer to the bottom-right of the cell and grab the autofill handle (small square) and then drag it across the other cells.

2.3 Using Flash Fill

Flash Fill is a feature that was introduced in Excel 2013 that enables you to split and rearrange data automatically. In the past, you would need to combine several Excel text functions like LEFT and MID to accomplish the same tasks that you can now do with the Flash Fill command.

For example, if you have a name field (made up of the *first name* and *last name*) that you would like to sort by *last name*. You would need to re-enter the names in another column with the last name first. This is because Excel starts its sorting with the first character of the field, and then the next, and so on.

With Flash Fill, you can insert a new column next to the name column and enter the first value with the last name first. When you enter the second value, Excel will figure out what you're trying to do and automatically Flash Fill the other cells in the format it predicts you want to enter the data. This will save you a lot of time as you only need to enter two cells to have the rest automatically completed for you.

Clipboard	Font		Alignment

B4		✕ ✓ *fx*	West, Peter		

	A	B	C	D	E	F
1						
2			Month 1	Month 2		
3	Jane Smith	Smith, Jane	$1,000.00	$1,100.00		
4	Peter West	West, Peter	$2,000.00	$1,500.00		
5	Derek Brown	Brown, Derek	$1,000.00	$1,200.00		
6	Jason Fields	Fields, Jason	$1,100.00	$1,300.00		
7	Mark Powell	Powell, Mark	$1,500.00	$1,600.00		
8	Julie Rush	Rush, Julie	$1,200.00	$1,300.00		
9						
10						

Steps in Flash Fill:

1. Enter the value in the first cell in the new format.

2. Start entering the second value in the next cell.

3. You'll see a preview of the rest of the column displaying the suggested entries.

4. Press **Enter** to accept the suggestions.

Another way to use Flash Fill is to select **Data** > **Flash Fill** from the Ribbon. The **Flash Fill** command button is in the **Data Tools** group on the **Data** tab.

Insert another column to the right of the one with the original data. Then enter the first value and click on the **Flash Fill** command button. This will automatically enter the rest of the data in the corresponding cells in the same format it was entered in the first cell.

Chapter 3: Design and Organize Workbooks

In this chapter, we'll cover various tasks to do with organizing your workbook.

These will include:
- Adding/removing worksheets.
- Moving, copying, hiding, and deleting worksheets.
- Freezing rows and columns.
- Applying themes to your worksheets.

3.1 Adding New Worksheets

We covered creating a new workbook in Chapter 1. When you first create a workbook, you'll have one worksheet in it named **Sheet1**.

To add a new sheet to your workbook, click on the plus sign (+) at the bottom of the worksheet area, to the right of Sheet1 and it will create a new worksheet named Sheet2. You can add more worksheets to your workbook this way.

The number of worksheets you can have in a workbook is unlimited. You're only limited by your computer resources like RAM and hard disk space. However, try not to have too many sheets in one workbook as the file can become very large, taking longer to open.

Naming a Worksheet

To name your worksheet, double-click on the name tab at the bottom of the screen and the name will become editable. For example, if you double-click on *Sheet1* the name will be selected with the cursor blinking, allowing you to type in the new name.

3.2 Moving and Copying Worksheets

You can move and reorder your worksheets by clicking on the name and dragging it to the left or right. You can also move a sheet by right-clicking on the name and selecting **Move or Copy** from the pop-up menu.

On the **Move or Copy** screen, select a name from the list and click OK. The selected worksheet will be moved to the front of the sheet selected.

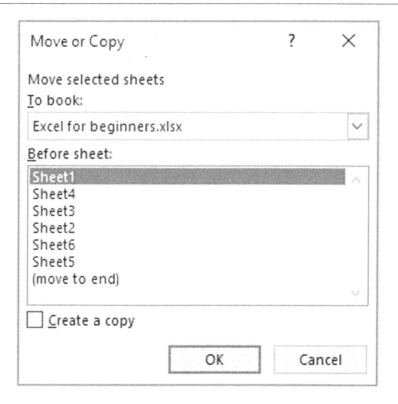

If you want it copied instead of moved, click on the **Create a copy** checkbox before clicking OK. A copy will be placed in front of the selected sheet.

Removing a Worksheet

On the Sheet tab, right-click the sheet you want to remove and click **Delete**.

If the sheet is empty, it will be deleted right away. If the sheet has data, then you'll get a pop-up message asking you to confirm the deletion. Click on **Delete** to confirm the deletion.

Hide a Worksheet

On the Sheet tab, right-click the sheet you want to hide and select **Hide**.

To unhide a sheet right-click on any of the sheet name tabs. If a sheet is hidden, the **Unhide** option will be available on the pop-up menu. Select **Unhide** to display a window listing the hidden sheets. You can select any sheet on the list and click **OK** to show it again.

3.3 Freezing Rows and Columns

When you have a large worksheet with lots of data, you may want your data headers (row and/or column) to remain visible as you scroll down or to the right of the page.

To make your column headings always visible you can freeze them on the page so that the scroll action does not take them out of view.

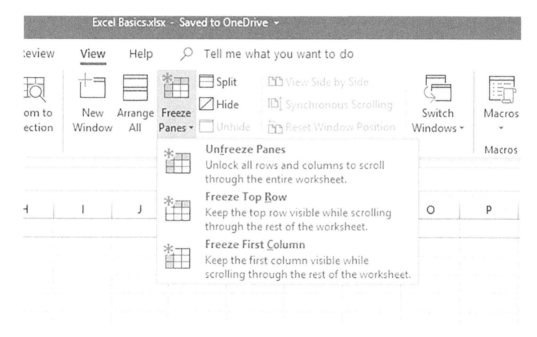

To quickly freeze the top row of your worksheet:

1.   Click on the **View** tab on the Ribbon.
2.   In the Window group click on **Freeze Panes** and select **Freeze Top Row.**

When you now scroll down the page the top row will always remain visible.

To quickly freeze the first column of your worksheet:

1.   Click on the **View** tab on the Ribbon.
2.   In the Window group click on **Freeze Panes** and select **Freeze First Column**.

When you now scroll to the right of the page the first column will always remain visible.

On some occasions, you may want to freeze rows and columns other than the first ones.

To freeze any row of your choosing:

1. Place the cell pointer directly under the row you want to freeze to make it the active cell.

2. Click on the **View** tab.

3. In the Window group click on **Freeze Panes** and select **Freeze Panes** from the pop-up list.

To freeze any column of your choosing:

1. Select a cell on the first row of the column that's to the right of the one you want to freeze. For example, if you want to freeze *column B* then you would select cell *C1*.

2. Click on the **View** tab.

3. In the Window group click on **Freeze Panes** and select **Freeze Panes** from the pop-up list.

Other examples:

- If you want to freeze the first row and first column of your worksheet, select cell **B2** and then select **View** > **Freeze Panes** > **Freeze Panes**.

- If you want to freeze only rows 1 and 2, select cell **A3** and select **View** > **Freeze Panes** > **Freeze Panes**.

- If you want to freeze only columns A and B, click on cell **C1**, and select **View** > **Freeze Panes** > **Freeze Panes**.

Unfreeze panes:

To unfreeze any frozen row or columns, click on Freeze Panes and select **Unfreeze Panes** from the pop-up menu.

3.4 Applying Themes to Your Worksheet

A theme is a predefined formatting package that you can apply to your worksheet that may include colours for headers, text fonts, the size of cells etc.

There are several themes in Excel that you can apply to your whole worksheet.

To change the look and feel of your worksheet with themes:

1. Click on the **Page Layout** tab on the Ribbon.

2. Click on the **Themes** button to display the drop-down list with many themes you can apply to your worksheet.

3. You can mouseover a theme on the list to get an instant preview of how your worksheet would look with that theme without selecting it.

4. When you find one that you're happy with, click on it to apply it to your worksheet.

Removing a Theme

If you apply a theme you don't like, simply click the **Undo** button on the Quick Access Toolbar (the left-pointing arrow) to undo the changes and return your worksheet to its previous state.

Chapter 4: Organising Your Data

I n this chapter, we will cover some essential tasks to do with organising your data in Excel.

These will include:
- Copying and pasting data.
- Moving data.
- Inserting/deleting rows and columns.
- Finding and replacing data.
- Sorting data.
- Filtering data.

4.1 Copying, Moving and Deleting Data

Selecting a Group of Cells

Method 1

1. Click on the first cell of the area.

2. Ensure your mouse pointer is a white plus sign.

3. Click and drag over the other cells in the range you want to include in the selection.

Method 2

1. Click on the top-left cell in the range, for example, A2.

2. Hold down the SHIFT key and click on the bottom-right cell in the range, for example, D10.

This will select the range A1:D10.

Deselecting Cells

Sometimes when you're selecting several cells or ranges, you might accidentally select more cells than you intended. You can deselect any extra cells within the selected range with the deselect feature.

To deselect cells within a selection, hold down the **Ctrl** key, then click, or click-and-drag to deselect any cells or ranges within the selection.

If you need to reselect any of the cells, hold down the **Ctrl** key and click on the cells to select them again.

Note This is a new feature starting from Excel 2019. If you are a Microsoft 365 subscriber, make sure you have the latest version of Office to activate this feature in Excel.

Copying and Pasting Data

Quick copy and paste:

1.   Select the range that you want to copy.

2.   On the **Home** tab, click on **Copy** (this is the double paper icon next to the Paste command).

3.   You will see a dotted line around the area. This is called the marquee.

4.   Click on the first cell of the area where you want to paste the contents.

5.   Click on **Paste**.

6.   The marquee remains active to let you know that you can carry on pasting the copied content if you wish to paste it in multiple areas. To get rid of the marquee hit the **ESC** key.

Other pasting options:

1.   To access other pasting options, after copying data, on the toolbar, click the **Paste** command button to display a pop-up menu with several pasting options. You can mouseover the options to see what each one does. You also see a preview of the paste action on your worksheet.

2.   For example, if you want to paste the contents and the column width, select the option that says **Keep Source Width (W)**. This is on the second row on the menu.

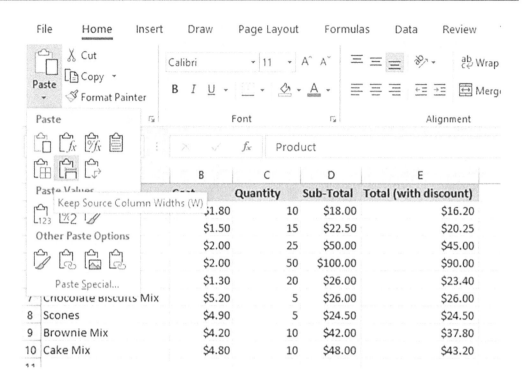

	B	C	D	E
	Cost	Quantity	Sub-Total	Total (with discount)
	$1.80	10	$18.00	$16.20
	$1.50	15	$22.50	$20.25
	$2.00	25	$50.00	$45.00
	$2.00	50	$100.00	$90.00
	$1.30	20	$26.00	$23.40
7 Chocolate Biscuits Mix	$5.20	5	$26.00	$26.00
8 Scones	$4.90	5	$24.50	$24.50
9 Brownie Mix	$4.20	10	$42.00	$37.80
10 Cake Mix	$4.80	10	$48.00	$43.20

3. Select that option to paste the data as well as the cell formatting and column width.

4. Once done, remove the marquee around the copied range by hitting the ESC key. This tells Excel that you're done with the copying.

Moving Data

To move content, you follow a similar set of actions as we did with copying, however, you would **Cut** the data instead of **Copy** it.

1. Select the range you want to move.

2. On the Home tab, click on the **Cut** button (this is the command with the scissors icon).

3. A scrolling marquee will appear around the area you've chosen to cut.

4. Place your cursor on the first cell of the area where you want to paste the content. You only need to select one cell.

5. Click on **Paste** on your toolbar. This will move the content from its current location and place it in the area you've chosen.

6. The cut and paste action automatically copies the format of the cells across but not the width. So, you need to adjust the width of the cells if necessary.

Insert or Delete Rows and Columns

To insert a column:

1. Click on the column letter immediately to the right of where you want to insert the column. For example, if you want to insert a column between columns A and B, select column B.

2. On the **Home** tab, in the Cells group, click the **Insert** button.

This will insert a new column to the left of the one you selected.

Whenever you need to insert a new column, ensure you select the column immediately to the right of the area where you want to insert a new column.

For example, let's say you have data in columns A, B, C and D, and you wish to insert a new column between C and D. You would select column D and then select **Home** > **Insert** to insert a new column between C and D. The new column will now be the new D.

Inserting a new column by using the pop-up menu:

1. Click the column letter to the right of the insertion point to select the whole column.

2. Right-click and select **Insert** from the pop-up menu. This will insert the new column.

Inserting a new row by using the pop-up menu:

1. Click on the row number directly below the insertion point to select the whole row.

2. Right-click and select **Insert** from the pop-up menu. This will insert a new row directly above the selected row.

You could also insert new rows and columns by using the **Insert** command button on the **Home** tab.

Inserting multiple rows or columns:

1. Hold down the CTRL key.

2. One by one, select the rows up to the number you want to insert. For example, if you want to insert 4 rows then select 4 rows directly under the insertion point.

3. Click on **Home** > **Insert** (or right-click and select **Insert**).

This will insert 4 new rows above the insertion point.

4.2 Find and Replace Data

An Excel worksheet can occasionally be very large. A worksheet can have over a million rows of data, for example, so in a large worksheet, it may be difficult to locate specific information. Excel provides a Find and Replace feature that enables you to quickly find data in your worksheet and replace it if needed.

If you have used the find function in other Microsoft Office applications before, then you should be familiar with this feature.

To display the **Find and Replace** dialog box, on the **Home** tab of the Ribbon, click the **Find & Select** button, and then click on **Find** from the pop-up menu.

The following dialog box will be displayed.

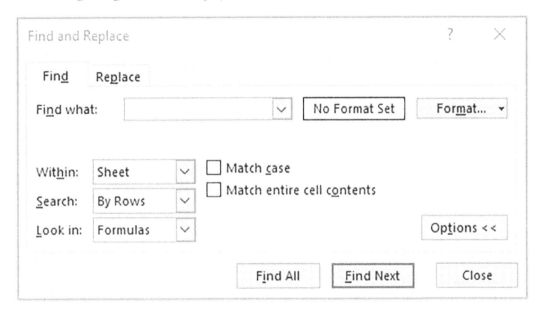

The **Find what** box contains the value you want to find.

You can click on the **Options** button to display more options to narrow down your search.

1. **Format** allows you to select the format of the data you're searching for.

2. **Within** allows you to search the current worksheet or the whole workbook.

3. **Search** allows you to search by rows (default) or columns.

4. **Look in** is used to search cell formulas, values, or comments. The default is formulas so to look for values change this option to Values from the drop-down list.

5. **Match case,** when selected, will only search for values that match the case of the entry in the **Find what** box.

6. **Match entire cell contents,** when selected, ensures that the cell contains the same value as in the **Find what** box.

Replacing Data

To replace data, click on the **Replace** tab of the Find and Replace dialog. On that tab, you get a **Replace with** box that allows you to enter the data you want to insert in place of what you find.

You get two additional buttons at the bottom of the screen:

1. **Replace All** – Automatically replaces all instances of the Find results.

2. **Replace** – Replace only the next one found.

All the other options on the screen remain the same on this tab.

-ᐤ-Tip   If you used **Replace/Replace All** to replace data by mistake you can use the **Undo** button on the Quick Access Toolbar to reverse the changes.

4.3 Sorting Data

Excel offers a wide array of methods to sort your data, from a quick and basic sort to more complex sorts using your own custom list. We will be covering the popular methods in this section.

Quick Sort

To quickly sort data in Excel, select any single cell in the column you want to sort.

Right-click the cell. From the pop-up menu, select **Sort A to Z** (for ascending) or **Sort Z to A** (for descending).

If your column is a number field you'll have, **Sort Smallest to Largest** (for ascending) or **Sort Largest to Smallest** (for descending).

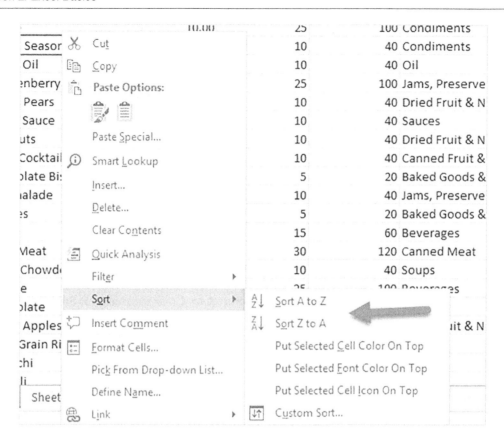

The sort does not change your data in any way. It simply reorders your rows according to the sort order and column you've chosen.

Custom Sort

In the example above, we sorted using just one column. However, you can sort using multiple columns, for example, in the data shown below, we may want to sort by *Category* and *Product name*. In this case, we would use the Custom Sort command on the Ribbon.

	A	B	C
1	Category	Product Name	Price
2	Beverages	Chai	18.00
3	Condiments	Syrup	10.00
4	Condiments	Cajun Seasoning	22.00
5	Cereal	Granola	4.00
6	Chips, Snacks	Potato Chips	1.80
7	Baked Goods & Mixes	Brownie Mix	12.49
8	Baked Goods & Mixes	Cake Mix	15.99
9	Beverages	Tea	4.00
10	Canned Fruit & Vegetables	Pears	1.30
11	Canned Fruit & Vegetables	Peaches	1.50
12	Canned Fruit & Vegetables	Pineapple	1.80
13	Canned Fruit & Vegetables	Cherry Pie Filling	2.00
14	Canned Fruit & Vegetables	Green Beans	1.20
15	Canned Fruit & Vegetables	Corn	1.20
16	Canned Fruit & Vegetables	Peas	1.50
17	Canned Meat	Tuna Fish	2.00
18	Canned Meat	Smoked Salmon	4.00
19	Cereal	Hot Cereal	5.00
20	Soups	Vegetable Soup	1.89
21	Soups	Chicken Soup	1.95
22			

Applying a custom sort:

Select a single cell anywhere in the data.

On the Home tab, in the Editing group, click **Sort & Filter**, then select **Custom Sort** from the pop-up menu. This will display the Sort dialog box.

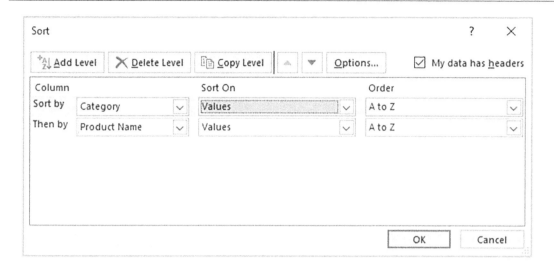

In the **Sort by** list, select the first column you want to sort.

In the **Sort On** list, you have the option of selecting Values, Cell Color, Font Color, or Cell Icon. If you're sorting by value, you'll leave this as the default (Value).

In the **Order** list, select the order in which you want to sort. For a text column, you can choose **A to Z** (ascending order) or **Z to A** (descending order).

For a number column, you can choose **Smallest to Largest** or **Largest to Smallest**.

Click **OK** when you're done.

Your data will now be sorted according to the criteria you've entered.

Sorting with a Custom List

When you click in the **Order** list, you can also select **Custom List** from the drop-down list and sort data by days of the week or months. You can add your own list (if the pre-defined ones do not meet your needs). This is useful when you want to sort using your own custom order rather than the standard ascending or descending order.

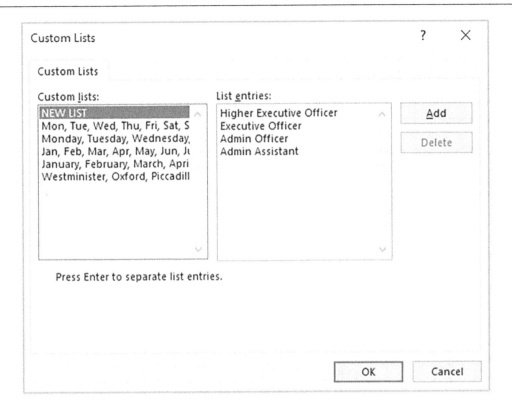

For example, if we wanted to sort our data by *employee grade* we could enter the grades in our list in the order we want the data sorted.

To add a new custom list, select NEW LIST in the left box. In the **List entries** box on the right, enter the items one item per line.

When you're done, click the **Add** button to add the list. You can now select the list and click **OK** to use it for your sort.

Your custom list will now be available to all Excel workbooks on the PC.

4.4 Filtering Data

Excel worksheets can hold a lot of data and you might not want to work with all the data at the same time. For example, you might want to only display a category of products or products within a certain price range.

Excel 2019 provides an array of options to filter your data so that you can only view data that meets a certain criterion. Filters provide a quick way to work with a subset of data in a range or table. When you apply the filter, you temporarily hide some of the data so that you can focus on the data you need to work with.

Excel tables would have column headings by default, however, if your data is not an Excel table, ensure you have column headings, like Category, Product Name, Price etc. This makes using sort much easier.

	Category	Product Name	Price	Reorder Level	Target Level
1					
2	Beverages	Chai	18.00	10	40
3	Condiments	Syrup	10.00	25	100
4	Condiments	Cajun Seasoning	22.00	10	40
5	Oil	Olive Oil	21.35	10	40
6	Jams, Preserves	Boysenberry Spread	25.00	25	100
7	Dried Fruit & Nuts	Dried Pears	30.00	10	40
8	Sauces	Curry Sauce	40.00	10	40

You can add column headings to your data by inserting a new row at the top of your worksheet and entering the headings. This is important because Excel will use the first row for the filter arrows.

How to filter data:

1. Select any cell within the data that you want to filter.

2. Click on **Home > Sort & Filter > Filter** (or click **Data > Filter**).

3. You will get a **filter arrow** at the top of each column. This is also called an **AutoFilter**. Note that in Excel tables, filter arrows are turned on by default.

4. Click the AutoFilter of the column you want to filter. For example, Price.

5. Uncheck **Select All** and check the values you want to use for the filter.

6. Click **OK**.

	A	B	C	D	E
1	Product Code ▼	Product Name ▼	Price ▼	Reorder Level ▼	Category ▼
16	NWTSO-41	Clam Chowder	$9.65	10	Soups
17	NWTB-43	Coffee	$46.00	25	Beverages
18	NWTCA-48	Chocolate	$12.75	25	Candy
19	NWTDFN-51	Dried Apples	$53.00	10	Dried Fruit & Nuts
20	NWTG-52	Long Grain Rice	$7.00	25	Grains
21	NWTP-56	Gnocchi	$38.00	30	Pasta
22	NWTP-57	Ravioli	$19.50	20	Pasta
23	NWTS-65	Hot Pepper Sauce	$21.05	10	Sauces
24	NWTS-66	Tomato Sauce	$17.00	20	Sauces
25	NWTD-72	Mozzarella	$34.80	10	Dairy Products
26	NWTDFN-74	Almonds	$10.00	5	Dried Fruit & Nuts
27	NWTCO-77	Mustard	$13.00	15	Condiments
28	NWTDFN-80	Dried Plums	$3.50	50	Dried Fruit & Nuts
29	NWTB-81	Green Tea	$2.99	100	Beverages
30	NWTC-82	Granola	$4.00	20	Cereal

The AutoFilter changes to a funnel icon to show that the column is filtered. If you look at the row heading numbers, you'll see that they're now blue, indicating which rows are included in the filtered data.

Applying a Custom Filter

Click on the AutoFilter of the column you want to use for the filter.

On the pop-up menu, you'll get a menu item and a pop-out menu. You'll get the following options depending on the datatype of the column:

1. **Text Filters** - this is available when the column has a text field or has a mixture of text and numbers: Equals, Does Not Equal, Begins With, Ends With, or Contains.

2. **Number Filters** - this option is only available when the column contains only numbers: Equals, Does Not Equal, Greater Than, Less Than, or Between.

3. **Date Filters** - this option is only available when the column contains only dates: Last Week, Next Month, This Month, and Last Month.

4. **Clear Filter from 'Column name'** - this option is only available if a filter has already been applied to the column. Select this option to clear the filter.

When you select any of the first 3 options you will get a dialog box – **Custom AutoFilter**. You'll be specifying your custom filter conditions using this screen.

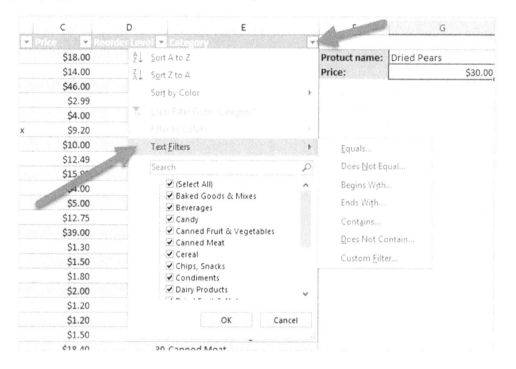

For example, if you wanted to display data with a price range between $2 and $10, you would:

1. Click on the **Price** AutoFilter and then select **Number Filters** > **Between...** from the pop-up menu.

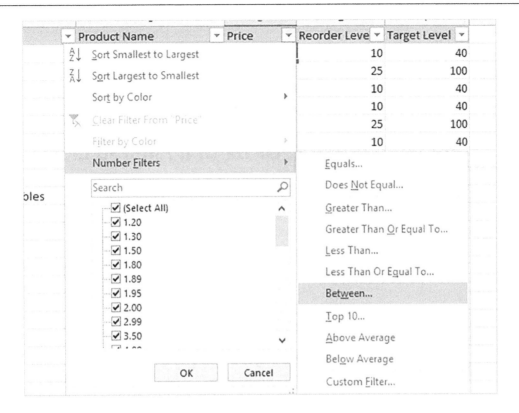

The **Custom AutoFilter** screen allows you to enter the criteria and specify the condition.

2. Enter the values you want to use for the filter. In our example, the values would be $2 and $10.

3. Select the logical operator. In this case, we'll need **And**, as both conditions must be true.

    Price >= $2 And <= $10. If only one of either condition needs to be true, then you would select Or.

4. Click OK when done.

The data will now be filtered to only show records where the Price is between $2 and $10.

Changing the Sort Order of a Filtered List

To change the sort order of the filtered results, click the **AutoFilter** icon that appears on the column used for the filter.

Select either, **Sort Largest to Smallest** or **Sort Smallest to Largest**. For a text column, it would be **Sort A to Z** or **Sort Z to A.**

Removing a Filter

Select any cell in the range/table and click on **Clear** in the **Sort & Filter** group. The filter will be removed, and all data will be displayed.

Chapter 5: Formatting Cells

In this chapter, we will cover various methods to format and resize cells in your worksheet to present your data in your desired format.

The topics covered will include, how to:
- Resize cells, rows, and columns.
- Hide and unhide rows and columns.
- Merge cells and align data.
- Hide and unhide worksheets.
- Apply predefined cell styles.
- Apply different types of number formats to cells.
- Create and apply custom cell formats.
- Apply conditional formatting to add visual representations to your data.

5.1 Arrange Cells, Rows and Columns

Resizing Rows and Columns

You can resize rows and columns with your mouse or by using the **Format** command on the toolbar.

To resize a column:

1. Click on any cell in the column.

2. Click on the right edge of the column letter and drag it to the right to widen the column.

To resize a row:

1. Click on any cell in the row.

2. Click on the bottom edge of the row number then drag it down to increase the height of the row.

Resizing Cells with the Cells Format Command

You can also increase column width and row height of a range of cells at once by using the **Format** command button on the **Home** tab of the Ribbon.

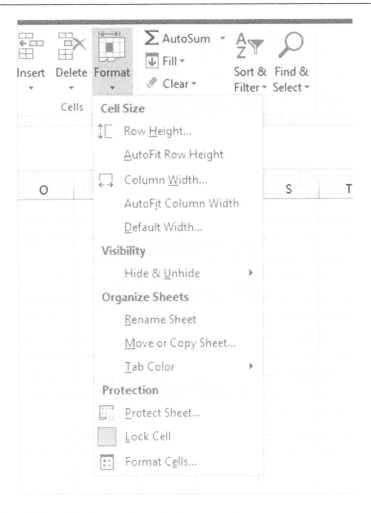

To increase the widths of columns A to E, for example:

1. Move your mouse pointer over the letter A until you see a downward pointing arrow.

2. Click on A to select the column and drag to column E to select columns A to E.

🔆Tip   Another way to select a range of columns is to select the first column, hold down the SHIFT key, and select the last column.

3. Click on **Home > Format > Column Width**.

4. Enter the **Column width** in the box.

5. Click **OK**.

To increase the height of rows 1 to 14, for example:

1. Move your mouse pointer over the header of row 1 until you get an arrow pointing right.

2. Click to select the whole row.

3. Hold down the SHIFT key and click on the header of row 14.

4. Click on **Home** > **Format** > **Row Height…**

5. The default row height is 15. So, you can enter any number higher than 15 to increase the height of the selected rows.

6. Click **OK**.

Automatically adjust columns to fit your data using AutoFit

Select the columns you want to apply AutoFit to. Click on **Format** > **AutoFit Column Width.** This will adjust each column to fit the length of all entries.

Automatically adjust row heights to fit your data using AutoFit

Select the rows you want to apply AutoFit to. Select **Format** > **AutoFit Row Height.** This will adjust each column to fit the height of all entries. This is useful if you have **Wrap text** enabled and some cells have more than one line of text.

Set the default column width for the whole workbook

Select **Format** > **Default Width** and then enter the figure in the **Standard column width** box.

Hide Rows and Columns

On some occasions, you may want to hide some rows or columns to make your worksheet easier to read.

To hide **rows,** select the rows and then click on **Format**. On the pop-up menu, under **Visibility**, select **Hide & Unhide** and then select **Hide Rows**.

To hide **columns**, select the columns and then click on **Format**. On the pop-up menu, under **Visibility**, select **Hide & Unhide** and then select **Hide Columns**.

Unhide rows and columns:

Navigate to **Home** > **Format** > **Hide & Unhide** and then select **Unhide Columns** to display hidden columns (or **Unhide Rows** to display hidden rows).

Hide and Unhide a Worksheet

You can use two methods to hide a worksheet:

Method 1: Right-click on the worksheet's name tab and select **Hide** from the pop-up menu.

Method 2: Ensure the worksheet you want to hide is the active one, then select **Home** > **Format** > **Hide & Unhide** > **Hide Sheet**.

To Unhide a worksheet:

Method 1: Right-click on any of the tabs at the bottom of the workbook and select **Unhide** from the pop-up menu. Select the worksheet name in the **Unhide** window and click **OK**.

Method 2: Navigate to **Home** > **Format** > **Hide & Unhide** > **Unhide Sheet**. Select the sheet name from the list box and click **OK**.

Applying Cell Styles

You can select a predefined colour format for your cells from a wide selection of styles from the **Styles** group on the **Home** tab.

To format a cell or range with a different style:

1. Select the cell or range.

2. Select **Home** > **Cell Styles**.

3. You can mouseover the different styles to get a preview on your worksheet before you select one.

4. Select a style from the pop-up menu.

Merging Cells and Aligning Data

To **merge** cells on your worksheet, select the cells you want to merge. On the **Home** tab, click **Merge & Center**. Alternatively, you can click on the drop-down button for Merge & Center and choose other merge options from the pop-up menu.

To **unmerge** cells, select the merged cells, then on the **Home** tab, click on the drop-down button for **Merge & Center**. Select **Unmerge Cells** from the pop-up menu.

Text Alignment and Wrapping

To align text in a cell, select the cell and click on one of the alignment options in the **Alignment** group on the **Home** tab. You can also wrap text and merge cells from the command options available.

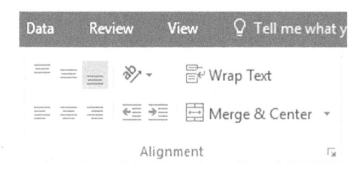

Shrink to Fit and Text Direction

The **Format Cells** dialog box provides additional formatting options like **Shrink to fit** and **Text direction**. To open the dialog box, click on the dialog box launcher on the bottom-right of the **Alignment** group.

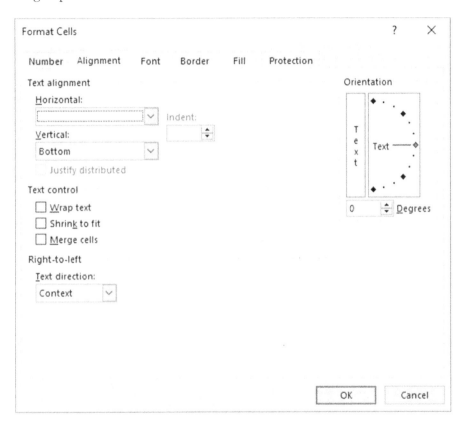

On the Alignment tab, you can:

1. Align text in your cells vertically and horizontally.

2. Wrap text so that it goes to a new line in a cell instead of continuing into other cells to the right.

3. Shrink text to fit one cell.

4. Merge cells.

5.2 Applying Number Formats

To quickly set the format for a range of cells:

1. Select the range of cells that you want to format.

2. On the **Home** tab, locate the **Number** group and click the drop-down list to display a number of formats.

3. Select one of the formats from the list, for example, Currency, Short Date or Time.

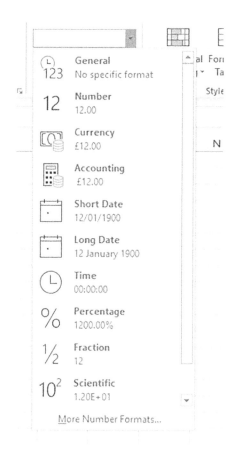

The selected cell/range will now be formatted in the format you selected.

Accessing More Formats

To choose a format that is not on the format drop-down list, for example, if you're in the US and you want to change the currency from US dollars to UK pounds:

1. Select **More Number Formats...** at the bottom of the drop-down list (shown above) or click on the **dialog box launcher** (the small diagonal arrow at the bottom-right of the **Number** group).

   The **Format Cells** window will be displayed.

2. On the left side of the dialog box under **Category**, select **Currency**.

3. Click on the **Symbol** field to display a drop-down list. Select the British pound sign (£) from the list.

   On this screen, you can also set the number of decimal places and the format you want for negative numbers. The **Sample** field gives you a preview of how the chosen format will look on your worksheet.

4. Click **OK** to confirm your changes when done.

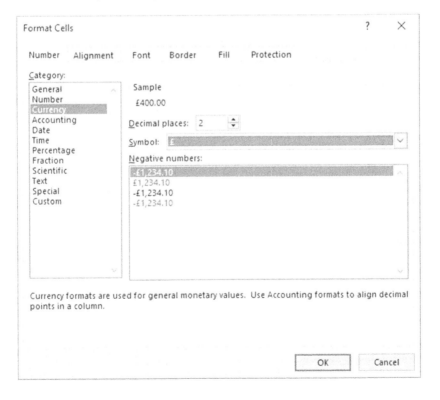

Creating Custom Numeric Formats

Excel has many predefined number formats you can select and then amend, to create your own custom format if none of the predefined formats meets your needs.

Let's say you have a column in your worksheet that you use to record a set of numbers. It could be product serial numbers, unique product IDs, or even telephone numbers. You may want the numbers to appear in a certain format regardless of how they've been entered.

In some applications like Microsoft Access, this would be called a *format mask*.

In Excel, you can create your own format for a group of cells, so that every entry is automatically formatted with your default format.

To create your own format:

1. Select the range of cells to be formatted.

2. Right-click any area in your selection and choose **Format Cells** from the pop-up menu. Alternatively, launch the **Format Cells** window by clicking the dialog box launcher in the **Number** group on the **Home** tab.

3. Under **Category,** select **Custom**.

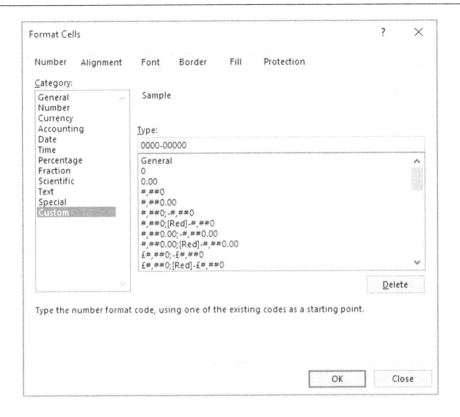

4. In the **Type** box, select an existing format close to the one you would like to create.

Note If you find a format on the list that meets your requirements, then you can just select that one and click **OK**.

5. In the Type box, type in the format you want to create. For example, *0000-00000*.

6. Click **OK**.

	A	B	C
1	**Serial Number**		
2	234401107	2344-01107	
3	234434589	2344-34589	
4	234466123	2344-66123	
5	234455692	2344-55692	
6	234234500	2342-34500	
7	234410976	2344-10976	
8	232310978	2323-10978	
9	234093419	2340-93419	
10	230923100	2309-23100	
11	234109035	2341-09035	
12	234102345	2341-02345	
13	234109093	2341-09093	
14			

In the image above, column A has a set of numbers. Column B shows the same numbers with a custom format (*0000-00000*) now applied to them.

5.3 Copy Cell Formatting

A quick way to format a cell or group of cells based on another cell is to use the **Format Painter**. This can be found in the **Clipboard** group on the **Home** tab. This can save a lot of time as you only create the format once and copy it to other cells in your worksheet for which you would like to apply that format.

To copy cell formatting with the Format Painter:

1. Click on the source cell, that is, the cell you want to copy the format from.

2. Select **Home > Format Painter**. The mouse pointer will turn into a plus sign (+) and a brush icon.

3. Click and drag over the destination cells i.e. the cells you want to copy the format to. The destination cells will now have the same format as the source cell.

An Example:

If cell A2 is formatted as **Currency** and you want to format A3 to A14 as currency with the **Format Painter**, you would carry out the following steps:

1. Click on cell *A2* to select it.

2. Click on **Format Painter**.

3. Select *A3* to *A14*. Click *A3* and drag to *A14*.

4. The currency format from *A2* will now be applied to A3:A14.

Clearing the Cell Format

To remove formatting from a cell or range, do the following:

1. Select the cells you want to clear.

2. Select **Home** > **Clear** (from the **Editing** group).

3. A pop-up menu with several options will be displayed - **Clear All, Clear Formats, Clear Contents, Clear Comments, and Clear Hyperlinks**.

4. To clear just the format and not the values, click on **Clear Formats**.

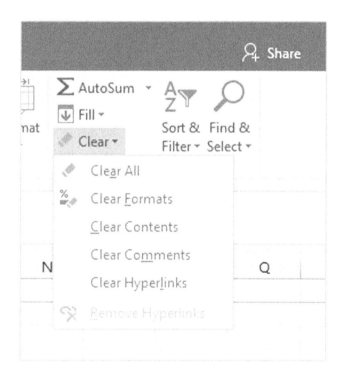

This will return the format of the selected cells to **General** which is the Excel default.

5.4 Conditional Formatting

With conditional formatting, you can format your data based on certain conditions to display a visual representation that helps you to spot critical issues and to identify patterns and trends. For example, you can use visual representations to clearly show the highs and lows in your data, and the trend based on a set of criteria.

In the example below, we can quickly see the trend in sales and how they compare to each other.

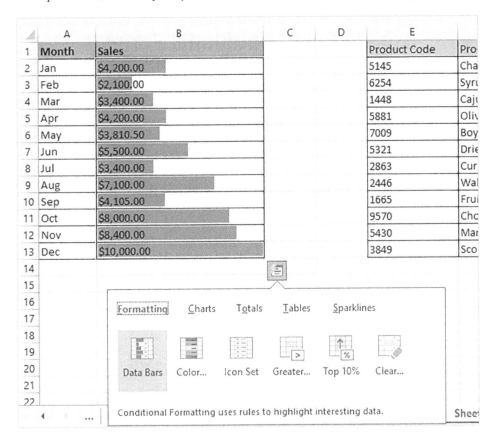

To quickly apply a conditional format:

1. Select the range of cells you want to format.

   The quick analysis button will be displayed at the bottom-right of the selection.

2. Click the Quick Analysis button, and use the default **Formatting** tab.

3. When you mouseover the formatting options, you'll see a live preview of what your data will look like when applied.

4. Click on **Data Bars** (or any of the other options) to apply the formatting to your data.

You now have a visual representation of the data that's easier to analyze.

Use Multiple Conditional Formats

You can apply more than one conditional format to the same group of cells. To do so, select the cells, click the Quick Analysis button, and click another format option, for example, Icon Set. The arrows are used to depict the upper, middle, and lower values in the set of data.

Formatting Text Fields

You can also apply conditional formatting to text, however, the formatting options for text are different from that of numbers.

For example, to if we wanted to highlight all the rows with "Sauce" in the name, we would...

1. Select the range.
2. Click the Quick Analysis button.
3. Select **Text...** from the Formatting options.
4. In the **Text That Contains** dialog, we would enter *Sauce* in the first box and select the type of formatting we want from the drop-down list.

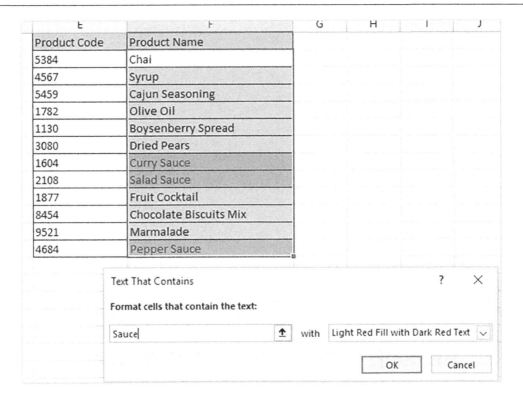

You can explore the formatting options for different data types by selecting the data to be formatted and clicking on the Quick Analysis button.

Conditionally Formatting Time

Let's say we had a task list and we wanted to see which ones are late, i.e. the ones with the due date before today.

1. Select the cells in the *Due date* column.

2. Click the Quick Analysis button, and then click Less Than.

3. Type in **=TODAY()**

    We could type in today's date, but that would mean we would need to update the conditional formatting daily, and that could get tedious fast! The TODAY function will always return today's date.

4. Select the formatting you'll like to use from the drop-down list.

5.   Click **OK**.

The tasks that are overdue now stand out in the list and are easy to identify at a glance.

Creating Conditional Formatting Rules

An alternative way to create conditional formatting is by creating Rules in Excel.

To launch the **New Formatting Rule** dialog:

1.   Select the range you want to apply the conditional formatting to.

2.   On the Ribbon, click on **Home** > **Conditional Formatting** > **New Rule**.

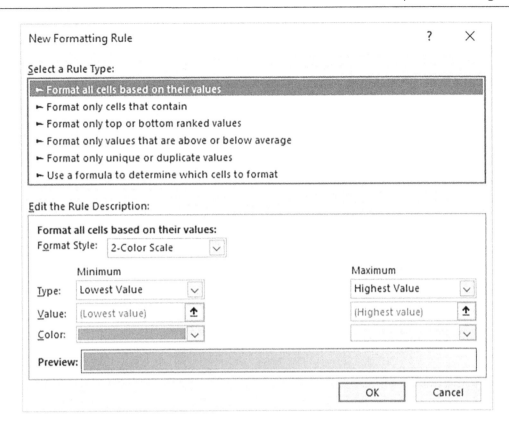

You can use this dialog box to create more complex rules using a series of conditions and criteria.

You can select a rule type from the following options:

1. Format all cells based on their values.
2. Format only cells that contain.
3. Format only top or bottom ranked values.
4. Format only values that are above or below average.
5. Format only unique or duplicate values.
6. Use a formula to determine which cells to format.

For each rule type, the bottom half of the screen, labelled **Edit the Rule Description**, gives you different fields to define your rule.

Example:

Let's say you had a products table and you wanted to format the whole row grey if the product stock fell below 10.

To do this, you select the range you want to conditionally format i.e. A2:C18. Note that A2 is the active cell.

On the Ribbon, you click **Conditional Formatting** > **New Rule** and select *Use a formula to determine which cells to format*.

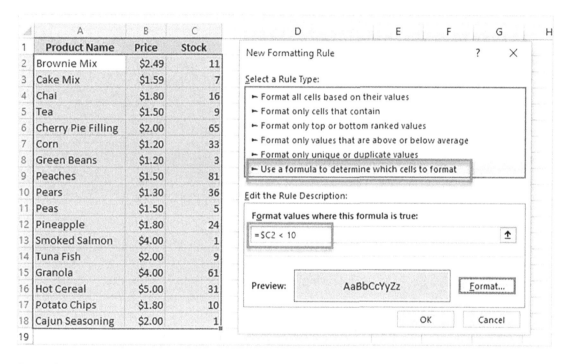

Since A2 is the active cell, you need to enter a formula that is valid for row 2 and will apply to all the other rows.

To do this, you type in the formula *=$C2 < 10*. The dollar sign before the C means it is an **absolute reference** for column C ($C). With this, the value in column C for each row is evaluated and used for the conditional formatting.

Note   The difference between an absolute reference and a relative reference is covered in chapter 6.

For the fill colour, click the **Format** button, select the fill colour you want and click OK and OK again to apply the rule.

The rows with Stock below 10 will now be filled with grey.

	A	B	C	D
1	**Product Name**	**Price**	**Stock**	
2	Brownie Mix	$2.49	11	
3	Cake Mix	$1.59	7	
4	Chai	$1.80	16	
5	Tea	$1.50	9	
6	Cherry Pie Filling	$2.00	65	
7	Corn	$1.20	33	
8	Green Beans	$1.20	3	
9	Peaches	$1.50	81	
10	Pears	$1.30	36	
11	Peas	$1.50	5	
12	Pineapple	$1.80	24	
13	Smoked Salmon	$4.00	1	
14	Tuna Fish	$2.00	9	
15	Granola	$4.00	61	
16	Hot Cereal	$5.00	31	
17	Potato Chips	$1.80	10	
18	Cajun Seasoning	$2.00	1	
19				

Chapter 6: Carrying out Calculations with Formulas

Excel provides tools and features that enable you to carry out different types of calculations from basic arithmetic to complex engineering calculations using functions.

In this chapter we will cover:

- Operator precedence in Excel and its effect on calculations.
- How to enter formulas in Excel.
- How to calculate percentages, dates, and time.
- How to use the AutoSum feature for automated calculations.
- The difference between relative and absolute cell references.
- How to access data in other worksheets in your formulas.

6.1 Operators in Excel

Arithmetic Operators

The following arithmetic operators are used to perform basic mathematical operations such as addition, subtraction, multiplication, or division.

Arithmetic operator	Meaning	Example
+ (plus sign)	Addition	=4+4
– (minus sign)	Subtraction	=4–4
		=-4
	Negation	
* (asterisk)	Multiplication	=4*4
/ (forward slash)	Division	=4/4
% (percent sign)	Percent	40%
^ (caret)	Exponentiation	=4^4

Comparison Operators

Comparison operators allow you to compare two values and produce a logical result i.e. TRUE or FALSE.

Comparison operator	Meaning	Example
=	Equal to	=A1=B1
>	Greater than	=A1>B1
<	Less than	=A1<B1
>=	Greater than or equal to	=A1>=B1
<=	Less than or equal to	=A1<=B1
<>	Not equal to	=A1<>B1

Operator Precedence

If you combine several operators in a single formula, Excel performs the operations in the following order.

Operator	Description
: (colon) (single space) ,(comma)	Reference operators
–	Negation (as in –1)
%	Percent
^	Exponentiation
* and /	Multiplication and division
+ and –	Addition and subtraction
&	Connects two strings of text (concatenation)
= < > <= >= <>	Comparison

At a basic level, you just need to remember that multiplication and division are carried out before addition and subtraction.

If a formula contains operators with the same precedence, for example, multiplication and division, Excel evaluates the operators from left to right.

Parentheses and Operator Precedence

You can change the order of evaluation by enclosing parts of your formula in parentheses (). The part of the formula in parentheses will be calculated first.

For example, the following formula produces 75 because Excel calculates multiplication before addition. So, Excel multiplies 7 by 10 first before adding 5 to the result.

=5+7*10

Answer = 75

In contrast, if we enclose 5+7 in parentheses, Excel will calculate 5 + 7 first before multiplying the result by 7 to produce 120.

=(5+7)*10

Answer = 120

In another example, we want to add 20% to 300. The parentheses around the second part of the formula makes Excel carry out the addition first before the multiplication to produce 360.

=300 * (1 + 0.2)

Answer = 360

6.2 Entering a Formula

To enter a formula in a cell, always start your entry with an equal sign (=) in the formula bar. This tells Excel that your entry is a formula and not a static value.

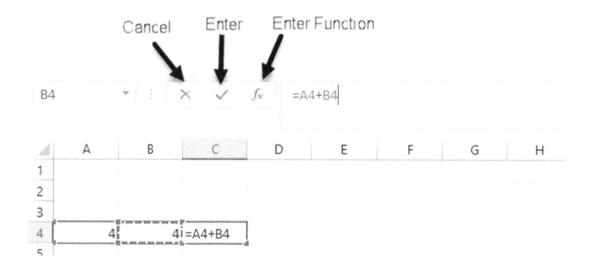

Next to the formula bar, you have the **Enter** command (check mark) that you use to confirm your formula. So, you enter your formula in the formula bar and then click on **Enter** to confirm the entry. If you wish to cancel the entry, then click on **Cancel** to discard it.

Let's say we want to add 2 figures, 300 + 400.

1. Enter 300 in cell **A4**.
2. Enter 400 in cell **B4**.
3. In cell C4, enter *= A4 + B4*.
4. Click on **Enter**.
5. C4 will now have the sum of the two figures which is 700.

-☼-Tip
         To minimise the possibility of errors, as much as possible, avoid typing cell references directly into the formula bar. After you type in the leading equal sign (=) in the formula bar, you can add cell references to your formula by selecting them on the worksheet with your mouse.

Whenever you want to reference a cell, select the cell on the worksheet with your mouse to automatically enter its reference in the formula bar.

So, for the basic calculation we performed above, the way you would enter it in the formula bar is as follows:

1. Select *C4*
2. Type "=" in the formula bar
3. Select on *A4*
4. Type "+"
5. Select *B4*
6. Click **Enter**

The sum of the two cells, i.e. 700, will now be displayed in cell C4.

6.3 Calculating Percentages

Let's say we want to calculate 20% of a value and then add it to the total, the way sales tax is calculated in invoices.

The price of the product is $2,900 and the sales tax is 20%.

Note
100 percent is 1 in Excel, so, anything less than 100 percent will be less than 1. Hence, 20 percent will be 0.2. Always enter a percent as a decimal place number, unless it is 100% or greater.

For the **Sales tax,** we then enter 0.2 in cell B3.

We can format the cell as a **Percentage** (although this is not a must when calculating percentages in Excel). On the Home tab, in the Numbers group, click on the % sign. This will change the 0.2 to 20%.

For the **Price**, enter $2,900.

For the Sales Tax formula, enter =*A6*B3* to calculate 20% of $2,900, which is $580.00.

For the **Total**, you can use the AutoSum tool to generate the sum, or you can enter the formula directly =*SUM(A6:B6)* to produce the total figure of $3,480.00.

| B6 | ▼ | ⋮ | ✕ | ✓ | *fx* | =A6*B3 |

	A	B	C	D
1	**Calculating percentages**			
2				
3	**Sales tax rate:**	20%		
4				
5	**Price**	**Sales Tax**	**Total**	
6	$2,900.00	$580.00	$3,480.00	
7				

You can use the same method above to subtract percentages. For example, if we wanted to subtract the Sales Tax from the Price we would enter =*A6-B6* in cell c6.

6.4 The AutoSum Tool

The AutoSum tool can be found on the **Home** tab of the Ribbon. It is the Greek Sigma symbol in the **Editing** group. AutoSum allows you to insert functions in your worksheet. The tool automatically selects the range to be used as the argument for you. You can use AutoSum with the SUM, AVERAGE, COUNT, MAX, and MIN functions.

AutoSum will default to the SUM function when clicked. However, you can use a different function with AutoSum by clicking the drop-down button next to the AutoSum sign to display a pop-up menu of the other functions you can use. Click on one of them, for example, **Average**, to insert that as the function to be used with AutoSum.

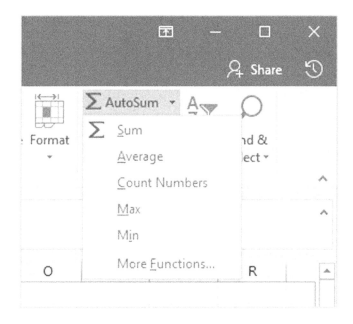

A *range* in Excel is a collection of two or more cells that contain the data you're working with. See chapter 8 for more on ranges.

A function *argument* is a piece of data that a function needs to run. The SUM function, for example, can have one or more arguments for the input ranges to be summed.

=SUM(A2:A10)

=SUM(A2:A10, C2:C10)

The great thing about AutoSum is that it selects the most likely range of cells in the current column or row that you want to use. It then automatically enters them in the function's argument.

For the most part, it selects the correct range of cells and marks the selection with a moving dotted line called the *marquee*. On occasions where there are blank rows or columns in your data, i.e. the data is not continuous, AutoSum may not automatically select everything. In those cases, you can manually correct the range by dragging the cell pointer over the other cells you want in the formula.

Let's say we have figures in B2 to B13 that we want to sum up. We can do so quickly using the AutoSum command.

SUM	▾	⋮	×	✓	fx	=SUM(B2:B13)

◢	A	B	C	D	E
1	Month	Expenses			
2	Jan	$400.00			
3	Feb	$500.00			
4	Mar	$300.00			
5	Apr	$700.00			
6	May	$800.00			
7	Jun	$750.00			
8	Jul	$800.00			
9	Aug	$600.00			
10	Sep	$550.00			
11	Oct	$420.00			
12	Nov	$350.00			
13	Dec	$800.00			
14	Sum	=SUM(B2:B13)			
15		SUM(**number1**, [number2], ...)			
16					

1. Click on the cell where you want the total displayed. For this example, this would be **B14**.

2. Click the **AutoSum** command button (**Home** > **Editing** group > **AutoSum**).

3. AutoSum will automatically select the range of cells with continuous data (above or to the side of the cell with the formula). In this case, it selects B2 to B13.

4. Click **Enter** (the check mark next to the formula bar) or hit the **Enter** key.

Cell B14 will now show the sum of the numbers.

Using AutoSum with Non-contiguous data

A non-contiguous range has blank rows or columns in the data. AutoSum will only select the contiguous range next to the cell with the formula. So, you have to manually drag the selection over the rest of the data.

1. Click on the cell where you want the total to be displayed.

2. Click the **AutoSum** command button.

3. AutoSum will automatically select the range of cells next to the cell with the formula.

4. Place your mouse pointer at the edge of the selection (over the cell pointer) until it turns into a double-headed arrow. Drag it over the rest of the cells in your range.

5. Click the **Enter** button or hit the **Enter** key on your keyboard.

The formula cell will now show the sum of the numbers.

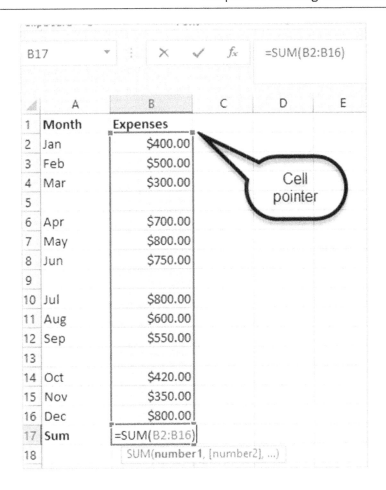

Using AutoSum with Different Ranges

Sometimes the data you want to calculate may be in different parts of your worksheet or even on different sheets in the workbook. With AutoSum, you can have arguments for individual values, cell references, ranges, or a mix of all three. So, to calculate different ranges you place the ranges as different arguments.

Summing up values in different ranges:

1. Click on the cell where you want the formula and then click on **AutoSum**.

2. If AutoSum does not select the first range for you then select it by clicking on the first cell and dragging to the last cell of the range.

3. Hold down the **CTRL** key and select any additional ranges you want to add to the calculation.

4. Click **Enter**.

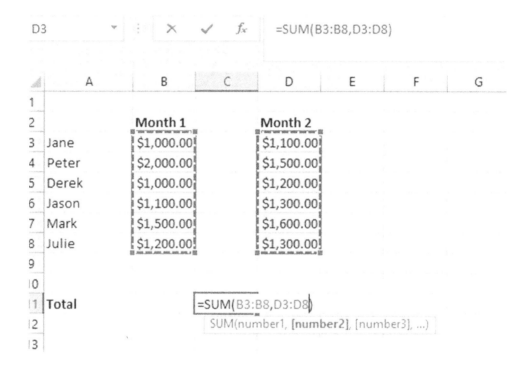

The sum of both ranges will now be entered. You can include up to 255 ranges as arguments in your SUM function.

Using AutoSum for Other Aggregate Functions

As mentioned previously, despite the name, you can use the AutoSum feature to also calculate the **Average**, **Count**, **Max**, and **Min**. To select these other functions, click on the drop-down arrow on the AutoSum command and select one of them.

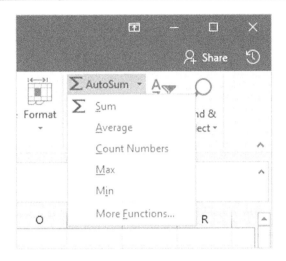

For example, to calculate the average of a row of numbers in cells B4 to I4, you would do the following:

1. Place the cell pointer in the cell where you want to display the average. This will be J4 for this example.

2. Click on **AutoSum > Average**.

3. AutoSum will automatically select all the contiguous cells next to the formula cell. For this example, it will be B4 to I4.

4. Click on **Enter** or press the **Enter** key.

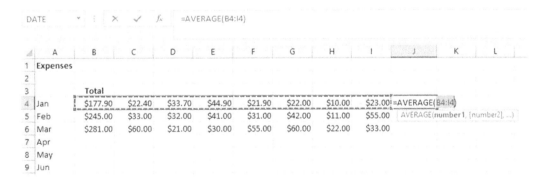

The average for B4:I4 will now be calculated and displayed in J4.

6.5 Quick Sum with the Status Bar

If you want to quickly see the sum of a range of cells, select the range and view the information on the Status Bar.

To select a range of cells, click on the first cell in the range, and hold down the SHIFT key, then click on the last cell in the range.

Once you have selected the range, look at the lower right-hand side of the Excel **Status Bar**. You will see displayed, the **Average**, **Count**, and **Sum** for the cells you have selected.

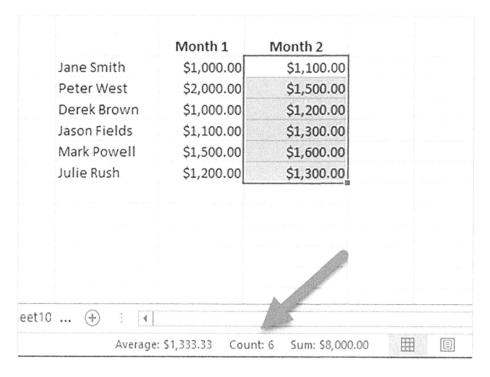

This provides a way of instantly viewing aggregate data for a range of values in a worksheet without needing to enter the formula(s).

6.6 Calculating Date and Time

Native support for date and time calculations have been vastly improved in Excel over previous editions. You can now carry out many date and time calculations in the worksheet area using arithmetic operators where functions were previously needed. The trick is to apply the right data format to the cells to get the right results. In this section, we will cover some of the most used date and time calculations.

Adding Time

When you enter two numbers separated by a colon sign, for example, 8:45, Excel recognises it as time and will treat it as such when you carry out calculations based on that cell.

Let's say we wanted to calculate how many hours and minutes it took to complete two trips. The first trip took 8 hours and 45 minutes and the second one took 6 hours and 30 minutes.

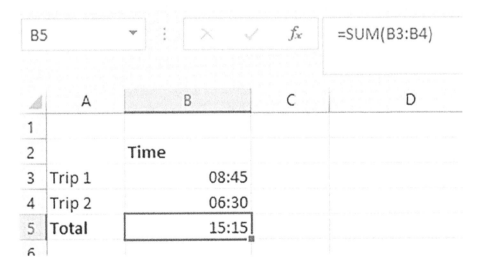

We enter **08:45** in B3 and **06:30** in B4.

The values are added in cell B5 with the formula **=SUM(B3:B4)** and it returns an answer of **15:15** (15 hours and 15 minutes).

As you can see from the example above, when we sum the two values, Excel uses hours and minutes to carry out the calculation rather than hundreds.

Note that Excel only recognises time up to 24 hours by default. If you want to calculate time that is greater than 24 hours, you'll need to format the cell to accept time over 24 hours.

To format the cell, click on the dialog box launcher on the Number group on the Home tab.

In the **Format Cells** dialog box, click on **Custom**, and in the **Type** field, enter **[h]:mm**. This tells Excel to display values beyond 24 hours.

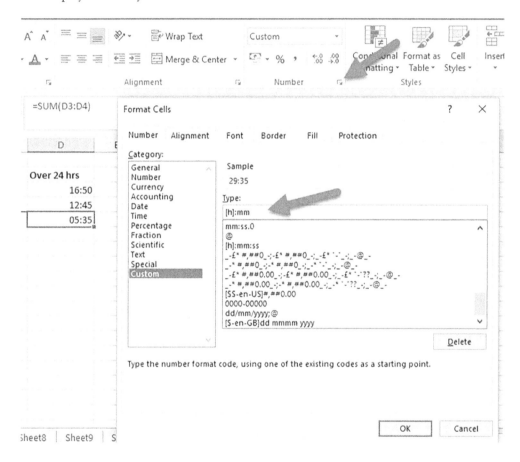

After this change to the cell format, if for example, you add 16:50 + 12:45 you now get 29:35 instead of 05:35.

C4				f_x	=SUM(C2:C3)	

	A	B	C	D
1		**Less than 24 hrs**	**Over 24 hrs**	
2	Trip 1	08:45	16:50	
3	Trip 2	06:30	12:45	
4	Total time	15:15	29:35	
5				
6				

Subtracting Time

You can calculate the number of hours between two times by subtracting one from the other, like in a work timesheet, for example.

E4				f_x	=(D4-B4)-C4

	A	B	C	D	E
1	**Timesheet**				
2					
3		**Start time**	**Break (hrs:min)**	**End time**	**Total (hrs:min)**
4	Mon	9:30 AM	1:00	7:30 PM	9:00
5	Tue	9:00 AM	0:40	5:00 PM	7:20
6	Wed	8:10 AM	0:50	4:30 PM	7:30
7	Thu	7:50 AM	1:30	4:30 PM	7:10
8	Fri	8:00 AM	0:30	4:30 PM	8:00
9					

If you enter the time with a colon between the hours and minutes, a simple subtraction can be used to calculate the difference between two times.

In the example above, the simple formula we need to calculate the total time worked per day is:

=(D4-B4)-C4

This formula first subtracts the **Start time** (B4) from the **End time** (D4), then it subtracts the **Break** (C4) from the difference, to create the total time worked for the day.

Just a few years back, you would need a series of nested IF functions to create the same solution we have achieved above. You would have to carry out all the calculations in hundredths and then use logical tests to derive the minutes. So, Excel (and spreadsheet technology in general) has come a long way since then!

Note To ensure the elapsed time is displayed correctly, format the cells showing hours and minutes, rather than AM/PM (in this case C4:C8 and E4:E8) with a custom time format - **[h]:mm**. On the other hand, the cells showing AM/PM time (in this case B4:B8 and D4:D8) have been given the custom format - **h:mm AM/PM**.

Calculating Time Across Days

You can use the same method above to calculate the time elapsed across days.

Let's say we have 2 times:

Time 1: *11/24/17 12:30 PM*

Time 2: *11/25/17 2:40 PM*

If Time 1 is in cell **B7** and Time 2 is in cell **C7**, the formula **=C7-B7** will produce the result **26:10** (if the results cell is formatted - **[h]:mm**).

Using the TIME function

You can use the TIME function to properly convert values to hours, minutes, and seconds, if directly entered in the formula bar, for example.

Syntax: TIME(hour, minute, second)

Let's say we want to subtract 1 hour 40 minutes from 8:20 AM and we want to just subtract the value in the formula bar rather than enter it in a cell. If the time is in cell A3, we could use the following formula to subtract 1 hour 40 minutes from it:

=A3 - TIME(1,40,0)

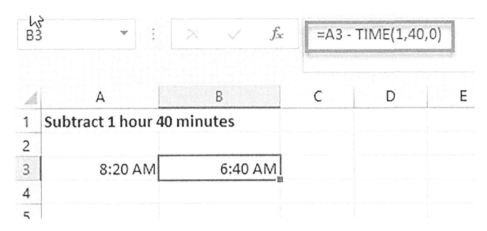

For more on date functions, see chapter 9 - Working with Functions.

Adding and Subtracting Dates

Excel now has improved native functionality for handling dates. For example, in the past, if we wanted to add a number of days to a date, we would need to use a specific function to make the calculation. Now we can just use basic addition and subtraction, and Excel handles all the complexity behind the scenes.

Example 1

Add 40 days to 12/14/2017

1. Enter *12/14/2017* in cell A2 and *40* in cell B2.

2. Enter the formula *=A2+B2* in cell C2

3. Click on Enter.

The result will be *01/23/2018*.

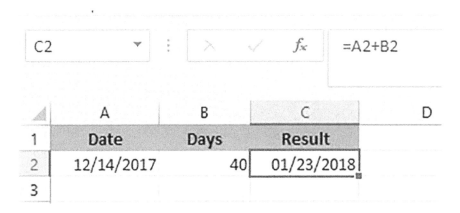

Example 2

Subtract 30 days from 12/14/2017

1. Enter *12/14/2017* in cell A2 and *30* in cell B2.
2. Enter the formula *=A2-B2* in cell C2
3. Click on Enter.

The result will be *11/14/2017*.

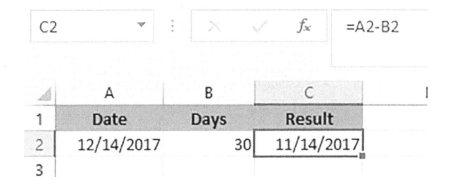

For more on calculating dates, see chapter 9 - **Working with Functions**.

6.7 Relative and Absolute Cell Reference

Relative Cell Reference

By default, a cell reference in Excel is relative. That means, when you refer to cell **B2** from cell **E3**, you are pointing to a cell that is three columns to the left (E minus B), and one row above (3-2). A formula with a relative cell reference changes as you copy it from one cell to another.

For example, if you copy the formula **=C2+D2** from cell E2 to F2, the formula will change to **=D2+E2**. The relative positions of the cells remain one column to the right of the formula.

Examples of relative references:

=D2+E2

=A3*B3

Absolute Cell Reference

If you want to maintain the original cell reference when you copy a formula, you need to make the cell reference *absolute* by inserting a dollar sign ($) before the column letter and row number, for example, **=$C$2 + $D$2**. The dollar sign before the column and row tells Excel that the cell reference does not change when the formula is copied to other cells. In this case, when you copy the formula **=$C$2 + $D$2** from E2 to F3, the formula stays the same.

To convert a cell reference to an absolute reference, select the reference in the formula bar (or place the flashing insertion point somewhere in its column letter and row number) and press the **F4** key. For example, if you have =C2 + D2 in the formula bar and you want to make C2 an absolute reference, select C2 in the formula bar and press F4. This will convert it to $C$2.

If you keep pressing F4, Excel will cycle through the different types of cell references available:

- Relative reference (default) - relative columns and rows, for example, A2.
- Absolute reference - absolute columns and rows, for example, $A$2.
- Mixed reference - relative columns and absolute rows, for example, A$2.

- Mixed reference - absolute columns and relative rows, for example, $A2.

Example

In the example below, we're calculating the Sales Tax on various items. The Tax Rate is **20%** and this has been entered in cell B3. The cell format of B3 is *Percentage*.

The formula in cell C6 is **=B6*$B$3**.

As you can see, cell B3 in the formula has been set to an absolute reference. So, when we copy the formula (using autofill) to the rest of the cells under Sales Tax (column C), the reference to cell B3 remains the same.

If the Tax Rate were to change at some point in the future, we would change the value in cell B3 only, and the Sales Tax for all the items will automatically be updated.

| C6 | | ▼ | ⋮ | ✕ | ✓ | *fx* | =B6*$B$3 |

◢	A	B	C	D
1	Sales Tax Calculation			
2				
3	Tax Rate:	20%		
4				
5	Product	Price (excl. tax)	Tax	
6	Item 1	$40.00	$8.00	
7	Item 2	$58.00	$11.60	
8	Item 3	$85.00	$17.00	
9	Item 4	$47.00	$9.40	
10	Item 5	$56.00	$11.20	
11	Item 6	$28.00	$5.60	
12	Item 7	$31.00	$6.20	
13	Item 8	$65.00	$13.00	
14	Item 9	$25.90	$5.18	
15	Item 10	$78.30	$15.66	

Mixed Cell Reference

In some cases, you may want to use a "mixed" cell reference. This is where you prefix either the column letter or row number with a dollar sign to lock it in place as an absolute reference, but then allow the other to be a relative reference.

For example, **=$B2 + $C2**

This formula says, the columns part of the cell references (B and C) are locked down as absolute, however, the row (2) is left free to be relative.

When this formula is copied from E4 to F5 (i.e. one column to the right and one row down) it will change to **=$B3 + $C3**. The columns remain the same, however, the row changed because the formula moved one row down. You can also lock down the row and leave the column as relative, for example, **=B$2**.

Examples of mixed references:

=$D2+$E2

=A$3*$B3

6.8 Using Data from Other Worksheets

On some occasions, you may be working on one worksheet and you want to access data on another worksheet in your formula. Or you may decide to separate your summary reports from your data using different worksheets. For example, you may want to have the raw data on **Sheet2** and the summary calculations on **Sheet1**.

Example 1

Let's say we want to create a formula in cell **A6** on **Sheet1** and we want to grab a value from cell **A1** on **Sheet2**.

1. Place the cell pointer in A6 on Sheet1.

2. Enter *=Sheet2!A1* in the formula bar.

3. Click **Enter**.

This will now reference cell A1 from Sheet2 as part of your formula in A6 on Sheet1.

Another way to grab the cell reference is to simply select it with your mouse:

1. Select **A6** on **Sheet1**.

2. Type the equal sign (=) in the formula bar.

3. Click on the **Sheet2** tab (at the bottom of the screen).

4. Select cell **A1** on **Sheet2**.

5. Click **Enter**.

The cell reference *Sheet2!A1* will automatically be entered in A6 on Sheet1. The same method applies for a range. Sometimes you may want your data on one sheet and your summary calculations on another sheet.

If you want to reference more than one cell i.e. a range, you click on Sheet2 and select the range of cells, for example, A1:A10. The reference **Sheet2!A1:A10** will now be added to the formula bar in Sheet1. If you have a named range then you can use the name of the range in place of the cell reference, for example, **Sheet2!MyRange**.

Example 2

In the following example, let's say we have our raw data on Sheet2, and we want to calculate the totals for each Quarter on Sheet1.

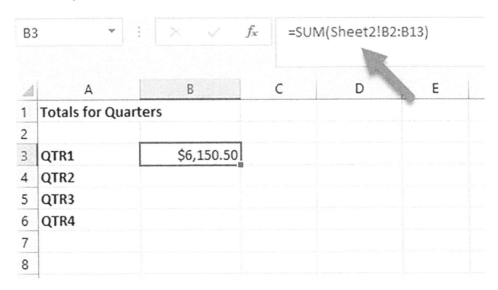

1. On **Sheet1**, select B3 and in the formula bar, enter *=SUM(*.

2. Click on **Sheet2**, using the tab at the bottom of the screen.

3. Select cells **B2:B13** by clicking on B2 and dragging down to B13. This will add *Sheet2!B2:B13* in the formula bar and your syntax should now look like this *=SUM(Sheet2!B2:B13*.

4. Click in the formula bar and enter the closing bracket. Your formula should now look like this *=SUM(Sheet2!B2:B13)*.

5. Click on **Enter** to confirm the entry.

The sum of the figures from B2 to B13 on Sheet2 will now be shown on sheet1.

Chapter 7: Use Drop-down Lists and Validation Rules

D rop-down lists and validation rules enable you to restrict the type of data or the range of values that users can enter into a cell. This can help in streamlining workflow and reduce errors.

In this chapter, we will cover:

- How to insert a drop-down list in your worksheet.
- How to add validation rules to cells.

7.1 How to Create a Drop-down List

There are occasions when you can make your worksheet more efficient by using drop-down lists in cells. Drop-down lists enable users to select an item from a list that you create instead of typing their own values. On occasions where you have a defined set of values from a lookup list or column, being able to select the value directly from the source data saves time and reduces errors.

In the following exercise, our source data will be from a worksheet named **SalesData.** Our drop-down list will be pulling data from the Product column (C4:C51). SalesData is a different worksheet in the same workbook as the worksheet with our drop-down list.

	A	B	C
1	Sales		
2			
3	Date	Salesperson	Product
4	4/25/2020	Anne Hellung-Larsen	Cora Fabric Chair
5	4/26/2020	Jan Kotas	Lukah Leather Chair
6	4/27/2020	Mariya Sergienko	Habitat Oken Console Table
7	4/28/2020	Michael Neipper	Hygena Fabric Chair
8	4/29/2020	Anne Hellung-Larsen	Harley Fabric Cuddle Chair
9	4/30/2020	Jan Kotas	Windsor 2 Seater Cuddle Chair
10	5/1/2020	Mariya Sergienko	Fabric Tub Chair
11	5/2/2020	Laura Giussani	Verona 1 Shelf Telephone Table
12	5/3/2020	Anne Hellung-Larsen	Floral Fabric Tub Chair
13	5/4/2020	Jan Kotas	Fabric Chair in a Box
14	5/5/2020	Mariya Sergienko	Slimline Console Table
15	5/6/2020	Nancy Freehafer	Martha Fabric Wingback Chair
16	5/7/2020	Nancy Freehafer	Slimline Console Table
17	5/8/2020	Nancy Freehafer	Fabric Wingback Chair
18	5/9/2020	Nancy Freehafer	Fabric Chair in a Box
19	5/10/2020	Nancy Freehafer	Fabric Chair in a Box

Follow the steps below to create a drop-down list:

1. On a blank worksheet, select the cell in which you want to create the drop-down list. For example, cell B3 in a blank worksheet.

2. On the **Data** tab, in the **Data Tools** group, click on the **Data Validation** command button and select **Data Validation** from the drop-down menu.

    This will open the **Data Validation** dialog box.

3. On the **Settings** tab, in the **Allow** box, select **List** from the drop-down list.

4. Next, click in the **Source** box, then select the data range you want to display in your list. For the example, in this chapter, you would click the SalesData sheet tab at the bottom of the workbook (this is the worksheet name), and then select range C4:C51 on the worksheet with your mouse. Excel will automatically enter the selected range in the Source box.

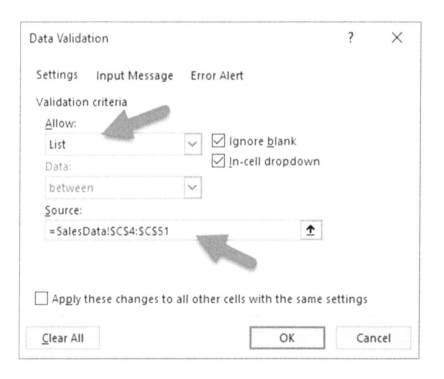

5. The **Ignore blank** and **In-cell** checkboxes should be checked by default. If not, then check both of them.

    We do not need the Input Message and Error Alert tabs for this exercise.

6. Click on **OK** to finish creating the drop-down list.

When done, the drop-down list will display a list of values from the selected source when you click the drop-down arrow.

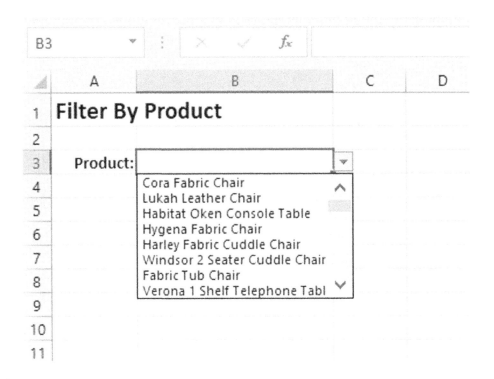

7.2 Creating Data Validation Rules

You can insert validation rules in cells to ensure that the data that is entered meets a certain criterion. For example, let's say we want to create a list that will be used by many people. The list has the following columns: *Product Code*, *Product Name*, and *Price*. We want to insert a validation rule to ensure the ***Product Code* is between 5 and 10 characters only**. We could also specify whether we want numbers only, letters only, or a combination of both.

For this example, we will make it a combination of letters and numbers.

Below is an example of how the list would look.

	A	B	C
1	Product Code	Product Name	Price
2	NWTB-1	Chai	$18.00
3	NWTCO-3	Syrup	$10.00
4	NWTCO-4	Cajun Seasoning	$22.00
5	NWTO-5	Olive Oil	$21.35
6	NWTJP-6	Boysenberry Spread	$25.00
7	NWTDFN-7	Dried Pears	$30.00
8	NWTS-8	Curry Sauce	$40.00
9	NWTDFN-14	Walnuts	$23.25
10	NWTCFV-17	Fruit Cocktail	$39.00
11	NWTBGM-19	Chocolate Biscuits Mix	$9.20
12	NWTJP-6	Marmalade	$81.00

How to Add a Data Validation Rule

Select the cells for which you want to apply the rule.

Click on the **Data** tab in the Ribbon, and in the **Data Tools** group, you will find the **Data Validation** command.

Click on **Data Validation** to launch the Data Validation dialog box. The box has three tabs, **Settings**, **Input Message**, and **Error Alert**.

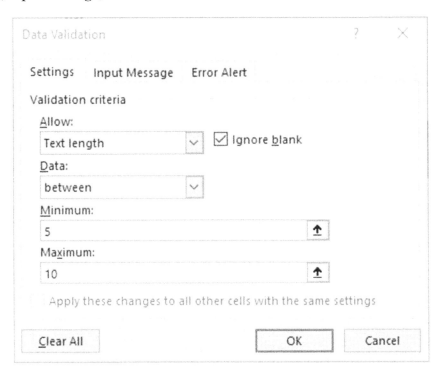

On the **Settings** tab, the **Allow** drop-down list gives us several options including, Text length, Whole number, and Decimal. In the **Allow** box, we choose **Text length**.

The **Data** drop-down list provides several comparison operators we can use in our validation criteria. For this example, we want the *Product Code* to be no less than **5** characters and no more than **10** characters.

Thus, for our validation criteria, we'll enter these entries:

- **Allow:** Text length

- **Data:** between

- **Minimum:** 5

- **Maximum:** 10

On the **Input Message** tab, we add a **Title** and the **Input message**. This help message will be displayed as a small pop-up message when the user clicks on a cell with the validation rule.

For this example, we can add a message like:

"The Product Code can be alphanumeric, and it should be between 5 and 10 characters."

In the **Error Alert** tab, we need to enter the message that is displayed when an entry fails the validation rule.

For the **Style,** we have 3 options. **Stop**, **Warning** and **Information**. We will choose the **Stop** icon for this example as a *Product Code* that does not meet the validation rule cannot be entered.

We can complete the **Title** and **Error Message** with the following:

Title: *"Invalid Entry!"*

Error Message: *"Invalid entry. Please enter a value between 5 and 10 characters in length."*

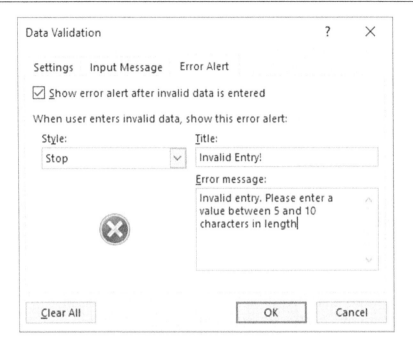

Once you have completed all the tabs, click **OK.**

Data validation will now be applied to the selected cells.

How to Edit or Remove Data Validation Rules

Occasionally you may want to change or remove data validation.

1. Select the cells where data validation has been applied.

2. On the **Data** tab, click on the **Data Validation** command to launch the Data Validation dialog box.

3. To change the validation rule simply edit the various entries and click OK when done.

4. To remove the validation rule, click **Clear All**.

5. Click **OK.**

Chapter 8: Named Ranges

When working with a lot of data, it is sometimes useful to identify your data as a group with one name to make it easier to reference in your formulas.

In this chapter, we will cover how to:

- Define a named range.
- Edit and rename a named range.
- Remove a named range.
- Use named ranges in your formulas.

8.1 What is a Named Range?

A Named Range is a group of cells in Excel that have been selected and given one name. After you give the selection a name, the whole range can now be referenced as one unit using that name in Excel formulas and functions. This is like a table with a name.

For example, we may have a list of contacts we would like to use in formulas. We could either use A1:G17 to identify the range of data or name the range "Contacts" and then use that name to reference the data from then on.

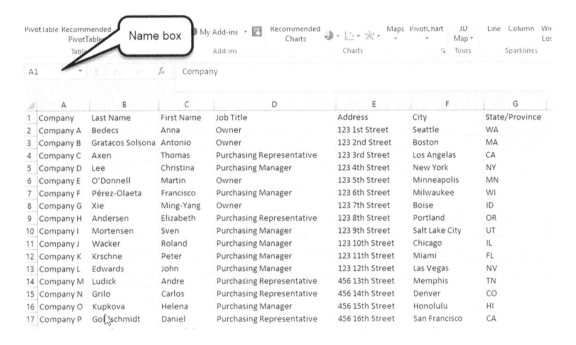

One of the benefits of using a named range is that the name is an absolute reference. When you create a formula with that name, you can copy and paste the formula in any part of your workbook, including different worksheets in the workbook, and the name will always point to the same group of cells.

8.2 Creating a Named Range

There are two ways you can create a named range:

Method 1

1.   Select the cells you want to include in the named range.

2.   Click in the Name box (this is the box on the left side of the screen, just above the worksheet area) and enter the name for your named range.

3.   Press **Enter** on your keyboard to save the name.

In the example below, I selected A1:G17 and entered "Contacts" in the name box to name that range. I can now use Contacts in place of A1:G17 in all formulas and functions in this workbook.

By default, when you create a Named Range it will be available across all worksheets in that workbook.

Method 2

1. Select the cells you want to include in the named range.

2. Click on the Formulas tab on the Ribbon. On the **Defined Names** group, click on **Define Name**.

3. A dialog box will be displayed that allows you to enter the name. Leave the Scope field as Workbook (which is the default) if you wish to reference the name in different worksheets in the workbook. You can also use the up-arrow next to the **Refers to** field to reselect the range.

4. Click **OK** when done.

Note

    If you set the Scope of a named range to 'Workbook', the name will be available for use throughout your workbook, and you can't create another named range using the same name in that workbook. If the scope is set to a particular sheet, then the name can be used within the sheet only. Also, you'll be able to use that name for named ranges within the scope of other sheets.

8.3 Editing a Named Range

1. On the Formulas tab, click **Name Manager** (in the Defined Names group).

2. The Name Manager dialog box will be displayed with a list of all the named ranges and tables in the workbook.

3. On the list, select the named range you want to edit and click on the **Edit...** button.

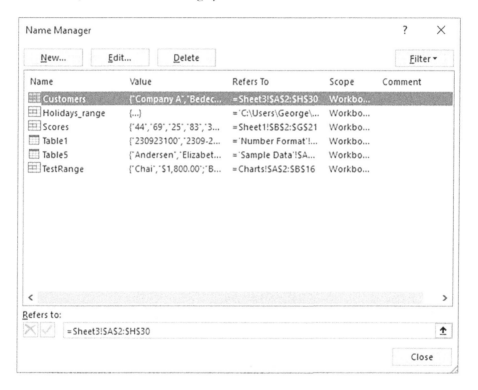

4. On the next screen, you can change the name of the range in the **Name** field.

5. To change the area that makes up the range, click in the **Refers to** field. A scrolling marquee will appear around the current range. You can now select a new area or hold down the **Shift** key and adjust the current selection with your mouse pointer.

6. Click **OK** on the Edit Name box.

7. Click **Close**.

Deleting a Named Range

1. On the **Formulas** tab, click **Name Manager**.

2. Select the named range you want to delete from the list.

3. Click the **Delete** button.

4. Click **Close** when done.

8.4 How to Use a Named Range

To select a named range, click the dropdown arrow of the name box and select the name from the drop-down list. This will display the worksheet with the range (if you're on a different worksheet) and select all the rows and columns in the range.

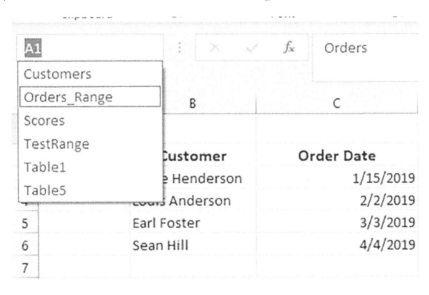

Example

The following example demonstrates the use of a named range called *Orders_Range* in place of the cell reference A1:D13. The example uses two formulas to count numeric values and blank cells in the range. The name of the range has been used as arguments in the functions instead of A1:D13.

=COUNT(Orders_Range)

=COUNTBLANK(Orders_Range)

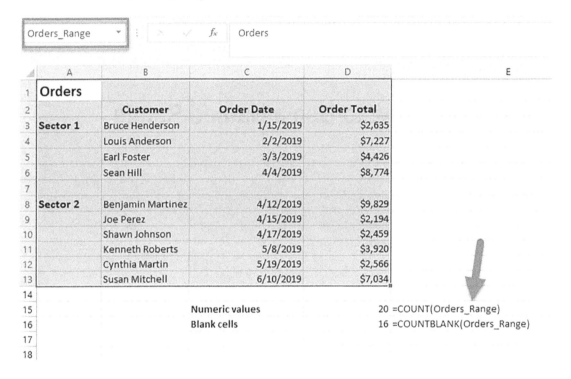

Chapter 9: Working with Tables

You can turn your Excel data into a table. When you create a table in Excel it is easier for you to manage and analyse your data. You also get built-in sorting, filtering, Banded Rows, and the ability to add a Total Row.

In this chapter, you'll learn how to:

- Convert a range to an Excel table.
- Apply different styles to a table.
- Sort and filter data in a table.
- Add a totals row to a table.
- Remove table attributes (if you want to convert your list back to a range).

9.1 Preparing Your Data

Before you create a table ensure there are no empty columns or rows in the data.

In the next example, we will convert the following range of data into a table.

	A	B	C	D	E
1	Last Name	First Name	Company	Job Title	Address
2	Bedecs	Anna	Company A	Owner	123 1st Street
3	Gratacos Solsona	Antonio	Company B	Owner	123 2nd Stree
4	Axen	Thomas	Company C	Purchasing Represen	123 3rd Street
5	Lee	Christina	Company D	Purchasing Manager	123 4th Street
6	O'Donnell	Martin	Company E	Owner	123 5th Street
7	Pérez-Olaeta	Francisco	Company F	Purchasing Manager	123 6th Stree
8	Xie	Ming-Yang	Company G	Owner	123 7th Street
9	Andersen	Elizabeth	Company H	Purchasing Represen	123 8th Stree
10	Mortensen	Sven	Company I	Purchasing Manager	123 9th Street
11	Wacker	Roland	Company J	Purchasing Manager	123 10th Street
12	Krschne	Peter	Company K	Purchasing Manager	123 11th Stree
13	Edwards	John	Company L	Purchasing Manager	123 12th Stree
14	Ludick	Andre	Company M	Purchasing Represen	456 13th Street
15	Grilo	Carlos	Company N	Purchasing Represen	456 14th Street
16	Kupkova	Helena	Company O	Purchasing Manager	456 15th Stree

First, check that there are no empty columns or rows in your data:

1. Select any cell within the data and press **CTRL + A**.

2. Then press **CTRL + "."** a few times to move around the data.

Note   **CTRL + A** selects the data range in question. **CTRL + "."** moves around the four edges of the data so you can see where the data starts and ends.

9.1 Create an Excel Table

To create a table from your data:

1. Click on any cell within the data.

2. Click on the **Insert** tab and click on **Table** (in the **Tables** group).

3. A dialog box will be displayed showing you the range to be used for the table. You can adjust the range here if necessary.

4. Click on the **My table has headers** checkbox to ensure that the first row of your table is used as the header.

-☼-Tip If your table has no column headers, create a new row on top and add column headers. This makes it easier to work with tables in Excel.

5. Click **OK**.

The table will be created with your first row used as column headers.

	A	B	C	D	E
1	**Last Name** ▾	**First Name** ▾	**Company** ▾	**Job Title** ▾	**Address**
2	Bedecs	Anna	Company A	Owner	123 1st Street
3	Gratacos Solsona	Antonio	Company B	Owner	123 2nd Street
4	Axen	Thomas	Company C	Purchasing Represen	123 3rd Street
5	Lee	Christina	Company D	Purchasing Manager	123 4th Street
6	O'Donnell	Martin	Company E	Owner	123 5th Street
7	Pérez-Olaeta	Francisco	Company F	Purchasing Manager	123 6th Street
8	Xie	Ming-Yang	Company G	Owner	123 7th Street
9	Andersen	Elizabeth	Company H	Purchasing Represen	123 8th Street
10	Mortensen	Sven	Company I	Purchasing Manager	123 9th Street
11	Wacker	Roland	Company J	Purchasing Manager	123 10th Street
12	Krschne	Peter	Company K	Purchasing Manager	123 11th Street
13	Edwards	John	Company L	Purchasing Manager	123 12th Street
14	Ludick	Andre	Company M	Purchasing Represen	456 13th Street
15	Grilo	Carlos	Company N	Purchasing Represen	456 14th Street
16	Kupkova	Helena	Company O	Purchasing Manager	456 15th Street

Another way to quickly format a range as a table is to select the cells in the range and on the Ribbon, select **Home > Format as Table.**

9.2 Choosing a Table Style

When you convert a range to a table, you will notice that a style with alternating row colours has been applied to the table. You can change this style if you want by selecting a new style from many options provided by Excel.

When you select any cell in the table, you'll see a **Table Design** tab on the Ribbon. On this tab, you'll find the groups **Table Styles** and **Table Style Options.** Table Styles provides a number of predefined styles you can apply to your table while Table Style Options provides further options to format your table.

How to Apply a Table Style

1. Select a cell within the table.

2. On the **Table Design** tab, locate the **Table Styles** group and click on the drop-down button for the styles. A drop-down menu will show you more styles.

3. Mouseover each style to see a preview of how it would look on your worksheet.

4. When you find a style you want, click on it to apply it to your table.

Configure Table Style Options

Here you have several options for configuring the style of your table.

For example, you can change your table from **Banded Row** to **Banded Columns**. Banded rows are the alternating colours applied to your table rows.

Banded Rows is the default but if you want banded columns instead, uncheck **Banded Rows** and check **Banded Columns** to have your columns alternate in colour instead of your rows.

Note that if a new column or row is added to the table, it will automatically inherit the current table style. When you add a new row, any formulas applied to your table will also be copied to the new row.

9.3 Sorting Data in a Table

Before you begin sorting data, ensure there are no blank rows and blank columns.

Tip To check for blank rows or columns, select a cell within the data and press **CTRL + A**. Then press **CTRL + "."** a few times. This moves the cursor around the four corners of the range so you can see the whole area.

Before you start sorting, also make sure your table header is a single row. If it is made up of more than one row, change it to a single row because it will make things a lot easier.

Sort by One Column

To quickly sort by one column in your table:

1. Select a cell in the column you want to use for the sorting, for example, *Last Name*.

2. On the **Data** tab, in the **Sort & Filter** group, click **AZ** (to sort the table in ascending order) or **ZA** (to sort the table in descending order).

Sort by Multiple Columns

A **Custom Sort** is required to sort a table by multiple columns.

Carry out the following steps to apply a custom sort:

1. Select any cell within the data.

2. On the Ribbon, navigate to **Home > Sort & Filter** (in the Editing group).

3. Select **Custom Sort...** from the drop-down menu. The sort dialog box will be displayed.

-☼-Tip Another way to launch the Custom Sort screen is to click on **Data** > **Sort** (in the Sort & Filter group).

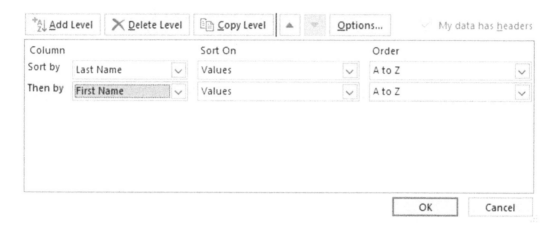

4. Click on **Add Level**.

5. Under **Column**, select the column you want to **Sort by** from the drop-down list. Select the second column you want to include in the sort in the **Then by** field. For example, Sort by Last Name and First Name.

6. Under **Sort On**, select **Values**.

7. Under **Order**, select the order you want to sort on i.e. **A to Z** for ascending order, and **Z to A** for descending order.

8. Click **OK** when done.

You can add additional columns to your sort. Starting with Excel 2016 you can have up to 64 sort levels. For each additional column that you want to sort by, repeat steps 4-7 above.

9.4 Filtering Table Data

Excel provides an array of options to filter your data so that you can view data that meets a certain criterion. Filters provide a quick way to work with a subset of data in a range or table. When you apply the filter you temporarily hide some of the data so that you can focus on the data you need to view.

How to filter data:

1. Select a cell within the data that you want to filter.

2. Click on **Home** > **Sort & Filter** > **Filter** (or click **Data** > **Filter**).

3. You will get filter arrows at the top of each column.

4. Click the drop-down arrow of the column you want to filter. For example, Price.

5. Uncheck **Select All** and check the values you want to use for the filter.

6. Click **OK**.

The filter drop-down arrow changes to a funnel icon to show that the column is filtered. If you look at the row heading numbers, you'll see that they're now blue, indicating which rows are included in the filtered data.

To remove the filter, click on **Clear** in the **Sort & Filter** group. The filter will be removed, and all data will be displayed.

Applying a Custom Filter

Select the filter drop-down arrow and then select one from the following:

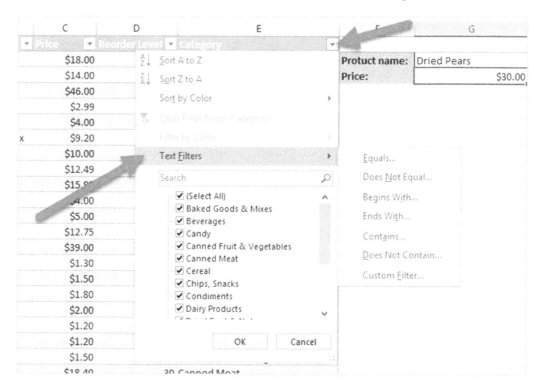

- **Text Filters** - this is available when the column has a text field or has a mixture of text and numbers: Equals, Does Not Equal, Begins With, Ends With, or Contains.

- **Number Filters** - this option is only available when the column contains only numbers: Equals, Does Not Equal, Greater Than, Less Than, or Between.

- **Date Filters** - this option is only available when the column contains only dates: Last Week, Next Month, This Month, and Last Month.

- **Clear Filter from 'Column name'** - this option is only available if a filter has already been applied to the column. Select this option to clear the filter.

When you select any of the first 3 options you will get a dialog box – **Custom AutoFilter**.

Select **And** if both conditions must be true. Alternatively, select **Or** if only one of the conditions needs to be true.

Enter the values you want to use for the filter.

For example, to view rows with a number that is within a certain range, select **Number Filters** > **Between** and then enter the values in the two boxes provided.

For the example in the image above, we're filtering the *Price* column so that only rows between $2 and $10 are shown.

To change the order of the filtered results, click the filter drop-down button, and then select either **Sort Largest to Smallest** or **Sort Smallest to Largest**.

For a text sort column, it would be **Sort A to Z** or **Sort Z to A.**

9.5 Adding a Totals Row to Your Table

You can add totals to a table by selecting the **Total Row** check box on the **Design** tab. Once added to your worksheet, the Total Row drop-down button allows you to add a function from a list of options.

To add totals to your table:

1. Select any cell in the table.

2. Select **Table Design** > **Total Row**. A new row is added to the bottom of the table. This is called the **Total Row**.

3. On the total row drop-down list, you have a choice of functions to select from, like **Average**, **Count**, **Count Numbers**, **Max**, **Min**, **Sum**, **StdDev**, **Var**, and more.

NWTS-65	Hot Pepper Sauce	$21.05	10 Sauces
NWTS-66	Tomato Sauce	$17.00	20 Sauces
NWTS-8	Curry Sauce	$40.00	10 Sauces
NWTSO-41	Clam Chowder	$9.65	10 Soups
NWTSO-98	Vegetable Soup	$1.89	100 Soups
NWTSO-99	Chicken Soup	$1.95	100 Soups
Total		$713.06 ▼	

> None
> Average
> Count
> Count Numbers
> Max
> Min
> Sum
> StdDev
> Var
> More Functions...

-ᗦ-**Tip**   If you need to add a new row of data to your table at some later point, you need to uncheck **Total Row** on the **Table Design** tab, add the new row, then recheck **Total Row**.

9.6 Removing Table Attributes

On some occasions, you may want to reverse a table back to a normal range.

Carry out the following steps to convert a table to a range:

1. Click anywhere inside the table so that the cell pointer is inside the table.

2. Click on the **Table Design** tab (this shows up when you click in the table).

3. In the **Tools** group on the Table Design tab, click on **Convert to Range**.

4. Click **Yes** at the prompt to confirm the action.

The table will now be converted to a normal range of cells without Excel's table attributes. Now, you may still have the banded-rows format that was applied as part of the table's format when it was converted. This formatting does not affect the behaviour of the range, but you can remove it if you want.

You can carry out the following steps to clear the formatting:

1. Select the range.

2. Click on the **Home** tab.

3. In the **Editing** group, click on **Clear** > **Clear Formats**.

Chapter 10: Creating Charts

Excel charts provide a way to present your data visually. As the saying goes, *a picture is worth a thousand words*. Some of us don't absorb numbers as easily as others because we're more visual and this is where charts come in. A visual representation may sometimes create more of an impact with your audience.

In this chapter, we will cover how to:

- Create charts quickly with the Quick Analysis tool.
- Create charts from the Insert tab
- Edit and format chart labels
- Apply different styles to your charts.
- Create mini charts called Sparklines to show data trends.

Preparing Your Data

To prepare your data for charting, you'll need to organize it in a list with only the items you want to report on. Leave out any extraneous data and grand totals you don't want on the chart. Ideally, you should have column headings. The example below has *Product Name* and *Total Sales* as column headings.

	A	B
1	**Product Name**	**Total Sales**
2	Chai	$1,800.00
3	Beer	$3,400.00
4	Coffee	$4,600.00
5	Green Tea	$200.00
6	Tea	$1,400.00
7	Chocolate Biscuits Mix	$900.20
8	Scones	$1,000.00
9	Brownie Mix	$1,200.49
10	Cake Mix	$1,500.99
11	Granola	$400.00
12	Hot Cereal	$500.00
13	Chocolate	$1,200.75
14	Fruit Cocktail	$3,900.00
15	Pears	$100.30
16	Peaches	$1,000.50

10.1 Creating a Chart via the Quick Analysis Tool

The Quick Analysis tool appears as a button on the bottom-right of your selection when you select a range of data in Excel. The Quick Analysis button offers a host of features for quickly adding conditional formatting, totals, tables, charts, and Sparklines to your worksheet.

To generate a chart using the quick analysis tool:

1. Select the data range you want to use for your chart. The Quick Analysis button is displayed at the bottom-right of the selection.

2. Click on the Quick Analysis button and then click on **Charts**. You'll get a list of recommended charts.

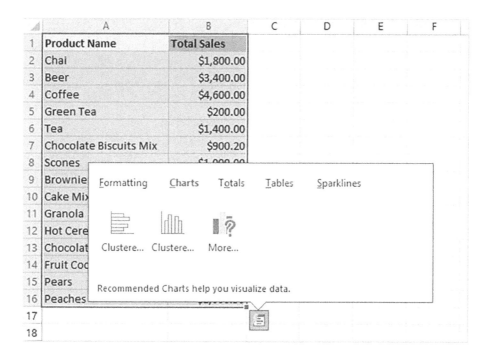

3. Click on the second option to generate a column chart.

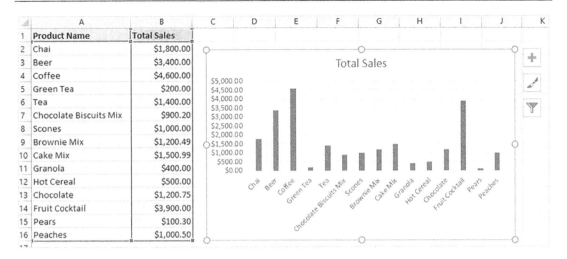

A floating chart will be created in the same worksheet as your data. You can click and drag this chart to another part of the screen if necessary.

To create another type of chart, like a pie chart, for example, you can click on the **More...** option on the Quick Analysis menu to show a list of all chart types.

Tip Another way to create a quick chart is to select the data and press the **F11** key to generate a chart of the default type on a new chart sheet. The default chart created would be the column chart unless you've changed the default chart. To create an embedded chart using this method (i.e. in the same worksheet as the data) press the **Alt + F1** keys together.

10.2 Creating a Chart via the Excel Ribbon

The **Charts** group in the Insert tab has several commands to create different types of charts. You can click on a chart type, for example, the pie chart icon, to display a list of charts options available for that chart type.

Alternatively, you can launch the **Insert Chart** dialog box that shows a list of all the chart types you can create in Excel.

To create a chart from the Insert Chart dialog box:

1. Select the range of data for your chart.

2. On the Ribbon, click on Insert > Recommended Charts > All Charts.

   The **Insert Chart** dialog box is displayed.

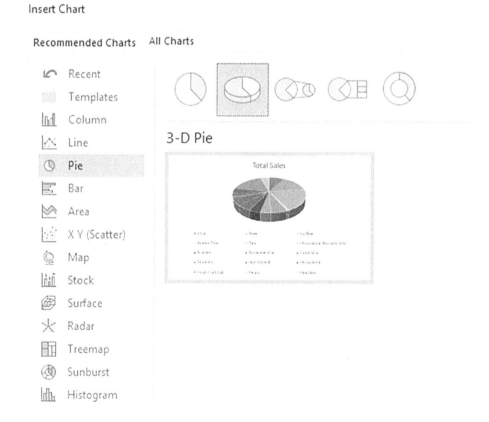

3. Select the type of chart you want to create from the list of charts on the left.

4. Click **OK**.

A floating chart will be created in the same worksheet as your data. You can click and drag this chart to another part of the screen if necessary.

To delete a chart, simply select the chart and press the **Delete** key.

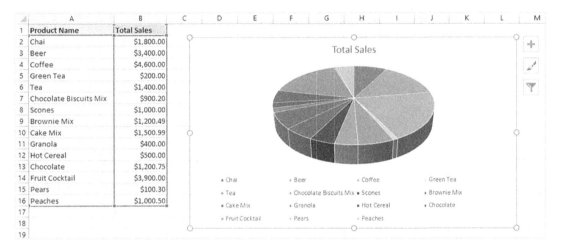

After creating the chart you'll get a new tab on the Ribbon called **Chart Design**. This tab provides many options to edit and style your chart. We will be covering editing the chart axis labels and style later in this chapter.

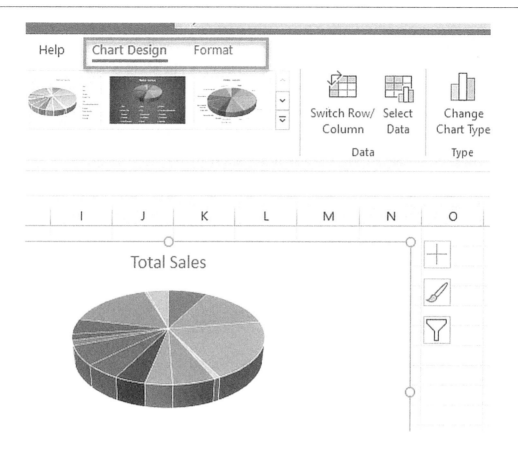

10.3 Customizing Charts

After creating a chart, you have several tools available for formatting and customizing the chart to your liking. For example, you can swap the axis, change/adjust the data source, update the chart title, adjust the layout, apply a chart style, and apply a theme colour to your chart.

To demonstrate some of these options, let's say we need to create a chart with four quarters of sales.

	A	B	C	D	E
1	Sales by Quarter				
2	Product	QTR1	QTR2	QTR3	QTR4
3	Chai	300	300	200	400
4	Beer	300	200	400	300
5	Coffee	350	400	500	500
6	Green Tea	250	150	100	300
7	Tea	100	400	100	500
8	Chocolate Biscu	320	200	100	300
9	Scones	250	500	200	100
10	Brownie Mix	350	400	550	200
11	Cake Mix	200	370	300	200
12	Granola	250	100	200	400
13	Hot Cereal	350	500	300	200
14	Chocolate	350	200	500	500
15	Fruit Cocktail	200	230	250	200
16	Pears	100	200	300	450
17	Peaches	200	300	200	600
18					

To create the chart:

1. Select the range with the data, including the column headers and row headers.

2. Click on **Insert > Recommended Charts.** You're presented with the **Insert Chart** dialog box with several chart recommendations for your data.

3. Select the **Clustered Column** option.

4. Click **OK**.

A chart will be created and added to your worksheet.

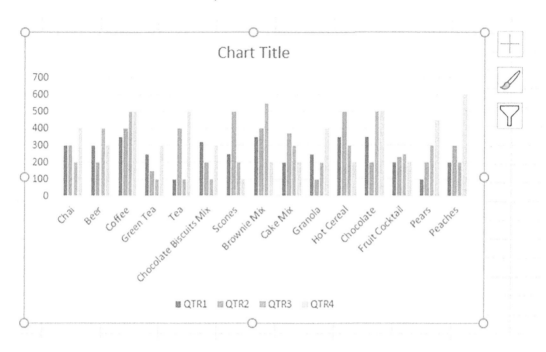

Switching the X and Y Axes

You can switch the values Excel applies to the vertical axis (also called the y-axis) and horizontal axis (also called the x-axis).

To switch the values applied to the axes:

1. Select the chart.

2. Click **Chart Design** > **Switch Row/Column**.

This will swap the values applied to the vertical and horizontal axes.

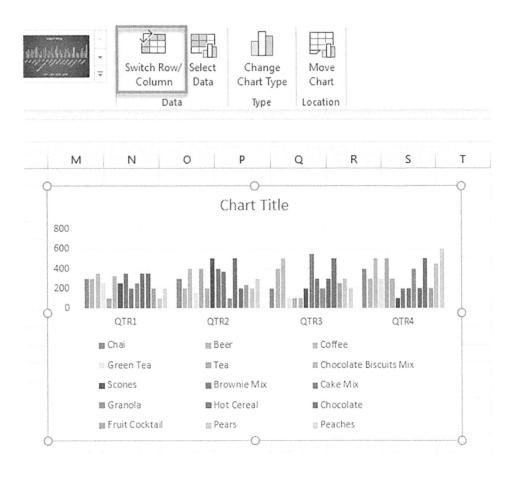

To swap the values back, simply click the **Switch Row/Column** button again.

Changing the Data Source

To change the data used as the source of the chart, do the following:

1. Click the **Select Data** button on the **Design** tab. The **Select Data Source** dialog box will be displayed.

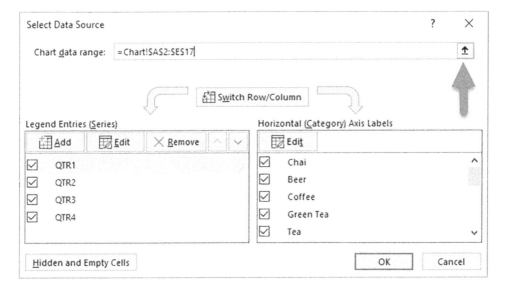

2. Select the up arrow that is on the **Chart data range** field. This will change it to a down-pointing arrow.

3. Select the cells you want in the worksheet area and click on the down-pointing arrow to return to the **Select Data Source** screen.

4. Click **OK** to confirm the change.

The new data source will now be used for the chart.

Adding Axis Titles

When you create a new chart, you'll see "Chart Title" as a placeholder that needs to be edited with the title of the chart. There are also no labels at the axis, and we may want to add them to the chart.

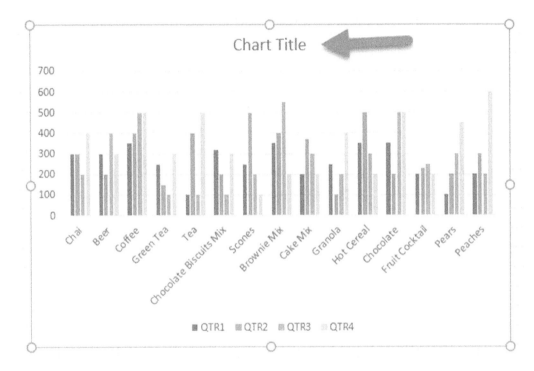

To change the **Chart Title,** you can simply click on it and type in the title. Alternatively, you can select the name from a field on your worksheet. For example, if we wanted our chart title to be *Sales by quarter,* which is in cell **A1** of our worksheet, we would click on the Chart Title label and in the formula bar, enter "**=A1**". This will use the value in cell A1 for our chart title.

We can also add titles down the left-hand side and at the bottom of the chart. These are called axis titles. The left side is the *y*-axis while the bottom is the *x*-axis.

To change the layout of your chart, click on **Chart Design** > **Quick Layout**.

You'll get a pop-up with several chart layouts. With the chart selected, you can mouseover each layout to view more details about it and get a preview of how your chart will look with that layout. A few of the options provide axis titles as well as moving the legend to the right of the chart. If you want a layout with both axis titles, then **Layout 9** would be a good pick.

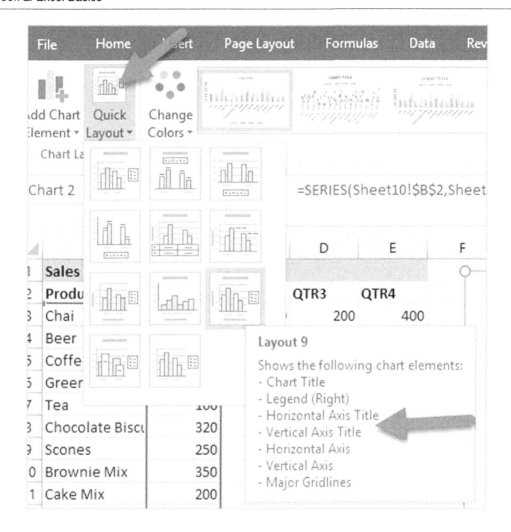

If we select **Layout 9**, we get a chart with labels that we can edit to add titles to the x-axis and y-axis.

You can edit the axis labels as described above. You can click on the labels and type in the text directly or pull the text from your worksheet area by typing in a cell reference, for example, **=A1**, assuming cell A1 as the text you want for that label.

Chart Styles

When you click on the chart, the **Chart Design** tab shows up on the Ribbon. On this tab, you have an array of **Chart Styles** you can choose from to change the look and colour of your chart.

To change the colour of the plot area:

1. Click on the plot area to select it (this is the centre of the chart) and it will be selected.

2. With the plot area selected, click on the **Format** tab on the Ribbon.

3. Click the drop-down button in the **Shape Styles** group.

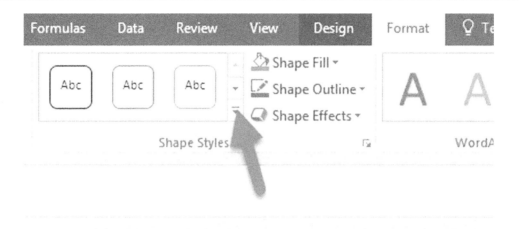

4. You'll get a pop-up with many **Theme Styles** to choose from for the format of the plot area. You can mouseover each one to see a preview of how your chart would look like if selected.

5. When you find the one you like, click on it to select it.

10.4 Creating Sparkline Charts

In the following example, we'll use the Quick Analysis tool to add sparklines to our worksheet. Sparklines are mini charts you can place in single cells to show the visual trend of your data. Excel 2019 allows you to quickly add Sparkline charts to your worksheet in a few steps.

Adding a Sparkline:

1. Select the data you want to create a Sparkline chart for. At the lower-right corner of the selection, you'll see the **Quick Analysis** tool.

2. Click on the Quick Analysis tool to open a pop-up menu of Quick Analysis options - **Formatting**, **Charts**, **Totals**, **Tables**, and **Sparklines**.

3. Click on Sparklines and then select one option from **Line**, **Column**, or **Win/Loss**.

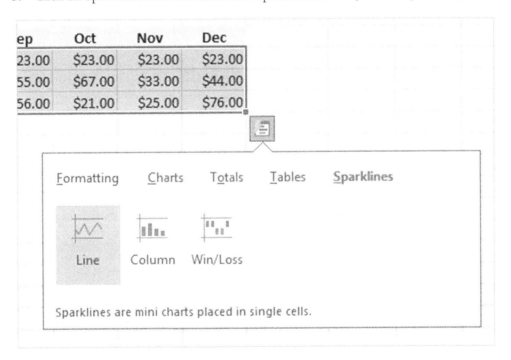

For this example, the **Line** option was selected. The sparklines will be created in the cells immediately to the right of the selected values.

	A	B	C	D	E	F	G	H	I	J	K	L	M	N
1	Expenses													
2		Jan	Feb	Mar	Apr	May	Jun	Jul	Aug	Sep	Oct	Nov	Dec	
3	Building 1	$45.00	$22.40	$33.70	$44.90	$21.90	$22.00	$10.00	$23.00	$23.00	$23.00	$23.00	$23.00	
4	Building 2	$31.00	$33.00	$32.00	$41.00	$31.00	$42.00	$11.00	$55.00	$55.00	$67.00	$33.00	$44.00	
5	Building 3	$34.00	$60.00	$21.00	$30.00	$55.00	$60.00	$23.00	$45.00	$56.00	$21.00	$25.00	$76.00	
6														

Formatting a Sparkline Chart

To format your Sparkline chart, click on it to select it.

On the Ribbon, click on the **Sparkline** tab. In the **Style** group, you'll see various options to edit and style your sparkline chart.

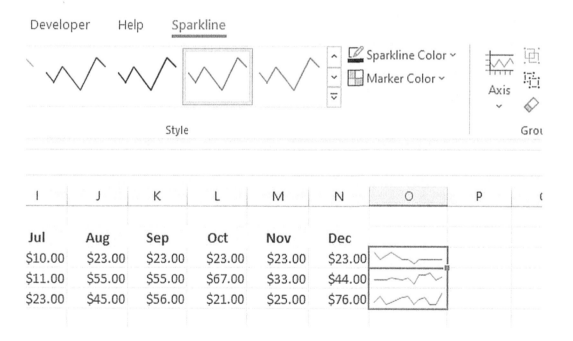

Use the following options to design your sparkline:

- On the Sparkline tab, click on **Line, Column,** or **Win/Loss** buttons to change the chart type.

- You can check **Markers** to highlight specific values in the Sparkline chart.

- You can select a different **Style** for the Sparkline.

- You can change the **Sparkline Color** and the **Marker Color**.

- Click on **Sparkline Color** > **Weight** to change the width of the Sparkline.

- Click on **Marker Color** to change the colour of the markers.

- Click on **Axis** to show the axis if the data has positive and negative values.

Chapter 11: Printing Your Worksheet

The world is increasingly becoming paperless, but on some occasions, you may need to print out a hardcopy of your worksheet. You may want to print it as part of a report or to present it to others. Excel provides a rich array of features that allow you to print your data in many ways.

In this chapter, we will cover how to:

- Select the page orientation for your printed document - portrait or landscape.
- Scale the width and length of the document.
- Set the Print Area so that you only print the data you want to see.
- Preview your document before printing to avoid printing blank pages.

Page Setup

Before you print your document, you may need to change some settings to get the page layout the way you want it. The **Page Setup** dialog box enables you to configure several page layout settings in one area.

To launch the Page Setup dialog box, click on the **Page Layout** tab, and in the **Page Setup** group, click on the dialog box launcher.

The Page Setup dialog box will be displayed.

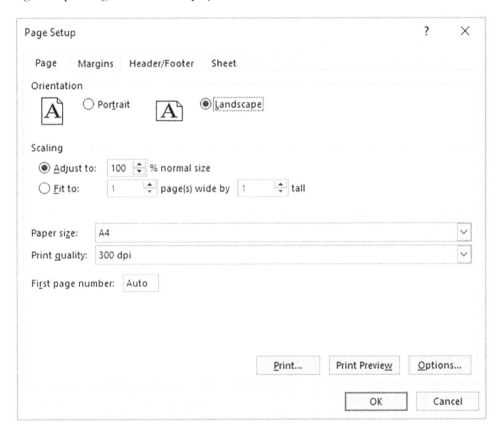

There are several settings on this page that you can configure to get the layout exactly how you want it for your printed document.

Orientation

On the **Page** tab, set the orientation to **Landscape**. This is best for printing worksheets unless you have specific reasons to use portrait.

Scaling

Under scaling you have two options:

1. **Adjust to:** This option enables you to scale the font size of your document up or down. 100% means it will print in normal size. For example, if the normal size of your content is larger than one page but you would like it to print as one page, you would reduce the percentage to less than 100%.

2. **Fit to:** This option enables you to choose how wide and how tall you want your document. So, for example, you may choose to fit the width to one page and have more than one page for the length.

Paper Size

The default paper size is A4. However, if you are printing to another paper size you can change it here.

Margins

On the Margins tab, you can change the size of the Top, Bottom, Left, and Right margins, including the size of the Header and Footer.

Header/Footer

You can insert a header or footer, e.g. a page number, in your document using this tab. You can either select an option from the drop-down list or enter a custom header/footer by clicking on **Custom Header** or **Custom Footer**.

When you're done, click **OK** to save your changes and close the Page Setup window.

Setting the Print Area

You need to set the Print Area so that unpopulated parts of the worksheet are not included in your print as this could result in blank pages. You can set the print area in the Page Setup screen, but it is easier to use the **Print Area** command button on the Excel Ribbon.

To set the print area:

1. Select the area in the worksheet that contains the data you want to print.

2. On the **Page Layout** tab, click on the **Print Area** button.

3. Select **Set Print Area**.

Note If you wish to clear the print area at any point, click on the Print Area button and select **Clear Print Area**.

Preview and Print Your Worksheet

Click on **File** to display the Backstage view, then click **Print** from the menu on the left.

This will display the Print screen. There are several settings you can adjust here to change the page layout, many of which are also available in the Page Setup screen.

The options on this screen are pretty much self-explanatory and similar for most Office applications. However, we'll touch on the ones you'll most likely need to set.

Printer

This option allows you to choose the printer you want to print to. If your printer is online (i.e. it has been configured in Windows and is turned on) then it will be available for selection here. You also have the option of printing to an electronic document like PDF, OneNote, Microsoft XPS Document Writer etc.

Settings

Print Active Sheets is the default. Leave this option selected if you want to print only the active worksheet. If your workbook has more than one worksheet and you want to print the entire workbook, then click on the drop-down list and select **Print Entire Workbook** from the list. If you have selected a range and you want to print only those cells, then use the **Print Selection** option.

The last option on this page is **scaling**. If you have not set the scale in the Page Setup dialog box, there are four predefined scaling options to choose from here.

- **No Scaling** - the document will be printed as it is with no scaling.

- **Fit Sheet on One Page** – all columns and rows in the print area will be scaled into one page.

- **Fit All Columns on One Page** – all the columns in the print area will be scaled down to fit one page, however, the rows can carry on into other pages.

-☼-Tip I find this option to be the most appropriate if you have many rows of data. Always try to scale the columns into one page, if possible, so that you can see a full row of data on one page.

- **Fit All Rows into One Page** – all rows in the print area will be scaled to fit one page, however, the columns can carry on into other pages.

Previewing Your Document

The right side of the screen provides a preview of how your printed document would look. If you have more than one page, use the navigation buttons at the bottom of the screen to view the other pages.

Note Always preview your document before printing it to ensure you're happy with the layout. This will save you a ton of ink and paper!

The other settings on the Print page are self-explanatory.

When you're happy with your settings and the preview, click on the **Print** button to print your document.

Book 2

Excel Advanced Topics

In Book 2

Excel Advanced Topics covers a selection of topics that will enable you to take advantage of more powerful tools in Excel to perform tasks that require more than a basic knowledge of Excel.

Contents at a Glance

Chapter 1: Working with Multiple Workbooks

There are occasions when you need to work with several open workbooks and Excel 2019 provides several features that make it easier to work with multiple windows.

In this chapter, we will cover how to:

- Switch between multiple open workbooks.
- View multiple workbooks side-by-side.
- Arrange all open workbooks on your screen.
- Split the screen of your worksheet.
- Move data between workbooks.
- Move worksheets between workbooks.

1.1 Managing Multiple Windows

To work with multiple workbooks, open the main one and then open all the others.

Switch Between Workbooks

To switch between workbooks, on the **View** tab, in the **Window** group, click **Switch Windows**. Select the workbook you want to switch to from the dropdown menu.

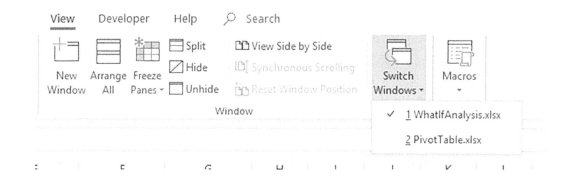

View Side-By-Side

To view worksheets from the different workbooks you've opened at the same time, you can manually arrange them on your screen or use an excel command to automatically tile them.

On the **View** tab, in the **Windows** group, click on the **View Side by Side** button. Toggle the **Side by Side** button to switch between a full screen of the active workbook and two workbooks.

If you have only two workbooks open, Excel will place the last one you opened above the earlier one. If you have more than two workbooks open, Excel will display the **Compare Side by Side** dialog box to allow you to select the workbook that you want to place side by side with the active one.

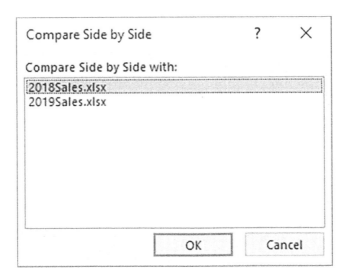

Arrange All

If you need to compare more than two workbooks on the same screen:

1. On the **View** tab, click the **Arrange All** button.

    The **Arrange Windows** dialog box will be displayed giving you the Arrange options of **Tiled**, **Horizontal**, **Vertical**, and **Cascading**.

2. Select one of the options, making sure you leave the **Windows of Active Workbook** unchecked and click **OK**.

New Window

To create a new window of the same document so that you can work in different places at the same time

On the **View** tab, in the **Window** group, click on the **New Window** button. This will open a new window of the same workbook (note that this does not create a new file).

To view the windows of the same workbook side-by-side:

1. On the **View** tab, in the Window group, click on the **Arrange All** button.
2. Select an Arrange option, for example, Vertical.
3. Click the **Windows of active workbook** checkbox to select it.
4. Click **OK** to complete the action and close the Arrange Windows dialog box.

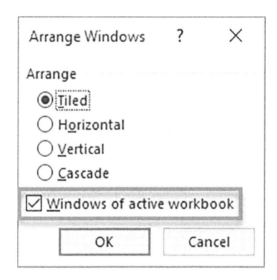

The windows of the same workbook will now the arranged side by side.

Split Screen

The split screen method allows you to split your worksheet so that you can see different parts of the worksheet in the same window. This comes in handy when you have a large amount of data and you would like to see different parts of the screen while working on the data.

To split the screen of a worksheet, do the following:

1. On the **View** tab, in the **Window** group, click on the **Split** button.

    A horizontal and vertical dividing line will split the screen into four parts with a scroll bar for each part. You can adjust the position of these dividers with your mouse pointer depending on how you want the layout.

2. To move a dividing line, for example, the horizontal one, place your mouse pointer over the divider and it will change to a double-headed arrow. You can now move the divider up or down, depending on how you want to view the split screen. You can do the same for the vertical line.

1.2 Moving Data Between Workbooks

There are two ways you can copy or move data between open workbooks.

Method 1

First, arrange the workbooks so that the worksheets you want to work with are visible side-by-side on the screen.

Select the range of cells in the source worksheet, then on the **Home** tab, click the **Copy** button (or press the **Ctrl+C** keys) to copy the data, or click the **Cut** button (or press the **Ctrl+X** keys) to move the data.

At the destination worksheet, select the top leftmost cell of the area where you want to paste the data and on the **Home** tab, click **Paste** (or press the **Ctrl+V** keys) to paste the data.

Method 2

The second method you can use to move or copy data between screens is to drag and drop the data from one workbook to the other.

Use the following steps to drag and drop data:

1. Select the data in the source worksheet.

2. Move the mouse pointer over the edge of the selected range until it turns into a crosshair (see image below).

$10,227	$8,343	$5,467	$9,?02
$13,263	$10,201	$6,199	$12,083
$13,680	$9,565	$14,089	$6,906
$5,610	$6,557	$5,756	$9,387
$11,335	$6,363	$5,980	$12,584
$10,214	$5,270	$11,708	$7,479
$5,746	$8,398	$6,390	$8,263
$5,594	$11,446	$7,794	$5,736
$14,537	$11,826	$8,848	$9,674
$9,118	$5,774	$7,533	$11,096
$13,417	$12,864	$13,032	$10,514
$6,573	$8,805	$13,254	$9,397

3. Once the pointer has changed to a crosshair, click and drag the selection to the other worksheet window.

4. At the destination worksheet window, you'll see a rectangle representing the area containing the data to be pasted. Drag it to the left topmost cell of the range where you want to place the data and release the mouse button.

Note   To copy the data instead of moving it, hold down the **Ctrl** key as you drag the data across to the other window.

5. After you release the mouse button, you may get a prompt that says: *"There's a problem with the clipboard, but you can still paste your content within this workbook."* Just click **OK** to dismiss the prompt and complete the action.

1.3 Moving Worksheets Between Workbooks

Method 1: Using Move or Copy

1. Open both the source workbook that contains worksheets to be moved or copied and the destination workbook where the worksheets will be placed. You need to open both the source and destination to copy or move worksheets between them.

2. On the **View** tab, use the **Arrange All** command to arrange the windows side-by-side, preferably using the **Vertical** option.

3. Click on the workbook with the worksheets that need to be moved or copied to activate it. Next, click on the sheet tab at the bottom of the screen to select it (to select more than one worksheet, hold down the **Ctrl** key as you click on the individual sheet tabs).

4. On the **Home** tab, click on the **Format** button and select **Move or Copy Sheet...** from the menu. This displays the **Move or Copy** dialog box.

5. In the Move or Copy dialog box, select the destination workbook in the **To Book** field. In the **Before sheet** field select where you want to place the worksheet inside the destination workbook.

   To create a copy of the worksheet, rather than move it, select the **Create a copy** checkbox.

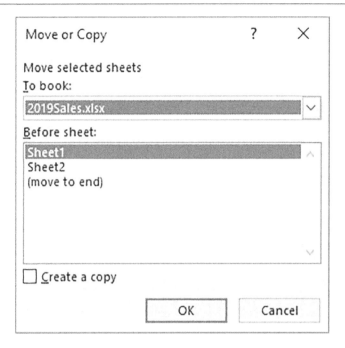

6.   Click **OK** to complete the move or copy action and close the dialog box.

Method 2: Using Drag and Drop

Just as you can copy data in a range between workbooks using drag-and-drop, you can also move or copy worksheets between workbooks using drag-and-drop.

To move or copy worksheets between workbooks using drag-and-drop do the following:

1.   Arrange the workbooks side-by-side so that you can see both on the screen. You can do this manually or use the **Arrange All** command described above. Preferably you should arrange them vertically.

2.   Click on the sheet tab in the destination workbook to select the worksheet to be moved or copied (to select more than one, hold down the **Ctrl** key as you click on the individual sheet tabs).

3.   Drag the sheet from the source workbook across to the destination workbook with your mouse. You'll see a little document icon representing the sheet you're moving.

Note   To copy the sheet (instead of moving it), hold down the **Ctrl** key as you drag the sheet from the source workbook to the destination workbook. The document icon will have a plus sign (+) if you're copying the sheet.

4. At the destination workbook, you'll see a small arrow, indicating where the sheet would be placed. You can move this arrow left and right to choose where you want to place the sheet before releasing the mouse button to place the sheet there.

This is a much faster way to move or copy worksheets between two open workbooks.

Chapter 2: Transform Data with Data Tools

In this chapter, we will cover how to use some of the data tools provided in Excel 2019 to quickly perform data organizing tasks.

In this chapter we will cover how to:

- Find and remove duplicate rows in your data.
- Find and delete blank rows in your data.
- Convert text to columns.
- Consolidate data from different worksheets into one worksheet.

2.1 Remove Duplicates

On some occasions, you may have a data set, for example, a list of customers you want to use for a mail merge. You want to make sure that you don't have duplicate records before you start the mail merge process so that you don't send the mail to the same customer more than once.

To remove duplicates in Excel, do the following:

1. Click in any cell in the range.
2. On the **Data** tab, in the **Data Tools** group, click on the **Remove Duplicates** button. The **Remove Duplicates** dialog box will be displayed.
3. Leave all the columns selected (if you want the full row checked against one another) and click on **OK**.
4. A message will be displayed telling you if any duplicates were found and how many records were deleted. Click **OK** to complete the process.

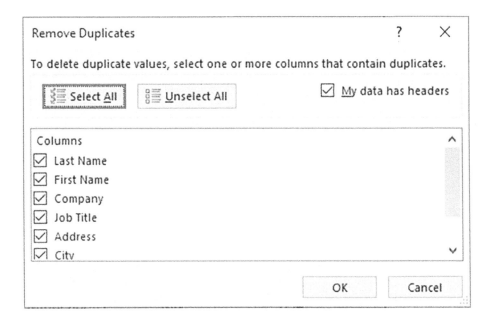

Note   You may have cases where you only want to use a few columns to check for duplicate records. For example, you may have more than one person on your list from the same address, but you only want each address once for the mail merge. In that case, in the Remove Duplicates dialog box, you should deselect all the other columns and only leave the columns you want to use to check for duplicates selected.

Tip You can also use the Power Query Editor to remove duplicate rows. See the section **Delete Blank Rows** below for how to open and use the Power Query Editor to transform your data.

2.2 Delete Blank Rows

There may be occasions when you have unnecessary blank rows in your data that you want to remove. If you have a large list with a lot of empty rows, it could be time-consuming to manually find and delete the empty rows. Thankfully, there are ways you can do this automatically. We will cover two methods for achieving this task here. The first will be using commands on the Excel Ribbon and the second method involves using the Power Query Editor, which has a command for deleting blank rows.

Method 1

There is no direct command for deleting blank rows on the Ribbon, but you can combine a couple of commands to achieve the task.

To delete blank rows, do the following:

1. Click on the **Home** tab, and then the **Find & Select** button in the Editing group.

2. Select **Go To Special** from the dropdown menu.

3. On the Go To Special screen select **Blanks** and click **OK.**

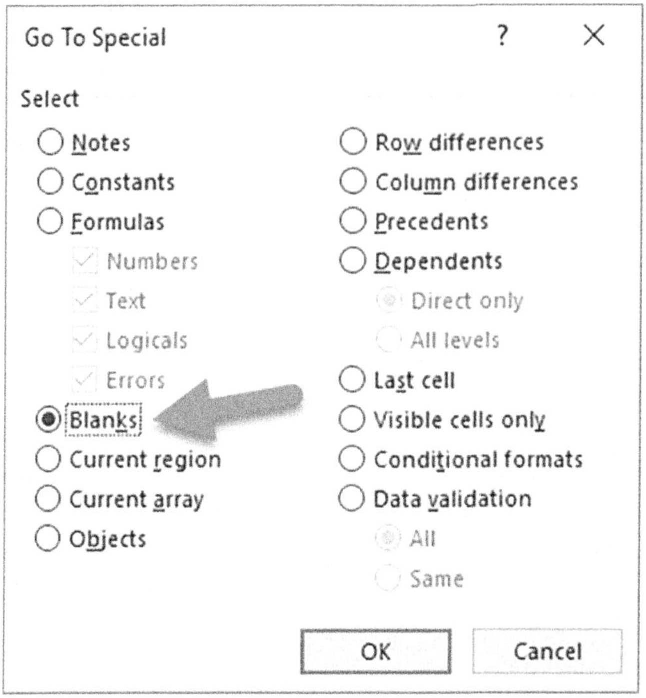

Excel will select the blank cells in the range.

	A	B	C	D	E
1		New York	Los Angeles	London	Paris
2	Jan	$547.00	$934.00	$412.00	$447.00
3	Feb	$880.00	$590.00	$961.00	$605.00
4	Mar	$717.00	$961.00	$460.00	$652.00
5					
6	Apr	$540.00	$542.00	$574.00	$754.00
7	May	$620.00	$497.00	$531.00	$462.00
8	Jun	$423.00	$874.00	$799.00	$699.00
9	Jul	$937.00	$755.00	$877.00	$446.00
10					
11	Aug	$683.00	$715.00	$792.00	$742.00
12	Sep	$633.00	$421.00	$877.00	$576.00
13	Oct	$551.00	$941.00	$675.00	$598.00
14	Nov	$680.00	$520.00	$867.00	$916.00
15	Dec	$766.00	$524.00	$401.00	$707.00

4. On the Home tab, in the Cells group, click **Delete** > **Delete Sheet Rows**.

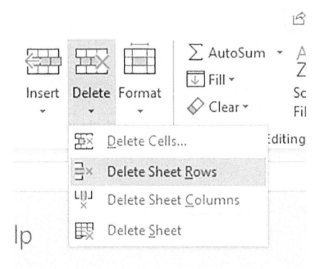

And that's it! This will delete all the rows that were identified and selected using the Go To Special command.

-ᄋᄼ-Tip
  If you mistakenly deleted rows that you don't want to delete, you can undo your changes by clicking the **Undo** button on the Quick Access Toolbar to reverse your changes.

Method 2

The second method involves using the Power Query Editor in Excel 2019.

To delete blank rows using the Power Query Editor, do the following:

1. Select the data list for which you want to remove blank rows.

-ᄋᄼ-Tip
  To quickly select a range, click on the top-left cell of the range, hold down the **Shift** key, and click on the bottom-right cell.

2. On the **Data** tab, in the **Get & Transform Data** group, click the **From Table/Range** command button.

   This will open and display your data in the **Power Query Editor**, which is a supplementary tool in Excel 2019 with a separate user interface and command buttons.

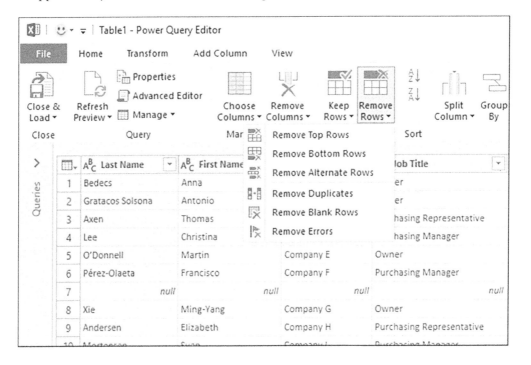

3. On the **Home** tab of the Power Query Editor, click the drop-down arrow on the **Remove Rows** command button, and select **Remove Blank Rows** from the drop-down menu.

    Excel deletes all the blank rows identified in the data list.

4. To save your transformed data, on the **Home** tab of the Power Query Editor, click the **Close & Load** command button to paste the transformed data in a new sheet in your workbook and close the Power Query Editor.

That's it! Your data list without the blank rows will now be in a new sheet with the original data list unchanged. Note that, among other commands, you can also use the Power Query Editor to remove duplicate rows.

2.3 Convert Text to Columns

If you work with a lot of data from different sources, there could be occasions where you receive a text file with values that are separated by commas. When you copy and paste the values in Excel, it would place them all in one column. You can separate these values into different columns using the text to columns command.

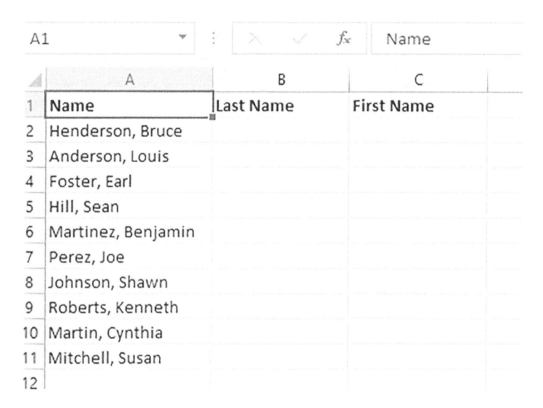

To convert delimited text values into separate columns, do the following:

1. Select the range that contains the text you want to split.

2. On the **Data** tab click on **Text to Columns**.

3. In the Convert Text to Columns Wizard, select **Delimited** and click on **Next**.

4. Select the **Delimiters** for your data. For our example (above), the delimiters are **Comma** and **Space**. You also have the options of Tab, Semicolon, and Other, which allows you to specify the delimiter if it's not one of the default options.

The **Data preview** portion of the screen shows you a preview of how your data would look after the conversion.

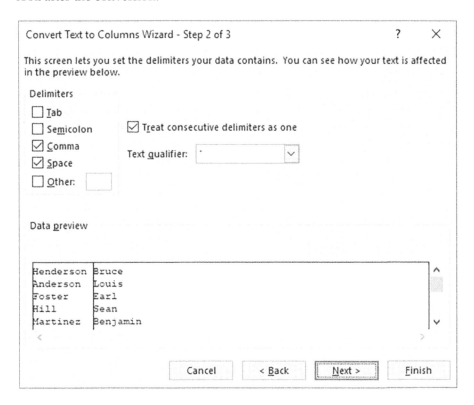

5. Click on **Next**.

6. At the next screen, select the **Column data format** or use what Excel chooses for you.

7. In the **Destination** field, click the up arrow, and on your worksheet, select the top leftmost cell where you want the split data to appear. The cell reference for the destination will be entered in the field.

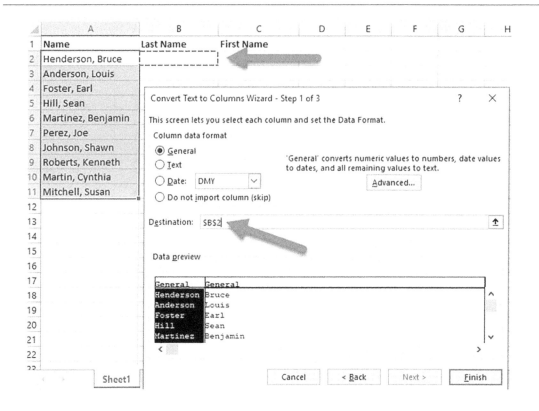

8. Click on **Finish**.

The delimited text will now be split into different columns. You can delete the initial column with the original text from the worksheet or move it to another sheet if you want to keep it.

	A	B	C
1	Name	Last Name	First Name
2	Henderson, Bruce	Henderson	Bruce
3	Anderson, Louis	Anderson	Louis
4	Foster, Earl	Foster	Earl
5	Hill, Sean	Hill	Sean
6	Martinez, Benjamin	Martinez	Benjamin
7	Perez, Joe	Perez	Joe
8	Johnson, Shawn	Johnson	Shawn
9	Roberts, Kenneth	Roberts	Kenneth
10	Martin, Cynthia	Martin	Cynthia
11	Mitchell, Susan	Mitchell	Susan
12			

2.4 Data Consolidation

Data consolidation provides an easy way to combine data from multiple worksheets in a single worksheet. You can consolidate data from different worksheets in the same workbook, different workbooks, or a combination of both. The process allows you to select the ranges you want to add to the consolidation from different sources and Excel will aggregate the data in another workbook.

To consolidate data, all the ranges to be included in the consolidation must be of the same shape and size. For example, let's say we have sales data from 2017 to 2019 that we want to consolidate from three worksheets into one worksheet named **Sales for 2017 – 2019**.

	A	B	C	D	E
1	Sales for 2017 - 2019				
2		New York	Los Angeles	London	Paris
3	Jan				
4	Feb				
5	Mar				
6	Apr				
7	May				
8	Jun				
9	Jul				
10	Aug				
11	Sep				
12	Oct				
13	Nov				
14	Dec				

The three workbooks we will be consolidating the data from are:

- 2017Sales.xlsx
- 2018Sales.xlsx
- 2019Sales.xlsx

To consolidate cell ranges from the three workbooks:

1. First, you need to open the destination workbook, that is, the workbook into which you want to consolidate your data. In our example, it will be 2017_2019Sales.xlsx.

2. Open the source workbooks, that is, the workbooks supplying the data you want to consolidate. For our example, the source workbooks are the three workbooks listed above.

3. Switch to the workbook into which you want to consolidate your data. Click on the **Data** tab and click the **Consolidate** button in the **Data Tools** group.

    The Consolidate dialog box will be displayed.

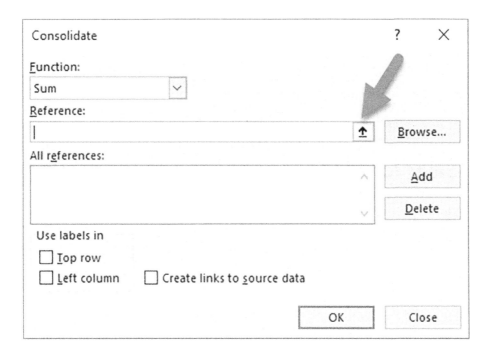

4. On the **Reference** field, click the **Collapse Dialog** button (at the right edge of the field) to collapse the dialog box. When you click this button, it will minimise the Consolidate dialog box.

5. Now you need to select the range from the first worksheet. On the **View** tab, in the **Window** group, click **Switch Windows**. This will display a list of all open workbooks.

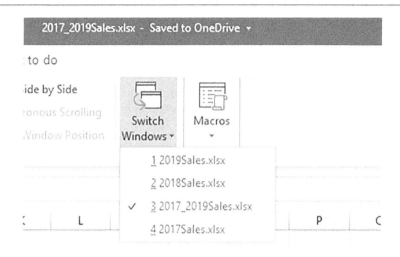

6. Click the first workbook that contains data you want to include in your consolidation. This will make the workbook the active window.

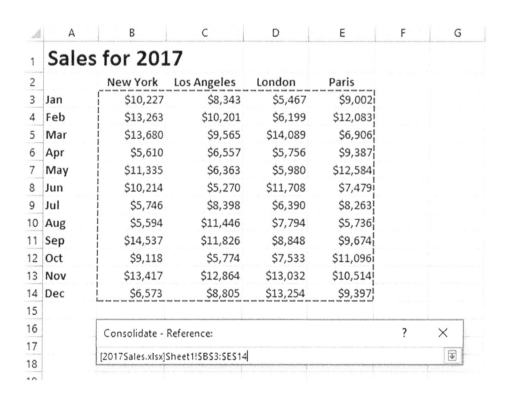

7. Select the cells you want to consolidate, then click the **Expand Dialog** button to return the Consolidate dialog box to its full size.

8. Click **Add** to add the selected range to the **All references** list box.

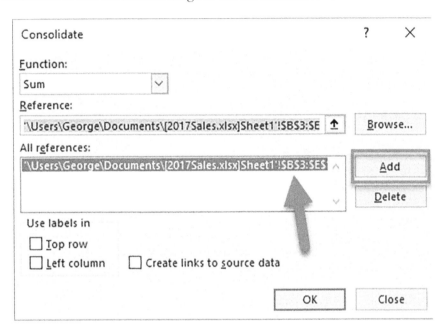

9. Repeat the steps 4 to 8 above to add additional ranges to the consolidation. These ranges can come from different workbooks or different worksheets in the same workbook. For our example, these would be from *2018Sales.xlsx* and *2019Sales.xlsx*.

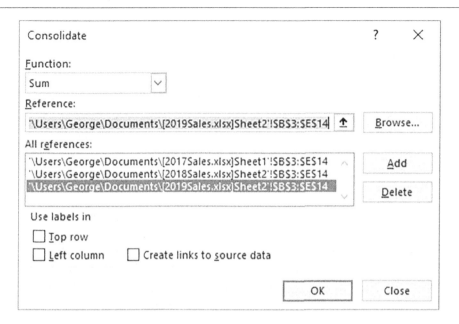

10. The default function used to aggregate the data in the consolidated workbook is **Sum**. You can change this to another function like Count or Average, for example, by clicking the **Function** drop-down list and selecting a different function.

11. Click **OK** when you've added all the ranges to be consolidated.

	A	B	C	D	E
1	**Sales for 2017 - 2019**				
2		New York	Los Angeles	London	Paris
3	Jan	$29,515	$27,631	$29,693	$19,726
4	Feb	$33,126	$30,064	$18,811	$26,229
5	Mar	$38,592	$34,477	$41,211	$30,876
6	Apr	$18,162	$22,023	$18,734	$22,527
7	May	$31,523	$29,097	$20,000	$25,832
8	Jun	$35,671	$23,079	$24,754	$36,707
9	Jul	$28,859	$34,226	$26,289	$27,339
10	Aug	$18,148	$39,842	$29,510	$29,486
11	Sep	$26,687	$32,604	$24,378	$33,720
12	Oct	$38,590	$19,248	$26,325	$29,174
13	Nov	$23,903	$30,672	$35,400	$38,724
14	Dec	$20,449	$33,015	$24,878	$24,997

Each cell in the consolidated data will now hold the sum for that cell from all the other worksheets.

Chapter 3: Using External Data

When working with Excel, you often have situations when you have to import data from other applications into Excel. The most common are comma-separated files (CSV) or some other form of delimitation.

In this chapter, we will cover how to import data into Excel from:

- A Microsoft Access database.
- A delimited text file, for example, a CSV file.
- A website with constantly changing live data, for example, Forex data.

3.1 Importing Data from Microsoft Access

To import data from an Access Database, do the following:

1. Click on the **Data** tab, in the **Get & Transform Data** group, click **Get Data**, then select **From Database** > **From Microsoft Access Database**.

2. At the **Import Data** dialog box, navigate to the Access database (this will usually be an *.accdb or *.mdb file) and then click the **Import** button.

   The **Navigator** dialog box is displayed. This dialog box is divided into two panes: On the left, there is a list of tables and queries and on the right, there is a preview. When you click an item on the left pane, a preview is displayed on the right showing the fields in the table.

   To import more than one table from the selected Access database, click the **Select Multiple Items** checkbox on the left pane. Excel will then display check boxes against each item on the list, which allows you to select more than one table from the list.

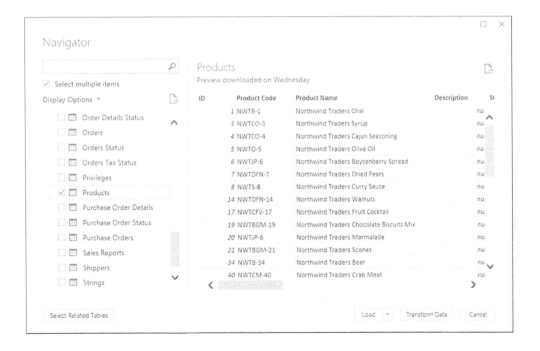

3. After you've selected the table(s) you want to import, click on the **Load** button to import the data. It will be imported into a new worksheet as an Excel table with all the Table tools available.

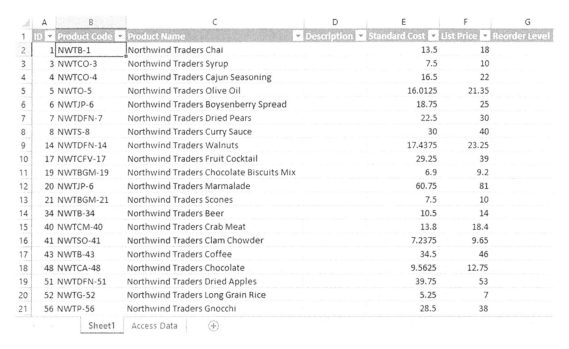

ID	Product Code	Product Name	Description	Standard Cost	List Price	Reorder Level
1	NWTB-1	Northwind Traders Chai		13.5	18	
3	NWTCO-3	Northwind Traders Syrup		7.5	10	
4	NWTCO-4	Northwind Traders Cajun Seasoning		16.5	22	
5	NWTO-5	Northwind Traders Olive Oil		16.0125	21.35	
6	NWTJP-6	Northwind Traders Boysenberry Spread		18.75	25	
7	NWTDFN-7	Northwind Traders Dried Pears		22.5	30	
8	NWTS-8	Northwind Traders Curry Sauce		30	40	
14	NWTDFN-14	Northwind Traders Walnuts		17.4375	23.25	
17	NWTCFV-17	Northwind Traders Fruit Cocktail		29.25	39	
19	NWTBGM-19	Northwind Traders Chocolate Biscuits Mix		6.9	9.2	
20	NWTJP-6	Northwind Traders Marmalade		60.75	81	
21	NWTBGM-21	Northwind Traders Scones		7.5	10	
34	NWTB-34	Northwind Traders Beer		10.5	14	
40	NWTCM-40	Northwind Traders Crab Meat		13.8	18.4	
41	NWTSO-41	Northwind Traders Clam Chowder		7.2375	9.65	
43	NWTB-43	Northwind Traders Coffee		34.5	46	
48	NWTCA-48	Northwind Traders Chocolate		9.5625	12.75	
51	NWTDFN-51	Northwind Traders Dried Apples		39.75	53	
52	NWTG-52	Northwind Traders Long Grain Rice		5.25	7	
56	NWTP-56	Northwind Traders Gnocchi		28.5	38	

Sheet1 | Access Data | (+)

The Navigator dialog box also provides other options for uploading the Access data:

Transform Data

At the bottom of the Navigator dialog box, there is a **Transform Data** button. When you click this button, it will open the **Excel Power Query Editor**, which provides several tools that enable you to transform the data before you import it. For example, you may choose to import only some columns or use a query to select only some of the data.

Load To

For more load options, at the bottom of the Navigator screen, click the **Load** button's drop-down menu, then click the **Load To** menu item to open the **Import Data** dialog box.

This box allows you to import the Access data as:

- An Excel Table (default)
- A PivotTable
- A PivotChart
- Only a connection to the database.

You can also choose to import the data into an existing worksheet or a new worksheet (default).

3.2 Importing Text files

As Excel stores data in cells, the text files you can import need to have a way of separating the content into different cells. The character that marks this separation is called a *delimiter* because it marks the "limit" of a value.

The most common delimiter used for text files is the comma. For example, you may have the sequence 200, 400, 100, 900 to represent data in four cells. The text files that use a comma as a delimiter are called comma-separated values (CSV) files.

There are occasions when text files need to use different delimiters when a comma might not be an appropriate delimiter. For example, using a comma delimiter may present a problem for financial figures (like $100,000) because commas are part of the values. Hence some financial data programs export their data by using the tab character as a delimiter and these files are referred to as Tab-delimited files.

Follow the steps below to import a text data file into Excel:

1. Click on the **Data** tab, in the **Get & Transform Data** group, select **From File**, then click **From Text/CSV**. This displays the Navigator screen.

   The Navigator examines the data in the text or CSV file and attempts to correctly split it up into separate columns for the worksheet based on the delimiter it identifies as the separator, for example, a comma or a tab.

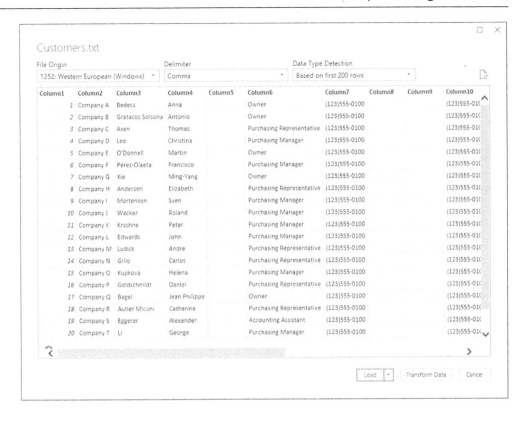

2. As depicted in the image above, on top of the Navigator screen you have three fields. For anything other than complex data requiring advanced knowledge, you should leave **File Origin** and **Data Type Detection** at their default values. The **Delimiter** drop-down list identifies the delimiter used in the text file. If this has been wrongly identified, for example, if your file is a Tab delimited file then you can select a different delimiter from the drop-down list.

3. If Excel correctly parsed the data in your text file as shown in the Navigator's preview, you can then select one of the following options to import the data into your worksheet.

   At the bottom of the screen, you have three options for uploading the data:

   - The **Load** button imports the data as seen in the Navigator preview into your workbook (in a new worksheet).

   - The **Load To** option (on the Load button's drop-down menu) gives you more options for how you want to import the data and where to place the data. The Load To dialog box is discussed above under importing data from Microsoft Access.

- The **Transform Data** button opens the data in the **Excel Power Query Editor**. This enables you to query and transform the data before importing it. For example, you may want to import only a few of the columns in the data set or data that meet some criteria. Transform data allows you to remove the columns you don't want to import.

Tip

If you only want a subset of the data, instead of using **Transform Data**, you can also import the full data into Excel and delete the columns you don't want within Excel.

Using the Convert Text to Columns Wizard

Occasionally, Excel may be unable to correctly parse the data into separate columns even after you change the Delimiter, File Origin, and Data Type Detection. If Excel still insists on importing each row as a single column, you can still import the data and use the **Text to Columns** tool in Excel to split the values into separate columns.

After importing the data into Excel, follow the steps below to split the data into separate columns:

1. In your worksheet, select the cells with the imported data.

2. On the **Data** tab, in the **Data Tools** group, click on the **Text to Columns** button.

   This will open the **Convert Text to Columns Wizard - Step 1 of 3** dialog box.

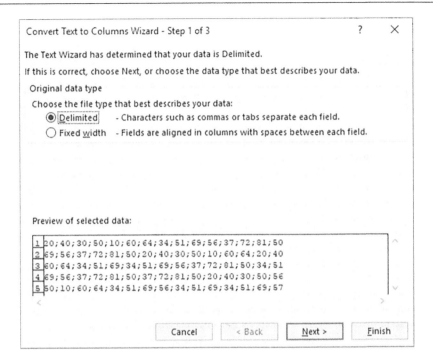

3. On step 1 of the wizard, choose between the **Delimited** and **Fixed width** option, depending on how your data is separated, then click the **Next** button to go to step 2.

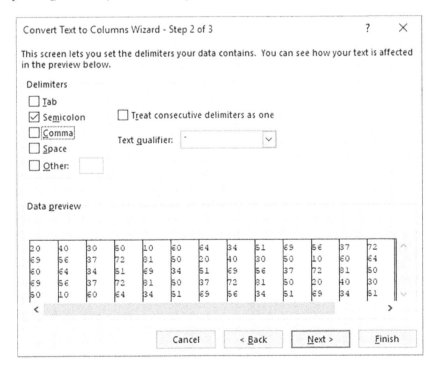

4. If you selected the Delimited option in Step 1 of the wizard, then In Step 2, under the **Delimiters** section, select the delimiting character for your text file. In the example above, the delimiter for our data is a semicolon.

5. If the delimiting character used in your text file is not any of the offered options under Delimiters, then select **Other** and enter the character in its text box. If your file uses more than one delimiting character, for example, a comma and a space, you need to select all their checkboxes including the **Treat Consecutive Delimiters As One** checkbox.

6. By default, the Convert Text to Columns Wizard treats characters enclosed in double-quotes as text entries and not numbers. If your text file uses single quotes, then you would select it from the **Text Qualifier** drop-down list.

    Fixed width files: If your file is a fixed-width separated file and you selected the Fixed width option in step 1 of the wizard, then in step 2, you'll see a preview that allows you to determine the column breaks by clicking in the text area to create column lines. You can drag and resize these column lines to match the column breaks in the text.

7. When you're happy with the preview of the text in step 2, click the **Next** button to go to step 3 of the wizard.

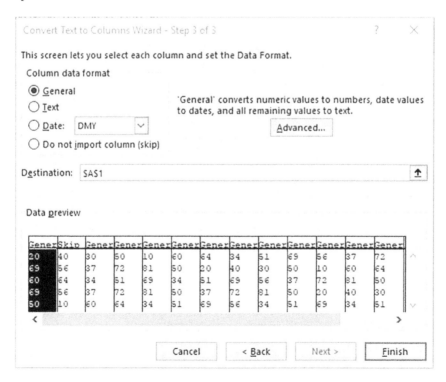

8. In step 3 of the process, you can click on each column in the preview area and select different settings for importing the data under **Column data format**. You can choose between the **General** (default), **Text**, and **Date** data formats, or skip importing the column altogether by selecting **Do not import column (skip)**.

-☼-Tip

You can always import the data using the **General** data format and change the data format within Excel for the columns you want to change.

9. The **Destination** field shows you the top-leftmost cell of the range where the text will be placed. If you want it in a different part of the worksheet then select a different destination by clicking on the up-arrow on the right of the field.

10. Once you're done, click on **Finish** to convert the data.

Excel splits the entries in the imported text file into separate columns in place of the previous data. You can now set the data format (if you didn't do that during the conversion) and adjust the column widths.

-☼-Tip

You can directly open some CSV files in Excel and convert them to Excel workbooks. If CSV files are associated with Excel on your computer, you can double click on the file to open it in Excel. Alternatively, you can open the file from within Excel even if the CSV extension is not associated with Excel on your PC. Once you have the file open in Excel and the data is displayed properly, you can then save the file as an Excel workbook.

3.3 Importing Data from a Website

To import data from the web, you first need to identify the web address (URL) of the website with the data you want to import. Then you can use the import tools in Excel to import the data directly from the webpage into your worksheet.

Let's say we want to import currency exchange rates from the web into our worksheet.

Below is how the data looks on the website after we've used the filters on the website to narrow down our search and display the data we want. We can now use this URL to import the data tables on the website.

https://www.xe.com/currencytables/?from=USD&date=2019-05-17

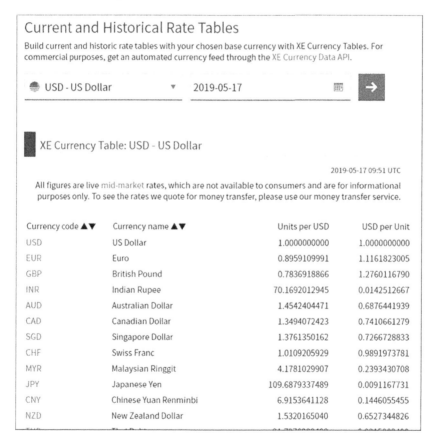

Current and Historical Rate Tables

Build current and historic rate tables with your chosen base currency with XE Currency Tables. For commercial purposes, get an automated currency feed through the XE Currency Data API.

USD - US Dollar ▼	2019-05-17 📅	→

XE Currency Table: USD - US Dollar

2019-05-17 09:51 UTC

All figures are live mid-market rates, which are not available to consumers and are for informational purposes only. To see the rates we quote for money transfer, please use our money transfer service.

Currency code ▲▼	Currency name ▲▼	Units per USD	USD per Unit
USD	US Dollar	1.0000000000	1.0000000000
EUR	Euro	0.8959109991	1.1161823005
GBP	British Pound	0.7836918866	1.2760116790
INR	Indian Rupee	70.1692012945	0.0142512667
AUD	Australian Dollar	1.4542404471	0.6876441939
CAD	Canadian Dollar	1.3494072423	0.7410661279
SGD	Singapore Dollar	1.3761350162	0.7266728833
CHF	Swiss Franc	1.0109205929	0.9891973781
MYR	Malaysian Ringgit	4.1781029907	0.2393430708
JPY	Japanese Yen	109.6879337489	0.0091167731
CNY	Chinese Yuan Renminbi	6.9153641128	0.1446055455
NZD	New Zealand Dollar	1.5320165040	0.6527344826

On the **Data** tab, in the **Get & Transform Data** group, click on the **From Web** button. Alternatively, on the Data tab, navigate to **Get Data** > **From Other Sources** > **From Web**.

Excel then opens the **From Web** dialog box with a URL field where you enter the address of the web page containing the data you want to import into Excel.

When you click **OK**, Excel will establish a connection to the website.

Note If this is the first time you've connected to the website, Excel may display an **Access Web-content** dialog box with different connection options. Connect with the default which is **Anonymous**.

Once connected, Excel will display the **Navigator** screen, listing the data tables on the Selection pane on the left. When you click on a table in the Selection pane the data is displayed on the preview pane on the right.

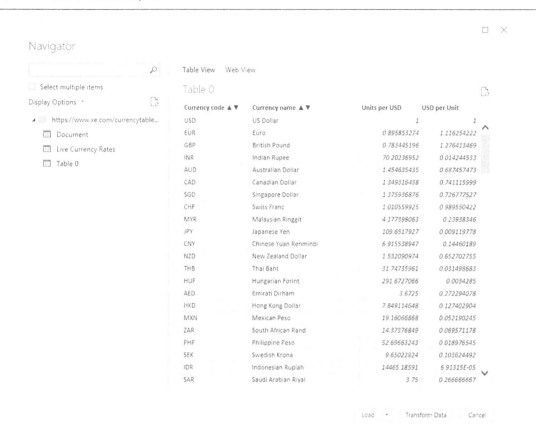

To import more than one table of data from the web page, select the **Select Multiple Items** check box and then click the checkboxes against the table names you want to import.

Once you've selected the table(s) you want to import on the page, you have the following three import options:

- The **Load** button imports the data as seen in the Navigator preview pane into your workbook (in a new worksheet).

- The **Load To** option (on the Load button's drop-down menu) opens the **Import Data** dialog box which gives you more options for how you want to import the data and where to place it. You can choose to import it as a worksheet data Table, Pivot Table, Pivot Chart, or to just establish a data connection without importing the data. You can also choose the worksheet where you want to place the data.

- The **Transform Data** button opens the data in the **Excel Power Query Editor**, which allows you to query and transform the data before importing it. For example, you may want to import only some of the data columns or filter the data with a criterion to only import a subset of the data.

After importing the data, you can manipulate and work with the data as you would with any other Excel table.

Refreshing Web Data

When working with tables imported from websites with live data, for example, financial websites like the Nasdaq or Dow Jones (while the markets are still open), you can refresh the data to reflect any changes in the data. When you import the data, Excel automatically stores information about the connection, so you just need one button click to refresh the data.

To refresh data imported from a website, on the **Data** tab, in the **Queries & Connections** group, click on the **Refresh All** button. This will automatically re-establish the connection and refresh the imported data with the latest data from the website.

3.4 Other Database Sources

Apart from Microsoft Access, the **Get Data** command on the **Data** tab also enables you to import data from a variety of database sources including:

- **From SQL Server Database:** To import data or create a connection to an SQL Server database.

- **From Analysis Services**: To import data from an SQL Server Analysis cube.

- **From SQL Server Analysis Services Database (Import)**: This is to import data from an SQL server database with the option to use an MDX or DAX query.

Chapter 4: Troubleshoot and Fix Formula Errors

Errors in simple Excel formulas are usually caused by syntax issues that can be easily fixed by correcting the syntax. For example, Excel may generate an error because a formula is missing a parenthesis and to fix the error you simply add the parenthesis to the syntax. On the other hand, a complex formula, for example, a nested formula with several levels, may not generate an error but fail to produce the expected result. This is called a logical error and they can be difficult to find.

Programming tools tend to have debuggers that can be used to step through the code to identify and fix logical errors. Fortunately, Excel 2019 provides several tools that you can use to step through complex formulas to troubleshoot and fix logical errors.

In this chapter, we will cover how to:

- Use Trace commands to trace the precedents and dependents in your formula values to identify the relationships between the results and cell references.

- Step through a nested formula one level at a time to see the evaluated result at each level.

- Use the Watch Window to display the value of a cell even when the cell is not in view.

4.1 Trace Precedents and Dependents

To help with troubleshooting your formula, you can use the **Trace Precedents** and **Trace Dependents** commands to show the relationships between the formula and any precedent or dependent cells using tracer arrows.

Note   The Trace commands on the Excel Ribbon are enabled by default. However, if they are disabled on your system, you need to enable them in Excel Options.

To enable Trace commands in **Excel Options**, do the following:
1. Click on **File** > **Options** > **Advanced**.
2. Scroll down to the section **Display options for this workbook** and select the workbook (if it is not already selected).
3. Under the **For objects, show** setting, select **All**.

Precedent cells are cells that are referred to by a formula in another cell. For example, if cell C2 contains the formula =A2+B2, then cells A2 and B2 are precedents to cell C2.

Dependent cells are cells that contain formulas that refer to other cells. For example, if cell C2 contains the formula =A2+B2, then cell C2 is a dependent of cells A2 and B2.

To Trace Precedents, do the following:

1. Select the cell that contains the formula that you want to trace.

2. On the **Formulas** tab, in the **Formula Auditing** group, click the **Trace Precedents** command button. This will display a tracer arrow to each cell or range that directly provides data to the active cell (cell with the formula).

| I15 | | | | | f_x | =SUM(B2:B13,D2:D13,F2:F13,H2:H13) |

	A	B	C	D	E	F	G	H	I	J
1	Month	Store1		Store2		Store3		Store4		
2	Jan	$547.00		$934.00		$412.00		$447.00		
3	Feb	$880.00		$590.00		$961.00		$605.00		
4	Mar	$717.00		$961.00		$460.00		$652.00		
5	Apr	$540.00		$542.00		$574.00		$754.00		
6	May	$620.00		$437.00		$531.00		$462.00		
7	Jun	$423.00		$874.00		$799.00		$699.00		
8	Jul	$937.00		$755.00		$877.00		$446.00		
9	Aug	$683.00		$715.00		$792.00		$742.00		
10	Sep	$633.00		$421.00		$877.00		$576.00		
11	Oct	$551.00		$941.00		$675.00		$598.00		
12	Nov	$680.00		$520.00		$867.00		$916.00		
13	Dec	$766.00		$524.00		$401.00		$707.00		
14										
15	Total								$32,081.00	

Blue arrows will show cells without errors while red arrows will show cells that cause errors. If the formula has references to a cell in another worksheet or workbook, a black arrow will point from the formula cell to a worksheet icon. If cells are referenced in other workbooks, they must be open before Excel can trace those dependencies.

3. If there are more levels of cells that provide data to the formula click on the Trace Precedents again.

To Trace Dependents, follow these steps:

1. Select the cell that contains the formula for which you want to trace dependents.

2. On the **Formulas** tab, in the **Formula Auditing** group, click **Trace Dependents**. This will display a tracer arrow to each cell that is dependent on the active cell.

3. To identify further levels of dependent cells, click Trace Dependents again.

Removing Tracer Arrows

To remove all tracer arrows, on the **Formulas** tab, in the **Formula Auditing** group, click the arrow next to **Remove Arrows**.

To remove only the precedent or dependent arrows, click on the down-arrow next to **Remove Arrows** and select **Remove Precedent Arrows** or **Remove Dependent Arrows** from the drop-down list. If you have more than one level of tracer arrows, click the button again.

4.2 Evaluate a Formula

Sometimes formulas can be complex, for example, a nested formula with several nested levels. Knowing how the formula is arriving at the final result may become difficult if there are several intermediate calculations and logical tests. Formulas that fail to produce the desired result may include logical errors that are difficult to spot at first glance.

The good news is, Excel has a tool called **Evaluate Formula** that allows you to step through a complex formula so you can see how the different levels of the formula are being evaluated, what the logical tests are doing, and the results being reached at each level. This will enable you to identify and resolve any logical errors in the syntax.

Example

In this example, we'll use the Evaluate Formula command to evaluate the following formula:

=IF(AVERAGE(E1:E8)>50,SUM(F1:F8),0)

The formula says:

If the average of E1:E8 is greater than 50, then sum F1:F8 in cell F9.

The way nested functions work is that the inner functions are evaluated first, then the results are used as input for the outer functions. With the Evaluate Formula command, we want to see the breakdown of the results of the individual evaluations before the formula returns the final result.

The data being evaluated is shown in the image below.

=IF(AVERAGE(E1:E8)>50,SUM(F1:F8),0)

E	F	G	H
45	47		
74	30		
26	40		
39	30		
30	77		
72	79		
28	48		
68	29		
	0		

Follow the steps below to evaluate a formula:

1. Select the cell that you want to evaluate. In our example, it would be cell **F9**. Note that only one cell can be evaluated at a time.

2. On the **Formulas** tab, in the **Formula Auditing** group, click on the **Evaluate Formula** button. This will open the Evaluate Formula dialog box.

First, we see the nested formula in the **Evaluation** box with the AVERAGE and SUM functions nested within the IF function.

=IF(AVERAGE(E1:E8)>50,SUM(F1:F8),0)

3. Click **Evaluate** to examine the underlined part of the formula. The result of the evaluation will be shown in italics.

=IF(47.75>50,SUM(F1:F8),0)

The average for the values in range F1:F8 is 47.75, so AVERAGE(F1:F8) returns that figure.

Note If the underlined part is a reference to another formula rather than a value, click **Step In** to show the other formula in the Evaluation box. Step Out takes you back to the previous cell and formula.

4. When you click on Evaluate again, you'll see the result of the logical test, which is false in this case =IF(False,SUM(F1:F8),0).

47.75 is not greater than 50, so the expression in the first argument of the IF function returns FALSE.

5. When you click on **Evaluate** again, you'll get 0 (zero) which is the final result returned by the IF function. The SUM function is not evaluated because the IF function executes the statement in the second argument only if the first argument evaluates to TRUE.

6. To go through the evaluation again, click **Restart**.

7. To end the evaluation, click **Close**.

Note Some functions are recalculated each time the worksheet changes, hence the Evaluate Formula tool could give results different from what appears in the cell. The following functions may not work well with Evaluate Formula: RAND, OFFSET, CELL, INDIRECT, NOW, TODAY, RANDBETWEEN, INFO, SUMIF (in some scenarios).

4.3 Using the Watch Window

Another way to troubleshoot logical errors in formulas is to use the **Watch Window** toolbar in Excel. You can use the Watch Window to inspect formula calculations and results in large worksheets. With the Watch Window, you don't need to continually scroll or go to different parts of your worksheet to see different results.

The Watch Window toolbar can be moved or docked like other toolbars in Excel. For example, you can move it and dock it at the bottom of the window. To undock the Watch Window toolbar, click on the top part of it and drag it up from the docking position.

The toolbar keeps track of the following properties of a cell: workbook, worksheet, name, cell reference, the value in the cell, and formula in the cell. You can only have one watch entry per cell.

You can change data on the worksheet and view the Watch Window for how the change is affecting other cells with formulas.

Use the following steps to add a Watch item:

1. Select the cells that you want to watch.

    To select all cells with formulas on your worksheet, navigate to: **Home** tab > **Editing** group > **Find & Replace** > **Go To Special**, and then click **Formulas**.

2. On the **Formulas** tab, in the **Formula Auditing** group, click the **Watch Window** button to display the Watch Window toolbar.

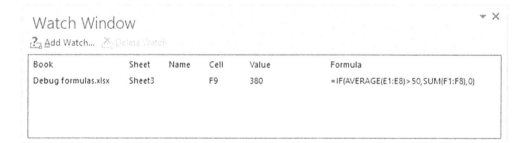

3. Click **Add Watch**.

4. Click **Add** on the **Add Watch** dialog box. Here, you can change the cell you want to add (if it is different from the one selected in step 1).

5. Move the Watch Window toolbar and dock it to the bottom, left, or right side of the Excel window. To change the width of a column, for example, the **Book** column, drag the boundary on the right side of the column heading.

6. To display the cell being referred to by an entry in the Watch Window, double-click the entry to select the cell. Note that cells that contain references to other workbooks are only displayed in the Watch Window when the referenced workbook is open.

7. To close the Watch Window toolbar, on the **Formulas** tab, in the **Formula Auditing** group, click the **Watch Window** button to toggle it off.

Removing cells from the Watch Window

1. If the Watch Window toolbar is not displayed, click the Watch Window button on the Formulas tab to display it.

2. Click the entry you want to remove to select it. To select multiple entries, press **Ctrl** and then click the entry.

3. Click **Delete Watch**.

4. To close the Watch Window toolbar, on the **Formulas** tab, in the **Formula Auditing** group, click the **Watch Window** button to toggle it off.

Chapter 5: Use Macros to Automate Excel Tasks

Macros enable you to automate pretty much any task you can carry out in Excel. You can use Excel's macro recorder to record tasks that you perform routinely. Macros enable you to do the work faster as Excel can play back keystrokes and mouse actions much faster than when you perform them manually. Also, macros ensure that you carry out the tasks the same way each time, which reduces the likelihood of errors.

Excel uses the Visual Basic for Applications (VBA) programming language to record all the commands and keystrokes that you make when you're recording the macro. VBA is a programming language developed and used primarily for Microsoft Office programs like Access, Word, Excel, PowerPoint etc. You don't need to have any knowledge of VBA to record and use macros in Excel, however, you have the option of using the Visual Basic Editor to view and edit your macros after recording them, if necessary.

In this chapter, we will cover:

- How to record and run macros in Excel.
- Add macro command buttons on the Ribbon and Quick Access Toolbar.
- Assign a macro to a graphics object in your worksheet.
- Macro security, including the Trust Center and Trusted Locations.
- How to view and edit your macros in the Visual Basic editor.

5.1 First Things First

Before we proceed to creating our first macro, we need to cover some essentials about macros in Excel and where to store them.

Two Ways to Create a Macro

There are two ways you can create a macro in Excel 2019:

1. You can use Excel's macro recorder to record your actions as you perform a task in the worksheet.

2. Use the VBA editor to directly write the code that performs the task. Visual Basic programming is outside scope of this book, but we will briefly look at the code editor.

Whichever method you use, Excel will create a special code module that holds the actions and instructions recorded in the macro. These are stored as Visual Basic code. In fact, one way to create VBA code for Excel is to simply start the recorder and manually perform the task for which you want to write code. Then you open the macro in the VBA editor and put the finishing touches to the code. This is how developers can quickly create code that automates Excel.

Where to Store Your Macro

The macro that you create can be stored in the following locations:

- The current workbook.
- A new workbook.
- The globally available **Personal Macro Workbook** called **PERSONAL.XLSB** that is stored in a folder called XLSTART in the AppData folder for Excel on your PC.

When you record a macro and store it in the Personal Macro Workbook, you can run that macro from any open workbook. Macros that are saved as part of the current workbook can only be run from within that workbook.

When recording a macro, you get to choose where you want to save the macro, what to name the macro, and what shortcut keystrokes to assign the macro.

When assigning a shortcut keystroke to run the macro, you can assign the **Ctrl** key plus a letter from A-Z, for example, Ctrl+M, or Ctrl+Shift and a letter from A-Z, for example, Ctrl+Shift+M.

There are some shortcut keystrokes you can't assign, for example, Ctrl+ (any number) or Ctrl+ (a punctuation mark). Also, you should avoid using known Windows shortcut keys like Ctrl+C or Ctrl+V (that is the shortcut keys for copy and paste).

The Three Ways to Start the Macro Recorder

There are three ways you can start the macro recorder in Excel:

1. On the Excel Status bar, click the **Record Macro** button (bottom left of the screen, next to the Ready indicator). Having the Record Macro button on the status bar is convenient because it means you don't have to switch from your current tab on the Ribbon to start and stop the recording.

2. On the View tab, click **Macros** and select **Record Macro** from the drop-down menu.

3. On the **Developer** tab, click the **Record Macro** command button. If you don't have the **Developer tab** on your Ribbon, follow the steps below to add it to the Ribbon:

   i. Click **File > Options** and then click the **Customize Ribbon** tab on the **Excel Options** dialog box.

   ii. Excel opens the **Customize the Ribbon** pane in the Excel Options dialog box.

iii. On the right side of the Customize the Ribbon pane, you'll see the **Main Tabs** list. Check the **Developer** check box and then click **OK**.

-☼-**Tip** Another way to open the **Customize the Ribbon** pane is to right-click anywhere on the Ribbon (below the tabs) and select **Customize the Ribbon** from the pop-up menu. This will take you directly to the **Customize the Ribbon** pane in Excel Options. For more on customizing the Excel 2019 Ribbon, see **chapter 1 in Book 1: Excel Basics**.

On the **View** tab of the Ribbon, the **Macros** button has three options on its drop-down list (you can also find these options as command buttons in the Code group in the Developer tab):

- **View Macros**: This opens the **Macro** dialog box which enables you to select and run a macro that has already been recorded. You can also choose to edit macros from here.

- **Record Macro**: This opens the **Record Macro** dialog box which allows you to define settings for the macro you want to record and then start the macro recorder.

- **Use Relative References**: This setting, which you can turn on before recording a macro, uses relative cell references when recording macros. Using relative cell references makes the macro more versatile because it enables you to run it anywhere on the worksheet rather than where it was originally recorded.

5.2 Recording a Macro

In the following example, we'll walk through recording a macro that carries out the following tasks:

- Enters the text "Microsoft Excel 2019"
- Increases the font to 14 points
- Bolds the text
- Autofits the column width so that the text does not flow into other columns

To start recording the macro, do the following:

1. Open an Excel workbook and a blank worksheet. On the **View** tab, click the drop-down button of the **Macros** button (not the command button itself), then select **Use Relative References** from the menu.

2. On the **View** tab, click the drop-down button of the **Macros** button and click **Record Macro**. This will open the **Records Macro** dialog box.

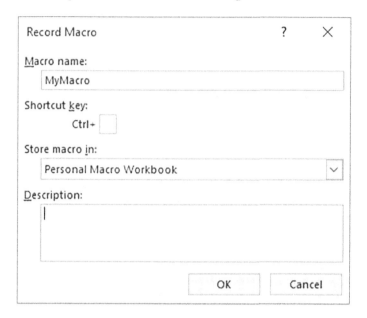

3. In the **Macro Name** field, enter the name of the macro, for example, Macro4.

4. For the **Shortcut key**, hold down the Shift key and press M. This will enter Ctrl+Shift+M for the shortcut key. This is the keystroke that you can use to run the macro. You can use other key combinations but avoid using popular Windows shortcut keys.

Note The shortcut key is optional, and you don't necessarily need to assign one to every macro you create.

5. In the **Store macro in** drop-down list, select **Personal Macro Workbook**. This ensures that the macro is saved in the global PERSONAL.XLSB workbook and not the current workbook.

6. In the **Description** box, you can enter a brief description of the macro. This is optional but if you're creating a lot of macros it would be a good idea to enter a description for each macro to make maintaining the macros easier.

7. When you're done, click **OK** to start recording.

    The Record Macro box is closed. On the status bar, next to Ready, you'll see a small square button which is the indicator that the macro recorder is currently running.

Next, we'll perform the Excel tasks we'll be recording.

8. On the Excel Ribbon, click on the **Home** tab then click in cell **A1**.

9. Type *"Microsoft Excel 2019"* in cell A1 and click the **Enter** button (this is a checkmark next to the formula bar).

10. On the **Home** tab, change the font size to 14 and make the text bold.

11. On the **Home** tab, in the **Cells** group, click the drop-down button of the **Format** command button, then select **Autofit Column Width** from the drop-down menu. This will increase the size of the column to fit the text.

12. On the status bar, to the immediate right of **Ready**, you'll see a square button (which is the Record Macro/Stop Recording button). Click that button to stop recording the macro.

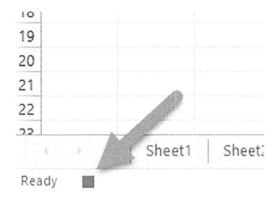

With that, your macro recording has been completed. Next, we'll run the macro.

5.3 Running a Macro

After recording a macro, there are three ways you can run it:

- On the **View** tab, click the drop-down button on the **Macros** button and select **View Macros**.

- On the **Developer** tab, in the **Code** group, click the **Macros** button.

- You can also use the **Alt+F8** shortcut keystroke to open the **Macro** dialog box.

Excel opens the **Macro** dialog box which has a list of all the macros you have created in the macro name list box.

To run the macro, click the macro name on the list and click the **Run** button.

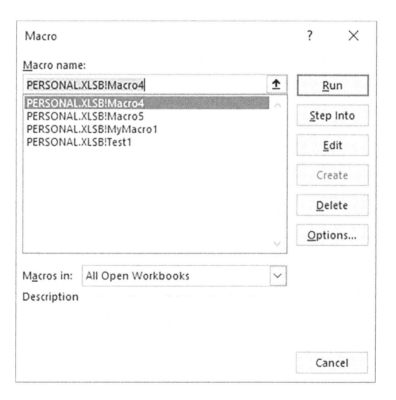

-ʘ-**Tip**   If you assigned a shortcut keystroke to the macro, for example, Ctrl+Shift+M, you can just press those keys to automatically run the macro without needing to open the Macro dialog box.

It is best to test a macro in a new worksheet (or a different range in the current worksheet) as you want to see if the macro replicates the actions you performed when recording it.

The macro recorder uses absolute references by default, which means that it will store specific cell references as part of the instructions. For example, if the macro was recorded in range A2:A5 in one worksheet, then when running in any worksheet, it will only perform the tasks in that range.

If you want the macro to perform the tasks in any range in a worksheet, you need to enable the **Use Relative Reference** setting on the **View** or **Developer** tabs of the Ribbon before you start recording the macro. With the reference type set to Relative, the macro will perform the actions relative to the active cell when the macro was started.

If you run the macro in a worksheet with existing data, there is a risk that the macro will overwrite your existing data or formatting. To ensure that you don't mistakenly overwrite data, always test the macro in a new worksheet. Only run the macro against actual data when you're satisfied that the macro is working as it should. For example, you may create a macro that adds formatting to existing data. In such cases, ensure you test the macro first against test copies of the data before running it against your live data.

5.4 Add a Macro Button to the Ribbon

To assign a macro to a custom command button, right-click anywhere on the ribbon, and select **Customize the Ribbon...** from the pop-up menu.

This will open **Customize the Ribbon** pane of the **Excel Options** dialog box.

On the **Customize the Ribbon** pane, you have two list boxes. On the right, you have the list box that shows your current tabs - **Main Tabs**. On the left, you have the command buttons that you can add to the ribbon. To expand a group in the **Main Tabs** list box, click on the plus sign (+) to the left of an item. To collapse a group, click on the minus sign (-).

⊜**Note**   You cannot add or remove the default commands on the ribbon, but you can uncheck them on the list to prevent them from being displayed. Also, you cannot add command buttons to the default groups. You must create a new group to add a new command button to an existing tab.

Creating a New Custom Group

You can add the macro button to a new custom group in one of the default tabs on the Ribbon or to a new custom tab you have created for your macro buttons. We'll go through creating a new tab and then adding a command button to it.

1. To create a **new tab**, click the **New Tab** button at the bottom of the Main Tabs list box. Inside the tab, you must create at least one group before you can add a command button from the left side of the screen.

2. To give the tab a display name, select the **New Tab (Custom)** item and click the **Rename** button at the bottom of the Main Tabs list box. Enter your preferred name for the tab in the **Rename** dialog box and click **OK.**

3. You can use the arrow buttons to the right of the Main Tabs list box to move your new tab item up or down the list, depending on where you want to place it.

4. To create a new **custom group**, select the tab in which you want to create the group. This could be one of the default tabs, for example, **Home**, or the new one you've created. Click on the **New Group** button (at the bottom of the screen, under the Main Tabs list box). This will create a new group within the currently selected tab.

5. To create a display name for the group, select the **New Group (Custom)** item and click the **Rename** button. Enter your preferred name, for example, *MyMacros* in the **Rename** dialog box and click **OK**.

You now have a custom group in which you can add your macro command buttons.

Follow the steps below to add a macro command button to the new custom group:

1. Select your custom group in the **Main Tabs** list box.

2. Click the **Choose commands from** drop-down list box (on the left of the dialog box) and select **Macros** from the drop-down list. In the list box on the left, you'll see a list of macros created in the current workbook and saved in the PERSONAL.XLSB workbook.

3. Select the macro name that you want to add to your custom group in the list box on the left, then click the **Add** button to add the macro command to the new custom group in the list box on the right.

Note If you mistakenly added the wrong command, you could select it in the list box on the right and click the **Remove** button to remove it.

4. Click **OK** on the Excel Options dialog box to confirm the change.

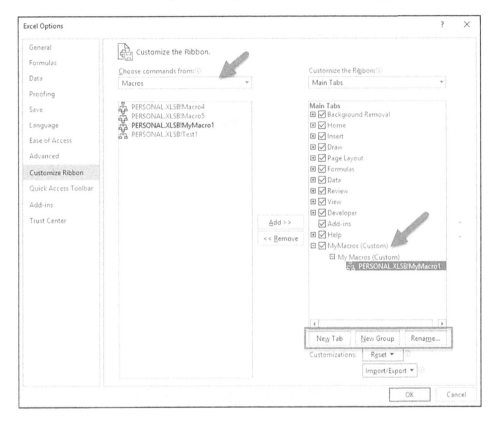

After adding the macro, the name of the macro appears on a button with a generic icon (a program diagram chart). When you click on the button it will run the macro.

5.5 Assign a Macro to a Button on the Quick Access Toolbar

Follow the steps below to add a custom macro button to the Quick Access Toolbar:

1. Click the **Customize Quick Access Toolbar** button at the end of the Quick Access toolbar. From the drop-down menu, click **More Commands**. This opens the **Customize the Quick Access Toolbar** pane in Excel Options.

2. Click the **Choose commands from** drop-down list box and select Macros from the drop-down list. In the list box on the left of the dialog box, you'll see a list of macros created in the current workbook and those saved in the PERSONAL.XLSB workbook.

3. In the list box on the left, select the macro name that you want to add to a custom button on the Quick Access Toolbar. Then click the **Add** button to add the macro command to the list on the right of the dialog box.

Note If you mistakenly added the wrong command, you could select it in the list on the right box and click the **Remove** button to remove it.

4. Click **OK** on the Excel Options dialog box to confirm the change.

A custom button with a generic macro icon will appear on the Quick Access Toolbar. A mouseover the button will display the name of the macro assigned to it. To run the macro, click the button.

5.6 Assign a Macro to a Graphic Object

You can assign macros to the graphic objects that you've inserted in your worksheet, including Pictures, Shapes, Icons that you can insert using **Insert** > **Illustrations**. You can also assign macros to graphic objects that you have drawn using tools on the **Draw** tab.

To assign a macro to a graphic object, do the following:

1. Insert the graphic object in the worksheet area, for the example, an icon from **Insert** tab > **Illustrations** > **Icons**.

2. Right-click the object and then click the **Assign Macro** option from its shortcut menu.

3. In the **Assign Macro** dialog box, select the macro name from the **Macro name** list box and click **OK**.

After you've assigned the macro to the graphic object, whenever you mouseover it, the mouse pointer changes to a hand with a pointing index finger, indicating that you can click it to run the macro.

5.7 Macro Security

Excel 2019 uses an authentication system called Microsoft Authenticode to digitally sign macro projects or add-ins created with Visual Basic for Applications. The macros you create locally on your computer are automatically authenticated so when you run them on your computer, Excel does not display a security alert.

For macros from an external source, the developer can acquire a certificate issued by a reputable authority or a trusted publisher. In such cases, Excel will run the macro if it can verify that it is from a trusted source.

If Excel cannot verify the digital signature of a macro from an external source because it perhaps doesn't have one, a security alert is displayed in the message bar (below the Excel Ribbon). This alert gives you the option to enable the macro or to ignore it. You can click the **Enable Content** button to run the macro if you trust the source and you're sure that the macro poses no security threat to your computer.

If you try to create a macro in an Excel workbook that was saved as an XLSX file, Excel will display a message on the message bar prompting you to save the workbook as a macro-enabled file first. When you get this message, click the **Save As** button on the message bar, and select the **Excel Macro-Enabled Workbook (*.xlsm)** file type from the filter list.

File type	File extension
Excel Workbook	xlsx
Excel Macro-Enabled Workbook	xlsm

If you choose to save the macro to the **Personal Macro Workbook**, it will be saved in the PERSONAL.XLSB file, which is an Excel Binary Workbook in the XLSTART folder. In this case, you'll not need to save your workbook as a macro-enabled workbook.

When creating a macro for use on your computer, as much as possible, you want to store the macro in the **Personal Macro Workbook.** This means the macro will be global and will work in any workbook on your computer. It also means that you don't need to convert your workbooks to macro-enabled files. Only use a macro-enabled workbook if there is a specific reason to do so, for example, you want to distribute the file to other people.

Trust Center Macro Settings

Microsoft Office security and privacy settings are located in the **Trust Center**. The Macro Settings tab of the Trust Center contains the macro security settings for your computer. Macro security is important to protect your computer against the threat of malicious code that can be inserted in Microsoft Office macros.

You can access the **Macro Settings** in the Trust Center in the following ways:

- On the **Developer** tab, in the **Code** group, click the **Macro Security** button. This will open the **Macro Settings** pane of the Trust Center dialog box.

- On the Ribbon, click the **File** tab and then click **Options** > **Trust Center** > **Trust Centre Settings** > **Macro Settings**.

By default, Excel 2019 disables all macros from external sources with a security alert on the message bar, giving you the option to enable the macro or ignore it. This is the default setting when you install Excel, but there are other security options from which you can choose.

You can also select one of these options in Macro Settings:

- **Disable all macros without notification**: This automatically disables macros in your computer. This setting means no macros will run on your computer and you'll not get a security alert giving you the option to run the macro. This option is useful for shared computers, for example, where you don't want anyone using the computer to run macros.

- **Disable all macros with notification**: This option is the default. All macros from external sources are disabled with a security alert showing on the message bar. With this option, you have to specifically choose to enable the macro before it can run.

- **Disable all macros except digitally signed macros**: This option disables all macros apart from the digitally signed macros from publishers that you have added to your **Trusted Publishers** in the Trust Center. When you have this option selected and you get a macro from a publisher that's not in your Trusted Publishers list, you will get an alert in the message bar with a **Trust All Documents from this Publisher** button that you can click to add them to the to your trusted publishers.

- **Enable all macros (not recommended; potentially dangerous code can run):** This option enables all macros without any notifications or security alerts, even those macros that are not digitally signed or authenticated. As stated in its label, this option is not recommended because you can inadvertently run malicious code that corrupts your data or damages your computer.

Trusted Locations

The **Trusted Locations** tab of the Trust Center dialog box enables you to add, remove or modify trusted locations. If you are receiving macros from an external source that you need to run on your computer without alerts, then you need to place them in a trusted location on your computer. In doing so, Excel knows that these files are safe, and you are not prompted with security alerts when you open them.

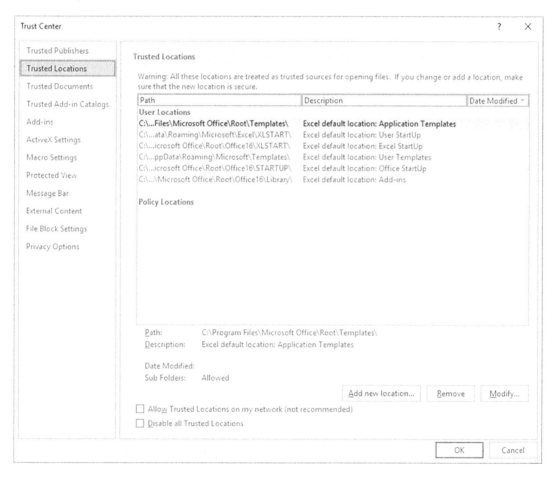

You can use the following options to change Trusted Locations settings:

- **Add new location**: To add a new trusted location, click the **Add new location** button at the bottom of the screen. On the **Microsoft Office Trusted Location** dialog box, click on the **Browse** button and navigate to the folder that you want to add to the list of trusted locations. After selecting the folder, click **OK** on the Browse dialog box, and **OK** again on the **Microsoft Office Trusted Location** dialog box to confirm the entry.

  This will add in a new trusted location on your computer and you can store any externally created macro-enabled files in that folder.

- **Allow trusted locations on my network (not recommended):** Click this option if you want to add folders on your network to your trusted locations. As indicated by the label, this is not recommended by Microsoft as you cannot entirely trust the safety of external locations. However, if you're working on a shared network drive that you trust, and that is the only way you can collaborate with others, then this may be an option for sharing macro-enabled files. Only use as a last option.

- **Disable all trusted locations**: Check this box if you want to immediately disable all trusted locations. This means macros in these locations would not run and only the macros that are digitally signed and recognised as trustworthy by Excel will run on your computer.

Note
The macro-enabled worksheets you create locally on your computer do not need to be stored in a trusted location to run on your computer. This is because they're automatically digitally authenticated by Excel.

5.8 Editing Recorded Macros

As mentioned earlier in this chapter, the macros recorded in Excel are stored as Visual Basic for Applications code instructions.

Visual Basic for Applications (VBA) programming is outside the scope of this book. However, being able to view the source code for your macro may help you identify and fix simple errors or make small changes. Often times, editing the macro in the Visual Basic Editor to change the way it behaves is more expedient than having to record the macro again.

Even if you have no programming skills, you may still be able to identify errors and make small changes, for example, spelling errors in the text, errors in the values, or errors in formulas. You don't need programming skills to make simple changes like these. Also, you may see something out of place in the code that helps you to avoid the error if you choose to re-record the macro.

Unhiding the Personal Macro Workbook

If the macro you want to edit is stored in your Personal Macro Workbook, you must unhide this workbook before you edit it in the Visual Basic Editor.

Follow the steps below to unhide the Personal Macro Workbook:

1. On the **View** tab, click the **Unhide** command button.

    Excel displays the **Unhide** dialog box showing the PERSONAL.XLSB workbook in the Unhide Workbook list.

2. Select PERSONAL.XLSB in the list box and click on **OK** to unhide the workbook.

With the Personal Macro Workbook unhidden, you can now edit its macros in the Visual Basic Editor.

Editing the Macro in the Visual Basic Editor

Follow the steps below to open a macro for editing in the Visual Basic Editor:

1. On the **View** tab, click the **Macros** command button then the **View Macros** option.

    This opens the **Macro** dialog box showing the names of the macros that you've created in the workbook, and your Personal Macro Workbook.

2. In the **Macro Name** list box, select the macro name that you want to edit and then click the **Edit** button.

Excel will display the macro in the Visual Basic Editor.

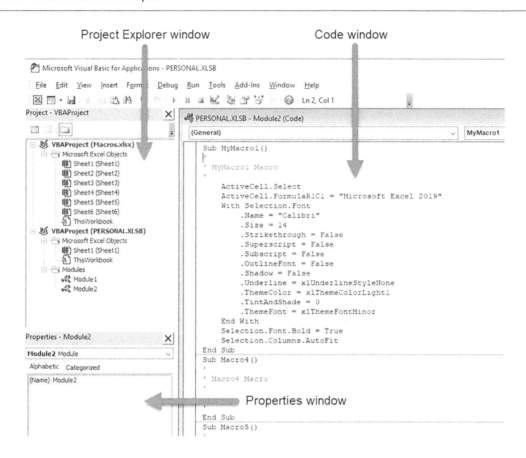

The **Code window** shows the code instructions for the macro. This is where you would edit the macro. The Project Explorer enables you to navigate to macros saved in different modules or in different workbooks that are currently open.

In the **Code window**, the macro code is between a starting keyword and an ending keyword. The beginning of the macro has the keyword **Sub** *MyMacro1()*, *w*here *MyMacro1* is the name you gave to your macro when you created it. The end of the macro is denoted by the keyword **End Sub**. To make changes to the macro, ensure you keep your edits within this area.

The code below was generated from the macro we created earlier in this chapter.

```
Sub MyMacro1()
'
' MyMacro1 Macro
'
    ActiveCell.Select
    ActiveCell.FormulaR1C1 = "Microsoft Excel 2019"
    With Selection.Font
        .Name = "Calibri"
        .Size = 14
        .Strikethrough = False
        .Superscript = False
        .Subscript = False
        .OutlineFont = False
        .Shadow = False
        .Underline = xlUnderlineStyleNone
        .ThemeColor = xlThemeColorLight1
        .TintAndShade = 0
        .ThemeFont = xlThemeFontMinor
    End With
    Selection.Font.Bold = True
    Selection.Columns.AutoFit
End Sub
```

After making your changes, save the changes by clicking the **Save** button on the Visual Basic Editor toolbar (the blue disk icon).

To close the Visual Basic Editor, simply click on the **Close** button on the top right of the window (x icon). You can also close the window by clicking on **File > Close and Return to Microsoft Excel**.

-ෛ-Tip   Another way to open the Visual Basic Editor is from the Developer tab on the Ribbon. On the **Developer** tab, in the **Code** group, click the **Visual Basic** command button. The Developer tab is not one of the default tabs on the Excel Ribbon so if you don't have this tab, follow the steps detailed in a previous section of this chapter for how to add the Developer tab to the Excel Ribbon.

Chapter 6: Analyze Alternate Data Sets with What-If Analysis

S preadsheet formulas are very good at automatically updating results based on your input. For that reason, spreadsheets are one of the best tools for carrying out financial projections based on assumptions. Excel provides a whole raft of tools for just this purpose.

In this chapter, we will be covering:

- What-If Analysis for one-variable and two-variable data tables.
- The Scenario Manager which you can use to create and compare different scenarios for your data.
- The Goal Seek tool to set a goal and allow Excel to adjust other values to meet the goal.
- The Solver add-in tool which can be used to generate scenarios for more complex data.

6.1 The Different Types of What-If Analysis

In Excel, there are different types of what-if analysis you can carry out. In this chapter, we will cover four types that are commonly used in Excel.

- **Data tables**: This feature enables you to generate a series of projections based on one or two changing variables.

- **Goal seeking**: This feature enables you to set a predetermined goal and then choose the variables that will change to meet this goal.

- **Scenarios**: In this type of What-If Analysis, you create different scenarios using alternate figures which you can then compare side-by-side in a generated report.

- **Solver**: The solver is an Excel add-in that you can use to create more complex What-If Analysis, enabling you to use multiple variables and constraints.

6.2 Data Tables

A data table gives you a projection of how your bottom line would look if one or two variables in your data are changed. For example, what would be our profit if we achieved a growth rate in sales of 1.5% rather than 1%? What would be our net profit next year if we reduced our expenses by 3%? These are the kinds of questions that can be answered by a data table.

Creating a One-Variable Data Table

The one-variable data table is a projection based on a series of values that you want to substitute for a single input value.

To demonstrate this type of data table, we will use an example where we create a series of projected sales for the next quarter.

In this example, we have the following figures:
- Sales for quarter one: $45,000.
- Projected growth in sales for quarter two: 2.0%.

- Projected sales for quarter two: 45,000 + (45,000*0.02).

For this projection, we want to substitute different growth rates into the projected growth for Qtr 2 to see a series of projected sales based on different growth rates.

For the column values, we enter rates ranging from 1% to 5% in cells B8:B16, with an increment of 0.5%. You can choose whatever increment you want here.

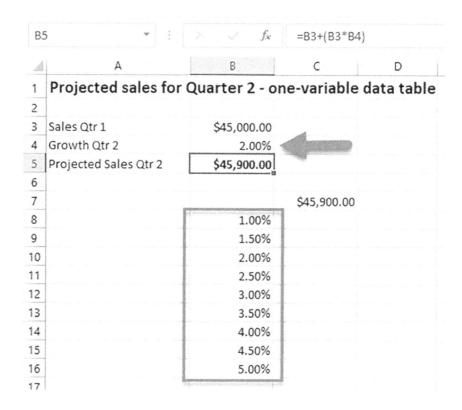

For the row value, that is, cell **C7**, we enter =B5 which is a reference to the master formula which calculates **Projected Sales Qtr 2**. This master formula will be used by the data table as the base figure for which to make the projections.

Once your data has been prepared, as shown above, follow the steps below to generate the data table:

1. Select the table. For this example, it'll be B7:C16.

2. On the Excel Ribbon, click on the **Data** tab, in the **Forecast** group, click on the **What-If Analysis** command button and select **Data Table** from the drop-down menu.

This will display the **Data Table** dialog box. As this is the one-variable data table, we need just one of the fields. Click the **Column input cell** field and then on the worksheet, select the growth percentage, which is cell **B4**.

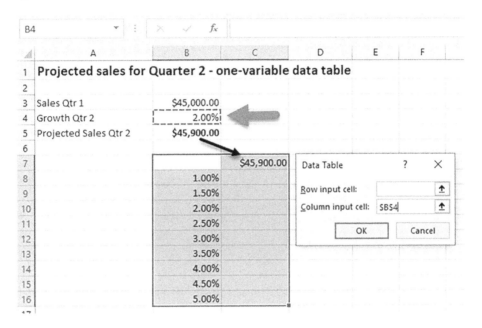

Click **OK** to generate the projected values in cells C8:C16.

| C8 | | | | | f_x | {=TABLE(,B4)} |

	A	B	C	D
1	**Projected sales for Quarter 2 - one-variable data table**			
2				
3	Sales Qtr 1	$45,000.00		
4	Growth Qtr 2	2.00%		
5	Projected Sales Qtr 2	**$45,900.00**		
6				
7			$45,900.00	
8		1.00%	$45,450.00	
9		1.50%	$45,675.00	
10		2.00%	$45,900.00	
11		2.50%	$46,125.00	
12		3.00%	$46,350.00	
13		3.50%	$46,575.00	
14		4.00%	$46,800.00	
15		4.50%	$47,025.00	
16		5.00%	$47,250.00	
17				

The data table is created as an array formula using the TABLE function. The TABLE function takes two arguments *row_ref* and/or *column_ref* but only needs one for a one-variable data table.

{=TABLE(,B4)}

The formula shows that the value in cell B4 represents its *column_ref* argument for which alternate values are provided in cells B8:B16. The process simply substitutes the original rate in B4 with the series of rates in B8:B16 to generate the projection.

As the data table uses an array formula, Excel will not allow you to delete only some of the values in the array. To delete values in the data table, you must select all the generated values, that is, cells C8:C16 and hit the **Delete** key.

Creating a Two-Variable Data Table

A two-variable data table enables you to create projections based on the changing values of two variables.

The method of creating a two-variable table is similar to the one-variable data table described above but, in this case, we have two variables that can change instead of one.

A two-variable data table requires input for the column and row fields, so we need a series of values for the first column and first row of the table. At the intersection of the row and column, we enter the master formula which would have the figure that we want to use as the bases of our projection.

To demonstrate this type of data table, we will use an example where we create a series of projected sales for the next quarter based on two variables.

In this example, we have the following figures:
- Sales for quarter one: $45,000.
- Projected growth in sales for quarter two: 2.0%.
- Expenses for quarter two: 15%.
- Projected sales for quarter two: 45,000 + (45,000*0.02).

We want to see a projection for how our sales would look with different growth rates (between 1% and 5%) and different expense rates (between 15% and 30%).

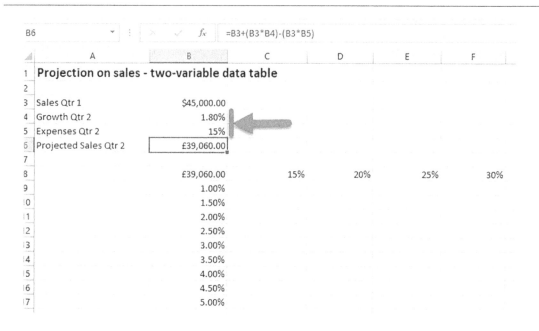

B6				f_x	=B3+(B3*B4)-(B3*B5)		
	A	B	C	D	E	F
1	Projection on sales - two-variable data table					
2						
3	Sales Qtr 1	$45,000.00				
4	Growth Qtr 2	1.80%				
5	Expenses Qtr 2	15%				
6	Projected Sales Qtr 2	£39,060.00				
7						
8		£39,060.00	15%	20%	25%	30%
9		1.00%				
10		1.50%				
11		2.00%				
12		2.50%				
13		3.00%				
14		3.50%				
15		4.00%				
16		4.50%				
17		5.00%				

For the row entries, to be substituted with **Expenses Qtr 2**, we enter a series of values ranging from 15% to 30% in cells C8:F8.

For the column entries, to be substituted with **Growth Qtr 2**, we enter a series of values ranging from 1% to 5% (increasing by 0.5%) in cells B9:B17.

In cell B8 we enter =*B6* which is a reference to the master formula that calculates **Projected Sales Qtr 2**.

Once your worksheet model has been prepared as shown in the image above, follow the steps below to generate the data table:

1. Select the table. For this example, it'll be B8:F17.

2. On the Excel Ribbon, click on the **Data** tab, in the **Forecast** group, click on the **What-If Analysis** command button and select **Data Table** from the drop-down menu.

   This will display the **Data Table** dialog box. As this is a two-variable data table, we need to enter both fields in the Data Table dialog box.

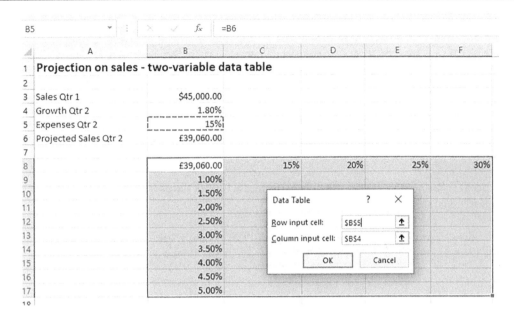

3. Click inside the **Row input cell** field and then on the worksheet, select the expenses for quarter two, which is cell **B5**.

4. Next, click in the **Column input cell** field and then on the worksheet, select the growth percentage, which is cell **B4**.

5. Click **OK** to generate the projected values in the data table.

	A	B	C	D	E	F
	C9		{=TABLE(B5,B4)}			
1	Projection on sales - two-variable data table					
2						
3	Sales Qtr 1	$45,000.00				
4	Growth Qtr 2	1.80%				
5	Expenses Qtr 2	15%				
6	Projected Sales Qtr 2	£39,060.00				
7						
8		£39,060.00	15%	20%	25%	30%
9		1.00%	£38,700.00	£36,450.00	£34,200.00	£31,950.00
10		1.50%	£38,925.00	£36,675.00	£34,425.00	£32,175.00
11		2.00%	£39,150.00	£36,900.00	£34,650.00	£32,400.00
12		2.50%	£39,375.00	£37,125.00	£34,875.00	£32,625.00
13		3.00%	£39,600.00	£37,350.00	£35,100.00	£32,850.00
14		3.50%	£39,825.00	£37,575.00	£35,325.00	£33,075.00
15		4.00%	£40,050.00	£37,800.00	£35,550.00	£33,300.00
16		4.50%	£40,275.00	£38,025.00	£35,775.00	£33,525.00
17		5.00%	£40,500.00	£38,250.00	£36,000.00	£33,750.00

The two-variable data table uses the TABLE function to create an array formula in the output range of C9:F17. The TABLE function takes two arguments *row_ref* and/or *column_ref*.

{=TABLE(B5,B4)}

The formula shows that cell B5 is the *row_ref* argument for which alternate values have been provided in cells B9:B17. The *column_ref* argument has cell B4 for which we have alternate values in cells C8:F8.

The process simply substitutes the original values with the series of values created in B9:B17 and C8:F8 to generate the projection.

As the data table uses an array formula, you can't delete only some of the values in the array. To delete the generated data in the table, you must select all values in cells C9:F17 and hit the **Delete** key.

6.3 Scenario Manager

Another tool provided by Excel that you can use to create a What-If Analysis is the Scenario Manager. The Scenario Manager enables you to create different scenarios where certain input values are changed to produce different results.

You can assign names the different scenarios in the scenario manager, for example, *Most Likely*, *Best Case*, and *Worst Case*. Once you've created the scenarios in the Scenario Manager, you can view the different scenario in your worksheet or generate a summary report with all the scenarios so that you can compare them side-by-side.

In the following example, we will create several projections for the next year based on figures from the current year. The scenarios will apply different growth rates to the current figures so that we can compare the scenarios together in a summary report.

Figures – Current Year

- Sales: $627,198.00
- Cost of production: $200,000
- Office supplies: $5,000
- Vehicle: $10,500.00
- Building: $50,000.00

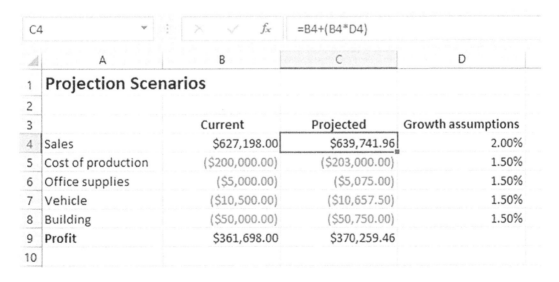

The projected value in C4 is calculated with the following formula:

=B4+(B4*D4)

The formula in **Projected** simply increments the **Current** value by the percentage rate in **Growth assumption**. The same formula is used to derive the values in cells C5:C8.

We want to create more scenarios using different growth assumptions without overwriting the original data as we want to be able to compare multiple scenarios together. This is where the Scenario Manager comes in.

Tip When using the Scenario Manager, it is a good idea to name each cell you intend to change. It makes it easier to know what each cell represents when you enter the new values in a subsequent dialog box. It also makes any subsequent reports you create of the scenarios easier to understand.

Follow the steps below to create different scenarios with the Scenario Manager:

1. Select the changing cells in the worksheet. In this case, the changing cells are D4:D8.

2. On the **Data** tab, in the **Forecast** group, click **What-If Analysis** command button and select **Scenario Manager** from the drop-down menu.

    The **Scenario Manager** dialog box will be opened.

3. Click on the **Add** button to add a new scenario.

4. Enter a name for the scenario in the **Scenario name** field. These can be names like *Most likely*, *Best case*, *Worst case* etc.

5. The **Changing cells** field should already have the reference to the cells you selected before opening the Scenario Manager dialog box. However, if the right cells have not been selected, click on the Expand Dialog box button on the field (up arrow) and select the cells in the worksheet.

6. The **Comment** box is optional. You can enter a short description for the scenario or leave the default text which is a log of when it was last updated.

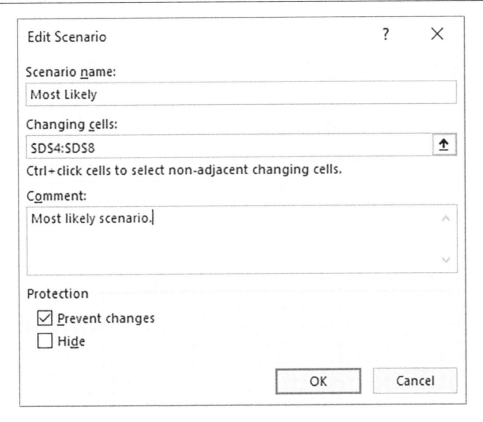

7. In the **Protection** portion of the screen, leave the **Prevent changes** checkbox selected if you want Excel to protect the scenario from changes when worksheet protection is turned on. If you don't want to protect the scenario when the worksheet is protected, uncheck Prevent changes.

8. If you don't want the scenario hidden when worksheet protection is on, leave the **Hide** check box unselected. Alternatively, if you want Excel to hide the scenario when the worksheet is protected, select the Hide check box.

Note Worksheet protection is a separate topic that's not related to What-If Analysis and covered elsewhere in this book.

9. Click **OK** to open the **Scenario Values** dialog box.

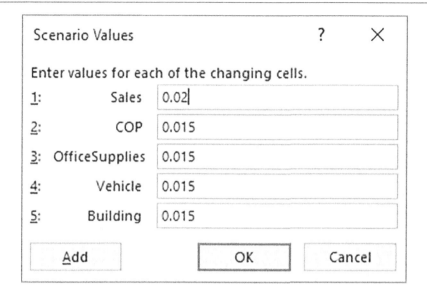

10. The Scenario Values dialog box contains several fields for the changing cells. As you can see from the image above, naming the changing cells becomes useful here as each field is labelled with a name rather than a cell reference.

    For the first scenario, you may want to accept the values already in the fields (if you had values in the cells before starting the Scenario Manager). If you want a different set of values for your first scenario, you can change them here.

11. When done, click the **Add** button to save the scenario and go back to the **Add Scenario** dialog box.

12. Repeat steps **4** to **11** above to add the other scenarios you want to create.

After you finish creating the different scenarios you want to add, you can close the Scenario Values dialog box and then return to the Scenario Manager dialog box. Now, in the Scenario Manager dialog box, you'll see the names of all the scenarios you've added in the **Scenarios** list box.

To show the scenario that you have entered, select the scenario in the **Scenarios** list box and click on the **Show** command button. You can also just double-click on the name of the scenario in the list box to show the scenario in the worksheet. For example, to display the *Best Case* scenario, double-click on *Best Case*. This will close the Scenario Manager dialog box and insert the rates we entered for the *Best Case* scenario in our table.

To delete a scenario, select it in the list box and click on the **Delete** button. This will remove that scenario from the scenario manager.

To edit a scenario, select the scenario in the **Scenarios** list box and click on the **Edit** button. This will take you through the editing process where you can change the name of the scenario, the changing cells, and the values for the cells. If you only want to change just the values, then click through until you get to the **Scenario Values** dialog box and change the values there.

The Scenario Manager dialog box also enables you to merge scenarios from other Excel workbooks that are open. Note that the workbooks must share the same data layout and changing cells for you to be able to merge their scenarios.

To merge scenarios from another workbook, do the following:

1. Click the **Merge** button in the Scenario Manager dialog box. This will display the **Merge Scenarios** dialog box.

2. Select the workbook name from the **Book** drop-down list box.

3. In the **Sheet** list box, select the worksheet and then click **OK**.

All the scenarios in that worksheet are then copied and merged with the current worksheet.

Summary Reports

After creating the different scenarios, you can compare them side-by-side in a summary report.

To generate a summary report for the scenarios you have entered:

1. In the Scenario Manager dialog box, click on the **Summary** button. This will open the **Scenario Summary** dialog box.

2. Select **Report type** if it is not already selected.

3. Click the **Results cells** text box and select the result cells in your worksheet. These would be the cells with the totals for your projection. For our example, our **Profit** cell is C9.

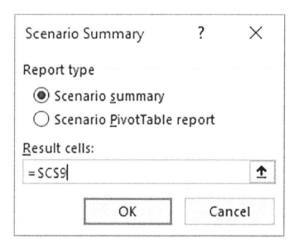

4. Click on **OK** to generate the report.

Excel will generate a report in a separate worksheet showing you all the scenarios you have created.

Scenario Summary				
	Current Values:	Most Likely	Best Case	Worst Case
Changing Cells:				
Sales	2.00%	2.00%	5.00%	1.00%
COP	1.50%	1.50%	1.00%	8.00%
OfficeSupplies	1.50%	1.50%	1.00%	2.50%
Vehicle	1.50%	1.50%	1.00%	5.00%
Building	1.50%	1.50%	1.20%	5.00%
Result Cells:				
Profit	$370,259.46	$370,259.46	$390,302.90	$348,819.98

Notes: Current Values column represents values of changing cells at time Scenario Summary Report was created. Changing cells for each scenario are highlighted in gray.

As you can see from the image above, assigning names to the changing cells and result cells in your worksheet comes in handy when producing a scenario summary.

Now, you may wonder why we need to use the scenario manager when we could have just entered the different scenarios directly in the Excel worksheet area. The example used here with the scenario manager is simple for demonstration purposes only. However, the scenario manager comes in handy when the complexity of the data model would make it difficult to enter the different scenarios side-by-side in Excel in a meaningful way.

6.4 Goal Seeking

On some occasions, when working with data in Excel, you already have the outcome that you want to achieve in mind, and you would like to know the various input values that will achieve that outcome or goal. For example, you may have a goal of $600,000 in revenue and to achieve that goal you need a certain amount for your sales against the cost of expenses. This is where the Goal Seek feature in Excel comes in.

The Goal Seek command in Excel enables you to set a goal in one cell and then choose the cell whose value you would like Excel to adjust in other to meet your goal. So, this is like working backwards, stating the results first and allowing Goal Seek to determine the inputs needed to meet that goal. The goal cell will have a formula which is based on the input from other cells, including the cell that Excel will be changing.

For example, let's say we want to find how much sales we need to generate to reach a certain level of income. Instead of making several adjustments to the sales figure in trying to produce the desired result, we can simply set the result we want and let Goal Seek work out the sales figure required to achieve the result.

To demonstrate the goal seeking feature in Excel, we'll use an example to forecast the income based on a range of input values.

B8		▾	⋮	✕	✓	f_x	=B6+B7

◢	A	B	C
1	**Income Forecast for 2020**		
2			
3			
4	Sales	$600,250.00	
5	Cost of production	($139,705.00)	
6	Gross Profit	$460,545.00	
7	Expenses	($84,267.00)	
8	Income	$376,278.00	
9			

In the table above, cell **B8** has a formula that calculates the *Income*, which is the sum of the *Gross Profit* and the *Expenses* (this is a negative value as denoted by brackets).

=B6+B7

Our goal seeking question is, what amount should our sales be if we want to generate an income of $500,000?

Once the data structure has been created in the worksheet, follow the steps below to get to perform the goal seeking:

1. On the Excel Ribbon, click the **Data** tab, then In the **Forecast** group, click the **What-If Analysis** command button and select **Goal Seek** from the drop-down menu. This will display the **Goal Seek** dialog box.

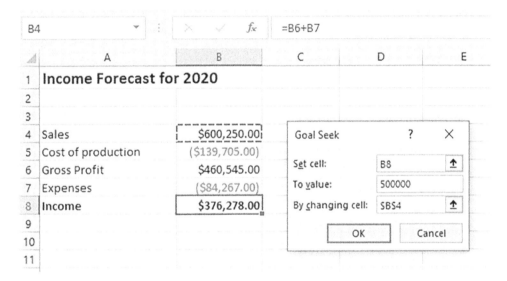

2. Click in the **Set cell** text box and select the cell in the worksheet that contains the formula that will return the value you're seeking. For our example, this is cell **B8**.

3. In the **To value** text box, enter the value that you want to set the cell to. For our example, the value will be 500,000.

4. Click in the **By changing cell** text box and select the cell that contains the value you want Excel to adjust to achieve the goal. For this example, this will be cell **B4**.

5. Click **OK** when done.

   Excel will display the **Goal Seek Status** dialog box which informs you that a solution has been found and that the result value is now the same as the target value.

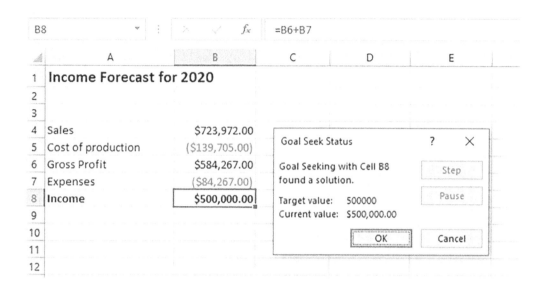

If the Goal Seek does not find a solution it will enable the **Step** and **Pause** buttons to enable you to step through different options to find a solution.

6. If you want to keep the solution found as a result of the goal seeking process, click **OK** to dismiss the Goal Seek Status dialog box. If you don't want to keep the result, simply click the **Cancel** button.

Note that if you accept the value by clicking OK, it will overwrite your existing values. You can switch back to the old the value by clicking the **Undo** button on the Quick Access Toolbar or by using the Ctrl+Z keystroke.

To switch back and forth between the previous value and the value returned by Goal Seek, you can use the **Undo** and **Redo** buttons on the Quick Access Toolbar. Alternatively, you can press Ctrl+Z to display the original values and Ctrl+Y to display the solution returned by the goal seeking command.

6.5 The Solver Add-in

The Data Table and Goal Seek commands are great for creating What-If Analysis solutions for simpler problems that require a direct relationship between the inputs and the outputs. However, for more complex problems, Excel provides another tool, which is the **Solver** add-in utility.

The Solver can be used when you need to create a solution that requires changing multiple input values in your model. The Solver also enables you to impose constraints on the input and output values.

The Solver uses an iterative method to find the optimum solution based on the inputs, the desired result, and the constraints you have set.

Complex problems can have different ways that they're solved and what the Solver does is try to present the best solution for you. However, this may not necessarily be the best one for your particular case. For example, if several variables need to be changed, the Solver may produce a combination of figures that may not suit your specific needs (even if the result meets the objective). This is why you may want to run the Solver multiple times to get the best solution for you.

To set up the problem in the Solver, you will need to define the following items:

- **Objective cell**: This is the target cell that is set to maximum, minimum, or a specific value. The objective cell needs to be a formula.

- **Variable cells**: These are the changing cells in your worksheet. The Goal Seek method, for example, enables you to only specify one cell that can be changed. The difference with the Solver is that you can have multiple cells that can be changed to achieve the objective.

- **Constraints**: These are the cells that contain the values you want to use to set a limit or restriction to the range of changes that can be made. For example, you could set a constraint that says the *Sales* figure cannot be increased by more than 10% to achieve the solution (perhaps because a sales figure of more than 10% would be unrealistic for this particular problem).

After setting the parameters in the Solver, Excel returns the optimum solution by changing the values in your worksheet. At this point, you have the option of retaining the changes in your worksheet or restoring your original values. The Solver also enables you to save the solution as a scenario which you can view at a later time.

The Solver can be used with the Scenario Manager to set up a problem to solve. The variable cells that you define when you use the Scenario Manager to set up a scenario are available and picked up by the Solver. The Solver also allows you to save solutions as scenarios which will then be available to the Scenario Manager.

Adding the Solver Add-in Utility to the Excel Ribbon

The Solver is an add-in and may not be available on your Ribbon if it hasn't been manually added as it is not added by default when you install Excel 2019.

Follow the steps below to add the Solver command button to your Excel Ribbon:

1. Click on **File > Options > Add-ins**.

2. At the bottom of the Add-ins tab, in the **Manage** drop-down list, select **Excel Add-ins** (if it's not already selected).

3. Click on **Go** to show the **Add-ins** dialog box.

4. In the Add-ins dialog box, select the **Solver Add-in** check box and click **OK**.

The **Solver** command button can be found on the **Data** tab, in the **Analyze** group.

In the following example, we will be using the Solver to find a solution to what combination of figures can generate an income of $680,500.00. The worksheet model created for the problem is shown below.

C4				f_x	=$B$4+($B$4*SalesGrowth)	

⊿	A	B	C	D
1	Sales Forecast			
2				
3		Qtr 1	Qtr 2	Assumptions
4	Sales	$800,250.40	$840,262.92	5%
5	Cost of production	($139,705.00)	($148,087.30)	6%
6	Gross Profit	$660,545.40	$692,175.62	
7	Expenses	($84,267.00)	($90,165.69)	7%
8	Income	$576,278.40	$602,009.93	
9				

The value in C4 is calculated with the following formula:

=$B$4+($B$4*SalesGrowth)

SalesGrowth is the name given to cell **D4** which is currently 5%. The formulas in the **Qtr 2** column simply increments the **Qtr 1** values by the growth rates under **Assumptions**.

For this example, the changing/variable cells will be those in the Assumptions column while the result/objective cell will be **C8** (which is named **Income_Qtr2**).

Once you have loaded the Solver add-in and created your worksheet model, follow the steps below to define a problem with the Solver:

1. On the **Data** tab, in the **Analyze** group, click the **Solver** command button. Excel opens the **Solver Parameters** dialog box.

2. In the **Solver Parameters** dialog box, the **Set Objective** textbox is the result you want to achieve. This needs to be a cell in the worksheet with a formula. Click the text box and then select the cell on your worksheet. For our example, this is cell **C8** on the worksheet. The name of the cell is **Income_Qtr2** so the name is inserted in the text box.

3. You have the option of setting the objective to a maximum (as large as possible based on the input values available), a minimum (as small as possible), or to a specific value. For this example, we are using a specific value for our objective, so, click **Value Of** and enter 680500.

4. Click the **By Changing Variable Cells** text box and select the cells you want to change in the worksheet. To select non-adjacent cells, simply hold down the **Ctrl** key while clicking on the cells. If you have given the variable cells names, the names will be entered in place of the cell references.

5. In the **Subject to the Constraints** list box, you can add constraints to place restrictions on the extent of changes the Solver can make. To add a constraint, click the **Add** button. This will display the **Add Constraint** dialog box.

6. Click the **Cell Reference** text box, then select the cell in the worksheet for which you want to create a constraint.

    Select the relationship from the drop-down list box in the middle. The options are: =, <=, >=, int (for integer), and bin (for binary). For our example, we select <= from the drop-down list.

    In the **Constraint** text box, enter the constraint. For our example, we don't want the *SalesGrowth* to be more than 15% so we enter 15%.

    Click **Add** to insert the constraint and continue adding more constraints (or click **OK** to return to the Solver Parameters dialog box if you're done).

    The constraint you added will now be listed in the **Subject to the Constraints** list box.

7. For our example, we'll leave the **Make Unconstrained Variables Non-Negative** checkbox selected, which is the default. Deselect this checkbox if you want to allow negative values in variable cells for which you've set no constraints.

8. The default value for the **Select a Solving Method** drop-down list will have the default value is **GRG Nonlinear**.

    There are three solving methods:

    - **GRG Nonlinear** is for solving smooth nonlinear problems.
    - **Simplex LP** method is for linear problems.
    - **Evolutionary** method is for non-smooth problems.

    Leave this selection as the default - GRG Nonlinear, unless you're sure one of the other methods is more optimal for your problem. There is a brief description of the solving methods in the label below the drop-down list box.

9. Once you've entered all the parameters in the Solver Parameters dialog box, click **Solve** button.

Solver Results

When you click Solve on the Solver Parameters dialog box, the box will disappear and depending on how complex your problem is, you may see an indicator on Excel's status bar informing you of the progress of the Solver. On most occasions, however, the solution would be generated quickly, and the **Solver Results** dialog box will be displayed.

Solver Results   ✕

Solver found a solution. All Constraints and optimality
conditions are satisfied.   Reports
                                                     Answer
  ⊙ Keep Solver Solution   Sensitivity
                                                     Limits
  ○ Restore Original Values

  ☐ Return to Solver Parameters Dialog   ☐ Outline Reports

      OK   Cancel   Save Scenario...

Solver found a solution. All Constraints and optimality conditions are satisfied.

When the GRG engine is used, Solver has found at least a local optimal solution. When Simplex LP
is used, this means Solver has found a global optimal solution.

The **Solver Results** dialog box informs you whether a solution was found for your problem or not. If a solution were not found, the dialog box will inform you that a solution could not be found, and you will have the opportunity to go back and adjust the parameters.

If a solution was found, the Solver will display the new values in your worksheet, but the Solver Results dialog box will give you the option to keep the values provided by the solution or restore your original values.

To keep the solution found by the Solver, select **Keep Solver Solution** (if it is not already selected), then click **OK**.

◢	A	B	C	D	E
1	**Sales Forecast**				
2					
3		Qtr 1	Qtr 2	Assumptions	
4	Sales	$800,250.40	$915,620.72	14%	
5	Cost of production	($139,705.00)	($145,790.62)	4%	
6	Gross Profit	$660,545.40	$769,830.10		
7	Expenses	($84,267.00)	($89,330.10)	6%	
8	Income	$576,278.40	$680,500.00		
9					
10					
11					
12					

From the worksheet model in the image above, you can see that the Solver changed the growth percentages for *Sales* (14%), *Cost of Production* (4%), and *Expenses* (6%), to achieve the target *Income* for *Qtr 2* of £680,500.00. You may also notice that the Solver stayed within the 15% constraint set for the *SalesGrowth* cell.

If you do not want to keep the solution and instead return to the original values in your worksheet, select the **Restore Original Values** option.

To save the solution as a scenario before restoring your original values, click the **Save Scenario** button and assign a name to it. Once you have saved it, you can then select the Restore Original Values option and click **OK** to close the Solver Results dialog box.

You can also click the **Cancel** button on the Solver Results dialog box to dismiss the Solver and return your original values.

Note   If you choose to keep the solution provided by the Solver, unlike the Goal Seek command, you can't undo the changes by clicking the Undo command on the Quick Access Toolbar. If you want to retain your original values, select **Restore Original Values,** and then click on **Save Scenario** to save the scenario for later viewing. That way, you can keep your original values in the worksheet and use the Scenario Manager (covered previously in this chapter) to display the solution generated by the Solver.

Solver Options

The default options used by the Solver is adequate for most problems, however, in some situations, you may want to change the options before generating a solution with the Solver.

To change the Solver options, click the **Options** button in the Solver Parameters dialog box. Excel opens the **Options** dialog box which has three tabs: All Methods, GRG Nonlinear, and Evolutionary.

The following settings apply to the Solver options.

- **Constraint precision**: This specifies the precision of the constraints added. To satisfy a constraint, the relationship between the cell reference and the value of the constraint cannot be more than this amount. The smaller this number is, the higher the precision.

- **Use automatic scaling**: Select this option if you want the Solver to automatically scale the results.

- **Show iteration results**: Select this option if you want the Solver to show the results for the iterations it followed in solving the problem.

- **Ignore integer constraints**: Select this checkbox if you want the Solver to ignore any constraints that you specified that use integers.

- **Integer optimality (%)**: This option specifies the percentage of integer optimality that the Solver applies when solving the problem.

- **Max time (Seconds)**: This value specifies the maximum number of seconds that you want the Solver to spend in finding a solution before it times out.

- **Iterations**: This value specifies the maximum number of iterations you want the Solver to make in recalculating the worksheet when finding the solution.

- **Max Subproblems**: This value specifies the maximum number of subproblems that you want the Solver to take when using the Evolutionary method in solving the problem.

- **Max feasible solutions**: This value specifies the maximum number of feasible solutions that you want the Solver to pursue when using the Evolutionary method in solving the problem.

Note that the Options dialog box also has the **GRG Nonlinear** and **Evolutionary** tabs where you can make additional changes to the settings.

After making changes to the Solver options, click **OK** to return to the Solver Parameters dialog box.

-☼-Tip
Only make a change to an option in the Solver if you understand what that setting represents and how the change will affect your worksheet model, otherwise the default values will suffice for most Solver problems.

Saving and Loading Solver Problem Models

When you save your workbook, the objective cell, variable cells, constraint, and Solver options that were last entered in the Solver Parameters dialog box are saved as part of the worksheet. These parameters will be loaded in the Solver Parameters dialog box the next time it is opened.

When you create other problem models for the worksheet that you want to also save, you must use the **Load/Save** button in the Solver Parameters dialog box to save them.

When you click the **Load/Save** button, Excel displays the **Load/Save Model** dialog box.

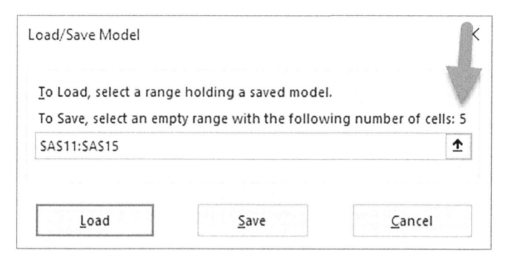

To **Save**, click the text box in the Load/Save Model dialog box and select an empty vertical range in your worksheet with enough cells to hold all the parameters you entered for the problem model. To help, the message in the Load/Save Model dialog box will tell you how many cells you need to select.

Once you have entered the range in the text box, click the **Save** button and the values will be saved to that range in your worksheet.

To **Load** a saved model, click the text box, and then select the range in your worksheet with the saved model, then click the **Load** button. The parameters saved in the range will then be loaded in the Solver Parameters dialog box.

Solver Reports

There are three types of reports you can create from the Solver Results dialog box:

- **Answer**: This report lists the result cell and the variable cells with their original values, final values, and any constraints used as parameters.

- **Sensitivity**: This report shows you how sensitive an optimal solution is to changes in the formulas behind the objective cell and constraints.

- **Limits**: This report displays the objective cell and the variable cells with their values, lower and upper limits, and results. The lower limit is the lowest value that the variable cells can have while still meeting the constraints. The upper limit represents the highest value that will do this.

To generate a report, in the Solver Results dialog box, select one or more of the reports in the **Reports** list box before clicking **OK**.

You can generate one or all of the reports as the Reports list box allows you to select more than one item on the list. When you click **OK**, Excel will generate the selected reports in separate worksheets, adding them to the beginning of the workbook.

Chapter 7: Analyze Data Dynamically with PivotTables and PivotCharts

There are different ways you can create pivot tables in Excel 2019. We will focus here on the different methods you can use to create pivot tables, including how to generate pivot charts from the pivoted data.

In this chapter, we will cover:

- How to create pivot tables with the Quick Analysis tool.
- How to create a Recommended PivotTable.
- How to create a pivot table manually.
- How to filter, sort and format pivot tables.
- How to create a pivot chart.

7.1 Creating PivotTables

An Excel PivotTable is a powerful tool that enables you to dynamically calculate, summarize, and analyze large data sets from different perspectives.

There are several ways to create a new PivotTable in Excel 2019:

- **Quick Analysis tool**: This option auto-generates a pivot table for you. When you select all the cells in your data list and click the Quick Analysis tool on the Tables tab, you get a list of pre-designed pivot tables for your data from which you can choose. When you select one, Excel inserts the pivot table in a new worksheet.

- **Recommended PivotTables button**: This option auto-generates a pivot table for you. When you select one cell in your data list and click on the Recommended PivotTables button on the Insert tab, you get a list of recommended pivot tables from which you can choose. When you select one, Excel inserts the pivot table in a new worksheet.

- **PivotTable button**: This option enables you to create a pivot table manually. When you select one cell in your data list and click on the PivotTable button on the Insert tab, Excel opens the Create PivotTable dialog box where you specify your data source and location of the pivot table before manually selecting the fields to use from the data.

Preparing Your Data

Some preparation is required to get a data list ready for a pivot table. The source data used for a pivot table needs to be organized as a list or converted to an Excel table (this is recommended although not compulsory).

A few steps to prepare the source data for a pivot table:

1. The data should have column headings in a single row on top.

2. Remove any temporary totals or summaries that are not part of the core data.

3. The data cannot have empty rows, so, delete any empty rows.

4. Ensure you do not have any extraneous data surrounding the list.

5. You may also want to convert the range to an Excel table (although it is not essential).

	A	B	C	D	E	F	G	H
1	Employee	Product	Customer	Order Date	Ship City	Item Cost	No. of Items	Total Cost
2	Anne Hellung-Larsen	Cora Fabric Chair	Acme LTD	11/24/2016	Las Vegas	$475.00	20	$9,500.00
3	Jan Kotas	Lukah Leather Chair	Elgin Homes	05/13/2016	New York	$345.00	9	$3,105.00
4	Mariya Sergienko	Habitat Oken Console Table	Mecury Builders	04/28/2016	Las Vegas	$36.00	28	$1,008.00
5	Michael Neipper	Hygena Fabric Chair	Infinity Homes	11/06/2016	Portland	$407.00	23	$9,361.00
6	Anne Hellung-Larsen	Harley Fabric Cuddle Chair	Elgin Homes	07/16/2016	New York	$803.00	20	$16,060.00
7	Jan Kotas	Windsor 2 Seater Cuddle Chair	B&B Seaside	04/27/2017	Denver	$302.00	8	$2,416.00
8	Mariya Sergienko	Fabric Chair	B&B Seaside	06/26/2016	Los Angelas	$425.00	11	$4,675.00
9	Laura Giussani	Verona 1 Shelf Telephone Table	Home Designers	04/07/2016	Milwaukee	$282.00	8	$2,256.00
10	Anne Hellung-Larsen	Floral Fabric Tub Chair	Acorn USA	08/17/2016	Memphis	$158.00	2	$316.00
11	Jan Kotas	Fabric Chair in a Box	Infinity Homes	04/20/2017	Portland	$857.00	28	$23,996.00
12	Mariya Sergienko	Slimline Console Table	Apex Homes	11/01/2016	Chicago	$534.00	29	$15,486.00
13	Nancy Freehafer	Collection Martha Fabric Wingback Chair	Empire Homes	09/24/2017	Boise	$137.00	15	$2,055.00
14	Nancy Freehafer	Slimline Console Table	Apex Homes	04/15/2017	Chicago	$433.00	16	$6,928.00
15	Nancy Freehafer	Fabric Wingback Chair	Express Builders	09/03/2016	Miami	$210.00	2	$420.00
16	Nancy Freehafer	Fabric Chair in a Box - Denim Blue	Impressive Homes	04/23/2016	Seattle	$634.00	14	$8,876.00
17	Nancy Freehafer	Tessa Fabric Chair	Acorn USA	02/10/2017	Memphis	$252.00	23	$5,796.00
18	Robert Zare	Collection Bradley Riser Recline Fabric Chair	Northern Contractors	01/05/2016	Salt Lake City	$281.00	5	$1,405.00
19	Michael Neipper	Fabric Wingback Chair	Home Designers	05/15/2017	Milwaukee	$405.00	30	$12,150.00
20	Mariya Sergienko	Tessa Fabric Chair	Infinity Homes	05/11/2017	Portland	$472.00	5	$2,360.00

Once the data has been prepared, you can now create a pivot table.

Create a PivotTable with the Quick Analysis Tool

In Excel 2019, you can quickly create a pivot table for your data list by using the Quick Analysis tool. If you're not that familiar with creating pivot tables but you have an idea of want you want to summarize, the Quick Analysis tool will recommend a series of pre-designed options from which you can choose.

Follow the steps below to create a pivot table from the Quick Analysis tool:

1. Select all the data in your data list (including the headings). Note that if you have assigned a range name to your data list, you can select the whole list by choosing the name from the Name box drop-down menu.

2. After you select the data list, the Quick Analysis tool appears on the lower-right of the selection. Click on the **Quick Analysis** tool to open the Quick Analysis palette.

3. Click on the **Tables** tab to display various PivotTable options for your data (after the Table button).

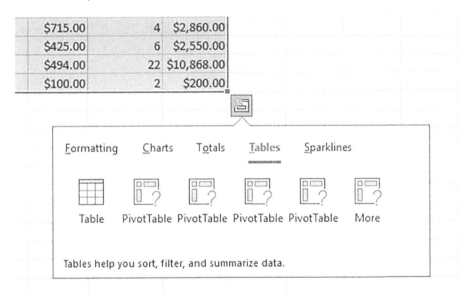

4. To see a live preview of each PivotTable option, move your mouse pointer over each button. You'll see a live preview (i.e. based on your data) of the type of pivot table that option will generate.

5. When you find a preview that you want, click on its button. Excel 2019 then generates the PivotTable in a new worksheet (inserted in front of the worksheet with the source data). You can rename and move this worksheet to a different part of your workbook if you want.

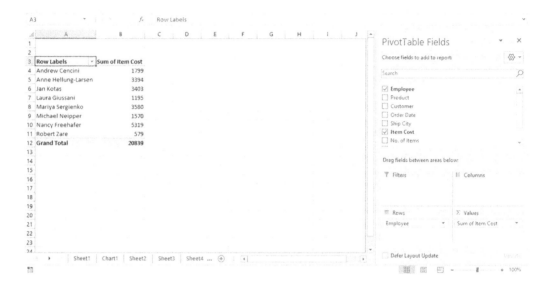

Notes:

- When you select any area in the new pivot table that has been created, the **PivotTable Fields** task pane will be displayed on the right side of the worksheet window.

- When you click any cell within the pivot table, two new contextual tabs will be displayed on the Ribbon - **PivotTable Analyze** and **Design.** These contextual tabs provide several tools and commands that you can use to modify and format your pivot table, just as you would if you had created it manually.

- On some occasions, Excel may not be able to suggest pivot table options with the Data Analysis tool, particularly if it can't analyze your data due to how your worksheet model is structured.

  When this happens, on the Tables tab of the Quick Analysis palette, a single blank PivotTable button will be displayed after the Table button. You can click that button to manually create your pivot table. We will cover how to manually create pivot tables later in this chapter.

Create a Recommended PivotTable

Another way to create a pivot table is by using the **Recommended PivotTables** command on the ribbon. This method is even faster than using the Quick Analysis tool (as long as you have prepared the data list with column headings as described earlier in this chapter).

Follow the steps below to use this method to create a pivot table:

1. Click anywhere within the data list for which you want to create a new pivot table.

2. On the **Insert** tab, in the **Tables** group, click on the **Recommended PivotTables** command button.

   Excel will open the **Recommended PivotTables** dialog box which presents a list of pivot table options for your data. You can click on each item on the list to see a live preview on the right pane of the dialog box.

3. Once you find one that has the type of summary you want to create, select the item, and click the **OK** button.

A new pivot table will be created in a new worksheet in front of the worksheet with the data source. With the pivot table selected, the **PivotTable Fields** task pane is displayed on the right side of the worksheet. Also, the **PivotTable Analyze** and **Design** contextual tabs will be available on the Ribbon.

Note If none of the recommended PivotTables meet your requirements, click on the **Blank PivotTable** button on the **Recommended PivotTables** dialog box to create the pivot table manually.

Creating a PivotTable Manually

To create a pivot table:

1. Click on any cell in your range or table.

2. On the **Insert** tab, click the **PivotTable** button.

   The **Create PivotTable** dialog box will be displayed.

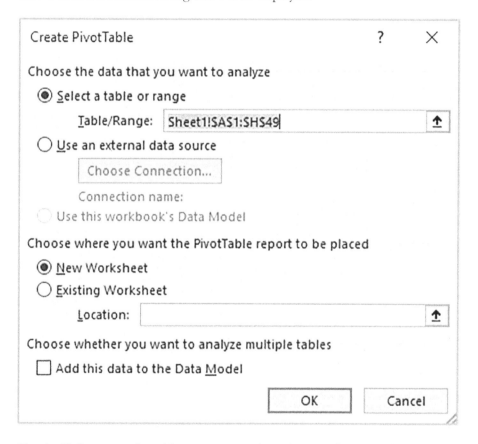

Excel will figure out the table or range you intend to use for your pivot table, and it will select it in the **Table/Range** field. If this is not accurate then you can manually select the range by clicking on the Expand Dialog box button (up arrow) on the field.

The next option on the screen is where you want to place the pivot table. The default location is in a new worksheet. It is best to have your pivot table on a worksheet separate from your source data, so select the **New Worksheet** option here if it's not already selected.

3. Click on **OK**.

A new worksheet will now be created with a PivotTable placeholder, and on the right side, you'll see a dialog box - **PivotTable Fields**.

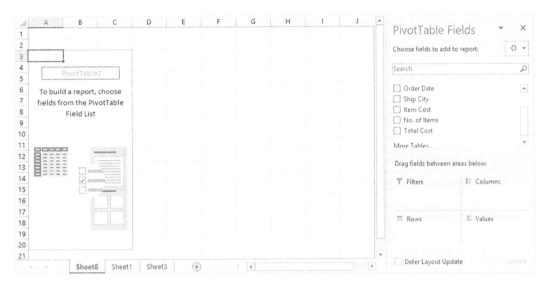

The PivotTable tool has four areas where you can place fields:

Rows, **Columns**, **Values**, and **Filters**.

To add a field to your PivotTable, select the checkbox next to the field name in the PivotTable Fields pane. When you select fields, they are added to their default areas. Non-numeric fields are added to the **Rows** box. Date and time fields are added to the **Columns** box. Numeric fields are added to the **Values** box.

You can also drag fields from the list to one of the four areas you want to place it. To move one field to another, you can drag it there.

To remove a field from a box, click on it and click **Remove Field** from the pop-up menu. You can also just uncheck it in the fields list or drag it away from the box and drop it back on the fields list.

Example

In this example, let's say we want a summary of our data that shows the total spent by each Customer.

1. Select the **Customer** field on the list and it will be added to the Rows box. The PivotTable will also be updated with the list of customers as row headings.

2. Next, select the **Total Cost** field and this will be added to the **Values** box.

The PivotTable will now be updated with the **Sum of Total Cost** for each Customer.

	Row Labels ▾	Sum of Total Cost
3		
4	Acme LTD	13226
5	Acorn USA	13292
6	Apex Homes	33082
7	B&B Seaside	48997
8	Elgin Homes	54504
9	Empire Homes	9355
10	Express Builders	11004
11	Home Designers	52322
12	Impressive Homes	14775
13	Infinity Homes	85612
14	Mecury Builders	17760
15	Northern Contractors	2001
16	Orion Spaces	4806
17	Grand Total	360736

So, as you can see, we have been able to get a quick summary of our data with just a few clicks. If we had hundreds of thousands of records, this could have taken many hours to accomplish, if done manually.

We can add more values to the table by dragging them to the Values box from the list.

For example, if we wanted to add the total number of items per customer, we'll select **No. of Items** on the list or drag it to the **Values** box.

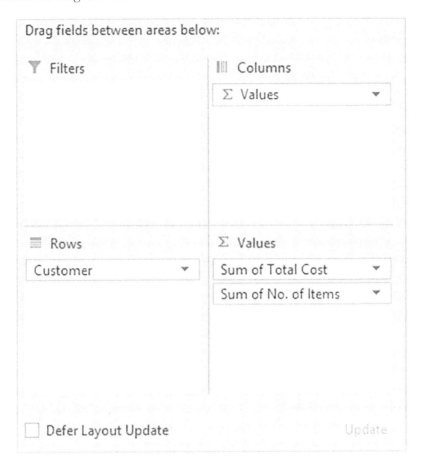

This will add the **Sum of No. of Items** for each customer to the PivotTable as shown in the image below.

Row Labels	Sum of No. of Items	Sum of Total Cost
Acme LTD	43	13226
Acorn USA	53	13292
Apex Homes	73	33082
B&B Seaside	88	48997
Elgin Homes	123	54504
Empire Homes	40	9355
Express Builders	14	11004
Home Designers	94	52322
Impressive Homes	31	14775
Infinity Homes	143	85612
Mecury Builders	52	17760
Northern Contractors	7	2001
Orion Spaces	33	4806
Grand Total	794	360736

To view the summary from the perspective of **Products**, that is, the total number of items sold and the total cost for each product, we would put **Product** in the Rows box and both **Total Cost** and **No. of Items** in the Values box.

To view the summary from the perspective of **Employees**, we would place **Employee** in the Rows box, and **No. of Items** and **Total Cost** in the Values box.

Here we see the data summarized by Employee, that is, how many items each employee sold, and the revenue generated.

Row Labels	Sum of No. of Items	Sum of Total Cost
Andrew Cencini	40	21418
Anne Hellung-Larsen	149	53969
Jan Kotas	110	70865
Laura Giussani	26	18690
Mariya Sergienko	176	78334
Michael Neipper	105	40203
Nancy Freehafer	181	75256
Robert Zare	7	2001
Grand Total	794	360736

If we want to see the number of items sold per city, we will place **Ship City** in the Rows box and **No. of Items** in the Values box.

	Row Labels	Sum of No. of Items
3		
4	Boise	40
5	Chicago	106
6	Denver	45
7	Las Vegas	95
8	Los Angelas	43
9	Memphis	53
10	Miami	44
11	Milwaukee	94
12	New York	93
13	Portland	143
14	Salt Lake City	7
15	Seattle	31
16	Grand Total	794

Summarizing Data by Date

To display the columns split into years, drag a date field into the Columns box, for example, Order Date. The PivotTable tool will automatically generate PivotTable fields for Quarters and Years. Once these fields have been generated, you should remove the Order Date field from the Columns box and place in the Quarter or Year field, depending on which one you want to use for your summary.

To display the row headings by date, place **Order Date** (or your date field) in the Rows box.

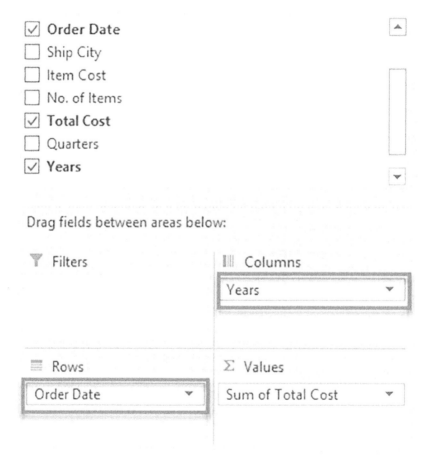

This will produce the following results.

Sum of Total Cost	Column Labels		
Row Labels	2016	2017	Grand Total
Jan	39569	7772	47341
Feb		22819	22819
Mar	5502	1854	7356
Apr	22724	57618	80342
May	3105	14510	17615
Jun	24021	596	24617
Jul	16060		16060
Aug	316	12141	12457
Sep	42763	9615	52378
Oct	16752		16752
Nov	34347	9756	44103
Dec	18896		18896
Grand Total	224055	136681	360736

Applying Formatting

As you can see, we can dynamically change how we want to view our data with just a few clicks. When you're happy with your summary, you can then apply formatting to the appropriate columns. For example, you could format **Sum of Total Cost** as **Currency** before any formal presentation of the data.

The good thing about PivotTables is that you can explore different types of summaries with the pivot table without changing the source data. If you make a mistake that you can't figure out how to undo, you can simply delete the PivotTable worksheet and recreate the PivotTable in a new worksheet.

Filter and Sort a PivotTable

On some occasions, you may want to limit what is displayed in the PivotTable You can sort and filter a PivotTable just like you can do to a range of data or an Excel table.

To filter a PivotTable:

1. Click on the AutoFilter (down arrow) on the Row Labels cell.

    The pop-up menu provides a list of the row headings in your PivotTable. You can select/deselect items on this list to limit the data being displayed in the PivotTable.

2. Uncheck **Select All.**

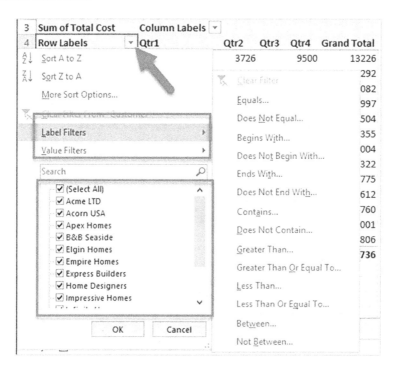

3. Scroll through the list and manually select the items you want to display.

4. Click **OK**.

The PivotTable will now show only the selected columns.

Applying a Custom Filter

You can also use the **Label Filters** and **Value Filters** menu commands to apply a custom filter to your PivotTable. This is done in the same way as you would do for a range or table. How to apply a custom filter to a data list is covered in **chapter 4 in Book 1: Excel Basics**.

Sorting PivotTable Data

To arrange the order of your data in a PivotTable, you use the same sorting methods you would use for a range or table.

- Click on the **AutoFilter** button on the column named **Row Labels**.

- Click on **Sort A to Z** (to sort in ascending order) or **Sort Z to A** (to sort in descending order). If your column headings are dates, then you'll get **Sort Oldest to Newest** (for ascending) and **Sort Newest to Oldest** (for descending).

7.2 Create Dynamic Charts with PivotCharts

Another way you can present and analyze your pivot data is by using charts. In Book 1, we covered creating, editing, and formatting regular Excel charts. Here we will be focusing on generating charts from pivot tables. A pivot chart is simply a chart based on a pivot table. So, instead of manually aggregating your data first before creating a regular Excel chart, you can simply generate a quick pivot table and pivot chart based on the pivot table. This makes the process much faster.

To create a pivot chart based on a pivot table, follow these steps:

1. Place the cell pointer anywhere in the pivot table. On the **Insert** tab, in the **Charts** group, click on the **PivotChart** command button.

   Note that you can also find the **PivotChart** command button in the **Tools** group of the **PivotTable Analyze** tab (which is displayed on the Ribbon when the cell pointer is in the PivotTable).

2. Excel opens the **Insert Chart** dialog box which allows you to select the type and subtype of the pivot chart you want to create.

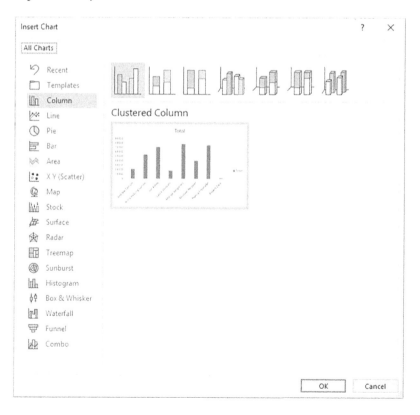

3. Select the type and subtype of the chart you want in the Insert Chart dialog box and click **OK**.

When you click OK, Excel inserts an embedded pivot chart in the worksheet with the pivot table used as the data source.

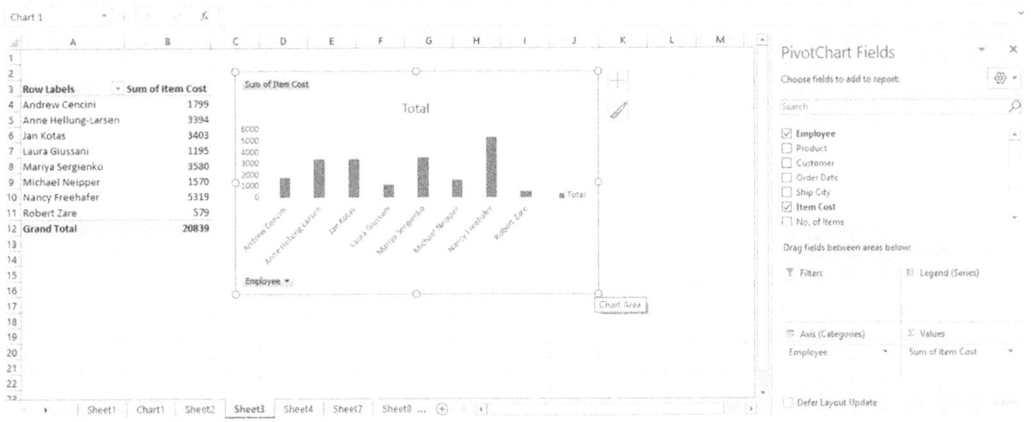

Tip

To move the chart around the screen, move your mouse pointer over the chart (the mouse pointer will change to a crosshair), then click and drag the chart to any part of the screen you want.

When you click on the PivotChart, three additional tabs appear on the Ribbon, **PivotChart Analyze**, **Design**, and **Format**. You can use commands on these tabs to redesign, modify, and format your pivot chart.

Filtering a PivotChart

After you generate a new pivot chart, you'll notice Field Buttons on the chart. These are drop-down list buttons for each of the fields represented on the chart. You can use these dropdown buttons in the pivot chart itself to filter what is represented on the chart in the same way you can do with the pivot table.

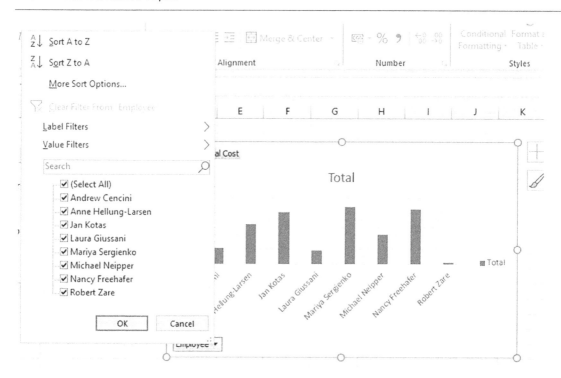

For our example above, we have the *Employee* drop-down button on the chart as that is the value being represented in the chart area.

To filter the chart, for example, if you want to exclude some names, you can click on the Employee drop-down button and uncheck **Select All**. Then you can individually select the names you want to represent in the filtered pivot chart.

To hide the Field Buttons on the chart, for example, if you want to print the chart without the buttons, do the following:

1. On the Ribbon, click the **PivotChart Analyze** contextual tab.

2. In the **Show/Hide** group, click **Field Buttons** (click the button's image rather than it's dropdown arrow). You can toggle this button to show or hide the field buttons on the chart.

Moving the PivotChart

To move the chart to another worksheet, do the following:

1. Click on the pivot chart and then click on the **PivotChart Analyze** tab.

2. In the **Actions** group, click the **Move Chart** command button. Excel displays the **Move Chart** dialog box.

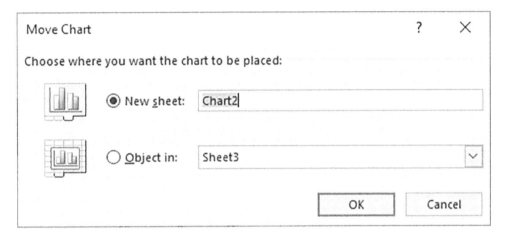

3. Select **New sheet** and in the corresponding text box, you can accept the default name provided for the new worksheet or type in another name of your choosing.

4. Click **OK** when done.

The pivot chart will be moved to a new worksheet.

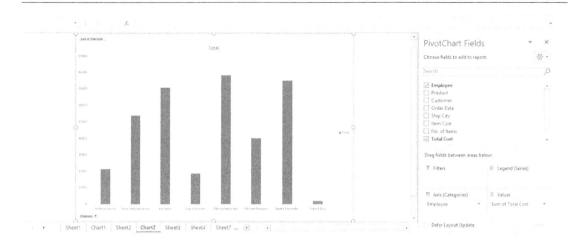

Generate a PivotTable and a PivotChart Simultaneously

You can generate a pivot table and a pivot chart simultaneously from your data list without having to generate the pivot table first.

To generate the pivot table and pivot chart together, do the following:

1. Click anywhere in the data list.
2. On the **Insert** tab click the drop-down arrow for the **PivotChart** command button.
3. Select **PivotChart & PivotTable** from the drop-down menu on the command button.
4. On the **Create PivotTable** dialog box, click the **OK** button.

Excel will create a new worksheet with the placeholders for a pivot table and a pivot chart. In the **PivotChart Fields** pane on the right side of the window, you can select the fields to go in your pivot chart, just as described in the section on manually creating a PivotTable in this chapter. As you select the fields you want for the chart in the PivotChart Fields pane, the pivot table and pivot chart will be created together.

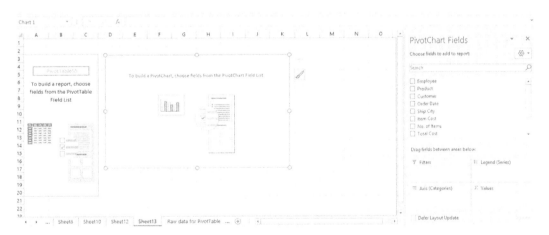

Formatting a Pivot Chart

Formatting a pivot chart is similar to formatting a regular Excel chart. This is covered in Book 1: Excel Basics. If you want to learn how to edit and format charts, look up **chapter 10, Creating Charts in Book 1**.

Chapter 8: Protect Workbooks, Worksheets, and Ranges

E xcel provides several methods at different levels that you can use to protect your workbooks and worksheets from unauthorised access, changes to the data, moving/deleting worksheets, or renaming worksheets in your workbook.

In this chapter, we will cover how to:

- Password-protect your Excel file.
- Set different access levels for your workbook with passwords.
- Protect your workbook structure from unauthorised changes.
- Protect individual worksheets within a workbook.
- Protect specific ranges within a worksheet.

⚠ **Important**

Before you protect your workbook with a password, ensure that you've got the password written down and stored in a safe place where it can be retrieved if necessary. Microsoft does not provide any methods to access a password-protected Excel file where the password has been lost. Without an advanced password cracking tool, it is impossible to gain access to an Excel file that has been password-protected, if the password has been forgotten.

8.1 Password-Protect Your Workbook

To quickly encrypt your workbook with a password on your Excel workbook:

1. Click **File** > **Info** > **Protect Document** > **Encrypt with Password**.

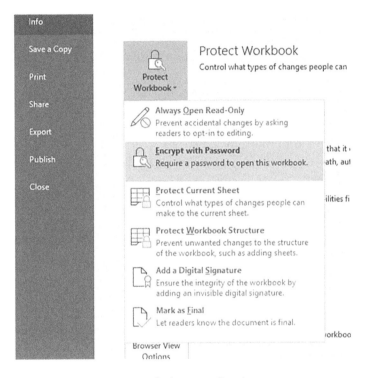

2. At the prompt enter your password, then confirm it.

3. Click on **OK** after confirming the password.

4. Save and close the workbook.

5. When you reopen the workbook, it will prompt you for the password.

Removing the Password

On some occasions, you may want to remove a password from an Excel file. The process of setting a password encrypts the file, so you'll need to remove the encryption to remove the password.

To remove the password of an Excel file, follow the steps below:

4. Open the workbook and enter the password in the Password box.

5. Click **File > Info > Protect Workbook > Encrypt with Password**.

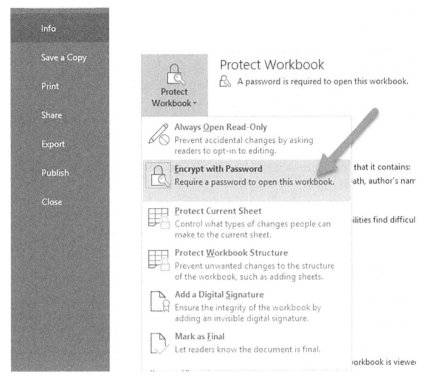

6. In the **Encrypt Document** dialog box, delete the contents of the **Password** text box.

7. Click **OK**.

8. Close and reopen the workbook. It will no longer challenge you for a password.

8.2 Set Different Access Levels

The password protection method described above enables you to quickly protect your Excel workbook from unauthorised access with a password. However, it does not provide a way to set different access levels, for example, **read-only** access and **read-write** access. To set different access levels with passwords, you need to use the older method where you save the file with a different name and insert the passwords during the process. This method allows you to set separate passwords for opening and modifying the file.

Note

        Only use this method (over the encryption method described above) if you want to create different access levels for different groups of users.

To set different passwords for opening and modifying an Excel file, do the following:

1. Click on **File** > **Save As** (or **Save a Copy** if your file is on OneDrive and AutoSave is set to **On**).

2. Click on the **More options** link (which is directly under the file type field). This will open the **Save As** dialog box.

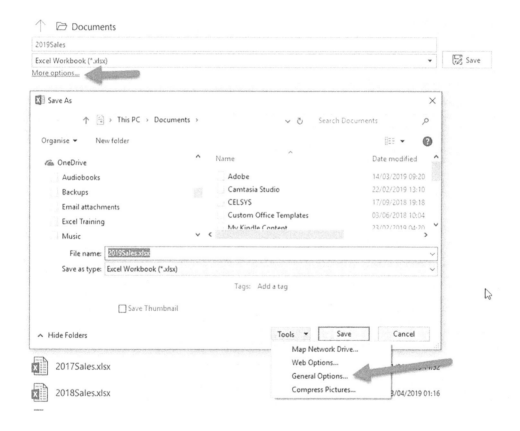

3. On the **Save As** dialog box, click on the **Tools** button and select **General Options** from the menu.

    This will display the **General Options** dialog box which enables you to set one password for opening the workbook and another for modifying the workbook.

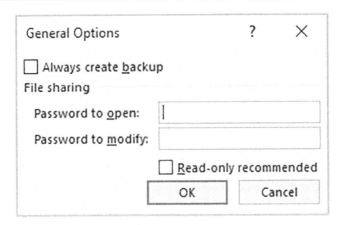

4. Enter different passwords in the **Password to modify** and **Password to open** boxes, and then click **OK**.

5. Two **Confirm Password** prompts will be displayed. Re-enter **Password to open** and **Password to modify** to confirm them.

6. In the **Save As** dialog box, in the **File nam**e field, enter a new name for the workbook and click **Save.** Note that you must save the file with a new name as Excel will not allow you to save it with the current name.

7. Close and reopen the workbook. This time Excel will challenge you with a prompt for a password to open the workbook. Enter the password and click **OK**.

8. Excel will display another password prompt for write-access to the workbook. Enter the write-access password in the **Password** field and click on **OK** (this is the password set in the Password to modify field).

Anyone with the password to open the workbook but not the password to modify it can open the file in read-only mode by clicking on the **Read Only** button.

Removing the Passwords Set in General Options

There may be occasions when you want to remove file protection and make the file accessible to all users. To remove the passwords set in General Options we need to delete them from General Options and save the file again.

Do the following to remove the passwords:

1. Open the Excel file with the current passwords.

2. Click on **File** to go to the backstage view and click on **Save As** (or **Save a Copy** if your file is saved on OneDrive).

3. Click on the **More options** link (which is directly under the file type text box). This will open the **Save As** window.

4. In the **Save As** dialog box, click on the **Tools** button and select **General Options** from the menu. This will display the **General Options** dialog box where you entered the passwords.

5. Delete the passwords from the **Password to modify** and **Password to open** fields and click on **OK** to dismiss the dialog box.

6. In the **Save As** dialog box, click on **Save** to save the file.

7. Close the workbook and reopen it. It will no longer prompt you for a password.

8.3 Protect the Workbook Structure

You can protect your workbook structure with a password to prevent other users from adding, moving, deleting, renaming, hiding, or viewing hidden worksheets. Note that, protecting the workbook structure is different from protecting an Excel file or worksheet with a password. When you protect your workbook structure, the file is still accessible to everyone with access to it, but they can't change the structure of the workbook.

To protect your workbook, carry out the following steps:

1.   On the **Review** tab of the ribbon, in the **Protect** group, click **Protect Workbook**.

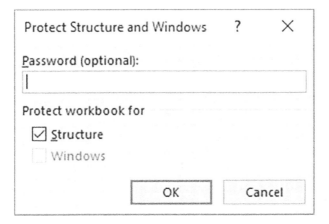

2.   In the **Protect Structure and Windows** dialog box enter a password in the **Password** field.

3.   Click **OK**.

4.   In the **Confirm Password** dialog box, re-enter the password and click **OK**.

With the workbook protected, all the commands that involve changing the structure of the workbook, for example, add, delete, move, or rename worksheets will be disabled. To re-enable these commands, you'll need to remove the password protection.

Unprotect the Workbook Structure

To unprotect your workbook's structure, do the following:

1. On the **Review** tab of the ribbon, in the **Protect** group, click **Protect Workbook**.

2. In the **Unprotect Workbook** dialog box, enter the workbook's password and click **OK**.

8.4 Protect Worksheets

Instead of protecting the whole workbook with a password, you can protect individual worksheets and even narrow it down to restricting certain actions within the sheet. For example, you can lock certain cells in the worksheet with formulas from being editable so that other users cannot accidentally delete formulas.

In a shared workbook, users could inadvertently delete formulas as they may not be aware that some cells are calculated values rather than ordinary values. To prevent this from happening, cells with formulas are often protected in shared worksheets.

Another reason to protect parts of your worksheet is that you may have some core data that you don't want users to change. You can protect those ranges only on the worksheet.

Worksheet protection involves two steps:

1. First, unlock the cells that you want to keep editable. If you don't take this step all cells in the worksheet will be locked when you protect it.

2. Protect the worksheet with or without a password.

Step 1 - Unlock any cells/ranges that need to be editable:

1. Click on the worksheet name tab that you want to protect to select it. In the worksheet area, select the range(s) that you don't want protected.

⌖-Tip You can select multiple ranges by holding down the **Ctrl** key while selecting additional ranges.

2. On the **Home** tab, in the **Cells** group, click on **Format > Format Cells**.

3. Click on the **Protection** tab and clear the **Locked** checkbox.

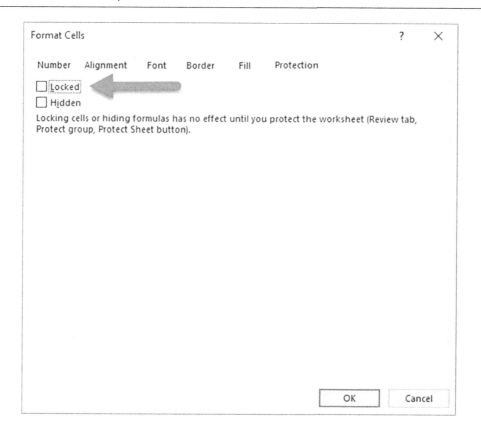

Step 2 - Protect the worksheet:

Next, you can choose specific actions that users are allowed to carry out in the worksheet.

1. On the **Review** tab, in the **Protect** group, click **Protect Sheet**.

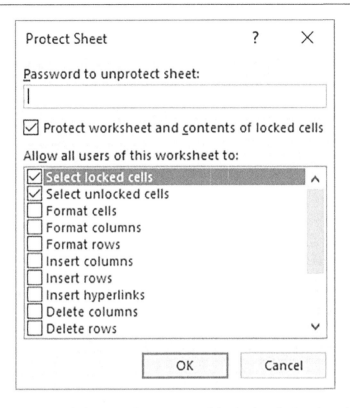

2. Ensure **Protect worksheet and contents of locked cells** is selected. This should be selected by default.

3. In the section named **Allow all users of this worksheet to**, check the actions you want users to be able to carry out on the worksheet. For example, you could allow users to insert rows and columns, sort data, format cells, use AutoFilter etc. among the many options on the list.

4. Optional: You can specify a password to lock your worksheet, but this is optional. You can protect the sheet without a password, but a user can click the **Unprotect Sheet** button to deactivate the sheet protection. If you want to prevent people from doing this, you can enter a password in the **Password to unprotect sheet** field and click **OK**. Re-enter the password at the **Confirm Password** prompt and click **OK** to complete the action.

⚠️ **Important**   If you set a password to protect your worksheet, you'll need the password whenever you want to unprotect it. Hence, it is critical that you remember your password. Ideally, you want to have it written down somewhere under lock and key for easy retrieval if needed. If the password is lost, there are no tools provided by Microsoft to retrieve it.

Unprotect a Worksheet

In a protected worksheet, in place of the **Protect Sheet** command button on the **Review** tab, you'll see an **Unprotect Sheet** command button.

To unprotect the sheet, click the **Unprotect Sheet** command button. If it was protected with a password, you'll get a password prompt. Enter the password, and then click **OK** to unprotect the worksheet.

8.5 Protect Specific Ranges

When you protect a worksheet, by default Excel locks all cells, unless you specifically unlock some cells before you enable protection (as described above). If all cells are locked, then to access the locked parts of the sheet you have to remove the sheet protection altogether.

What if we have occasions where we want to enable some users to have access to locked ranges without removing the sheet protection?

Excel provides a solution with the **Allow Edit Ranges** command. You can password protect specific ranges in the worksheet rather than the whole sheet.

Also, if you're using a Microsoft Windows machine that is on a network domain, you can give specific users in your domain permission to edit ranges in a protected worksheet.

The process involves two steps:

1. Specify the ranges to be password protected.

2. Protect the worksheet.

Step 1 - Follow these steps to specify the ranges to be password protected:

1. If the worksheet is already protected, you need to unprotect the sheet first.

2. Select the worksheet that you want to protect by clicking on the sheet tab at the bottom of the screen.

3. On the **Review** tab, in the **Protect** group, click **Allow Edit Ranges**. Note that this command button is only available when the worksheet is unprotected.

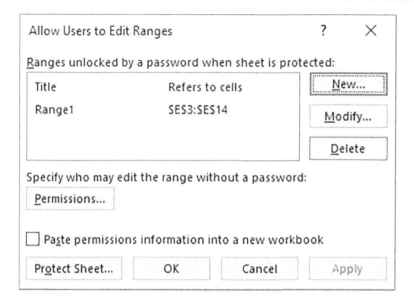

4. To add a new range that you want to be editable using a password, click **New**.

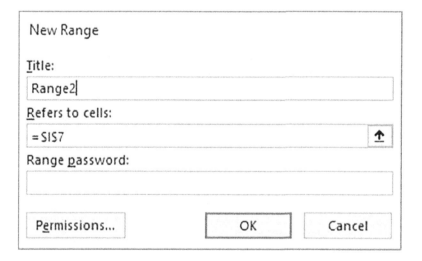

5. On the **New Range** dialog box, in the **Title** field, type the name for the range that you want to unlock.

6. In the **Refers to** cells field, you can type in the cell reference of the range, starting with an equal sign (=). Alternatively, you can click on the Collapse Dialog button (the up arrow on the field) and select the range on the worksheet. Click the Collapse Dialog button again to return to the New Range dialog box.

7. In the **Range password** field, enter a password that allows access to the range.

Note   To use domain permissions, click the **Permissions** button and follow the process to add a domain user. This only applies to network domains with multiple user accounts.

8. Click **OK** to return to the **Allow Users to Edit Ranges** dialog box.

Step 2 - Protect the worksheet:

1. In the **Allow Users to Edit Ranges** dialog box, click the **Protect Sheet** button.

Note   If you have closed the **Allow Users to Edit Ranges** dialog box, then click **Protect Sheet** on the **Review** tab of the Ribbon.

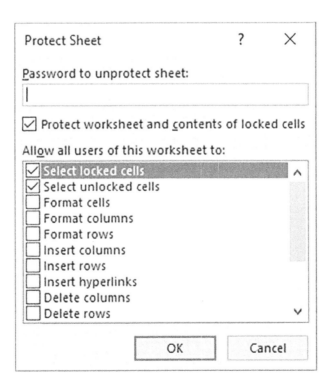

2. The **Protect worksheet and contents of locked cells** check box should be selected by default. If it is not you should select it.

3. In the **Allow all users of this worksheet to** list, select the actions you want users to be able to carry out on the worksheet. For example, you could allow users to insert rows and columns, sort data, format cells, or use AutoFilter, among the many options on the list.

4. In the **Password to unprotect sheet** field, enter a password and click **OK**. Re-enter the password to confirm it and click **OK** again.

    As mentioned previously, the password is optional. If you don't set a password, any user can click the **Unprotect Sheet** button on the Ribbon to unprotect the sheet.

Once a range has been protected, the user will be prompted to enter a password when they try to edit it. They'll only need to enter the password once per session.

⚠ **Important**
This has been mentioned earlier in this chapter but is worth repeating. If you set a password to protect your worksheet, you'll need the password whenever you want to unprotect it. Hence, it is critical that you remember your password. Ideally, you want to have it written down somewhere under lock and key for easy retrieval if needed. If you forget the password, there are no easy tools provided by Microsoft to retrieve it.

Book 3

Excel Functions

In Book 3

Excel Functions covers over 70 of the most useful functions in Excel from several categories. The functions covered in this book have been carefully selected based on data from Microsoft on how often they're used in common Excel tasks and specialized work. Each function is covered in detail - the syntax, description of arguments, and examples to demonstrate its use. You also learn how to combine functions in your formulas to create answers.

Contents at a Glance

Chapter 1: How to Enter a Function

Chapter 2: Lookup and Reference Functions

Chapter 3: Logical Functions

Chapter 4: Math Functions

Chapter 5: Statistical Functions

Chapter 6: Date and Time Functions

Chapter 7: Text Functions

Chapter 8: Financial Functions

Chapter 1: How to Enter a Function

To insert a formula/function:

1. Click the cell where you want to display the result.
2. Click in the formula bar.
3. Enter your formula, starting your entry with the equal sign (=). This specifies that your entry is a formula and not a static value.

For example:

=SUM(A2:A10)

Function Library

| A11 | ▾ | ⋮ | ✕ | ✓ | *fx* | =SUM(A2:A10) |

◢	A	B	C	D	E	F
1						
2	12					
3	40					
4	68					
5	96					
6	124					
7	152					
8	180					
9	208					
10	236					
11	A10)					
12						
13						

Tip As much as possible, avoid typing cell references directly into the formula bar as it could introduce errors. Instead, enter the name of the formula and then open bracket, for example, enter **=SUM(**. Then select the cells you want for your argument in the worksheet itself, then enter the closing bracket.

The Insert Function Dialog Box

A second way you can enter a function is by using the **Insert Function** dialog box.

Click in the formula bar to place the cursor there and click the **Insert Function** command on the **Formulas** tab, or the Insert Function button next to the formula bar.

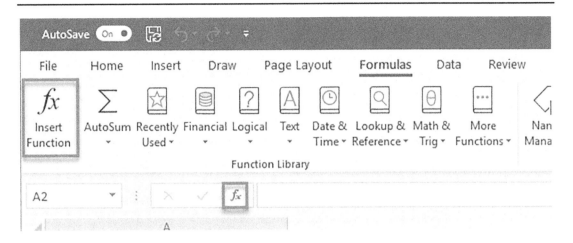

This will display the **Insert Function** dialog box. This dialog box provides the option to search for the function or select it from a category.

To search for the function, enter the name of the function in the **Search for a function** box. For example, if you were searching for the IF function you would enter IF in the search box and click **Go**. The **Select a function** list will display all the functions related to your search term.

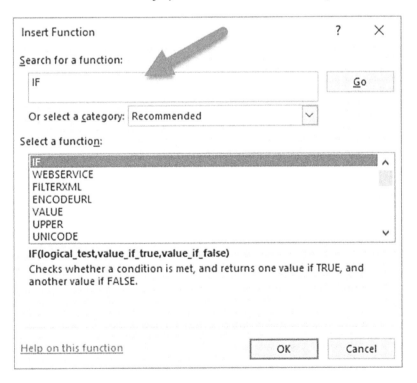

You can also use the **category** drop-down list to select a function if you know its category in Excel. For example, you can find the IF function in the **Logical** category.

If you have used a function recently it'll be listed in the **Most Recently Used** category.

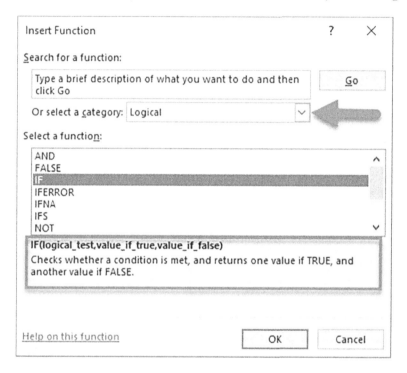

When you select a function on the list, you'll see the syntax for the function and a description of what the function does below the list.

Once you've selected the one you want, click **OK** to go to the **Functions Arguments** screen.

The Functions Arguments screen enables you to enter the arguments for the function. A function argument is a piece of data that the function needs in order to run.

The Functions Arguments screen is particularly useful if you are not familiar with a function because it provides a description of each argument, a preview of your entries, and the result returned by the function.

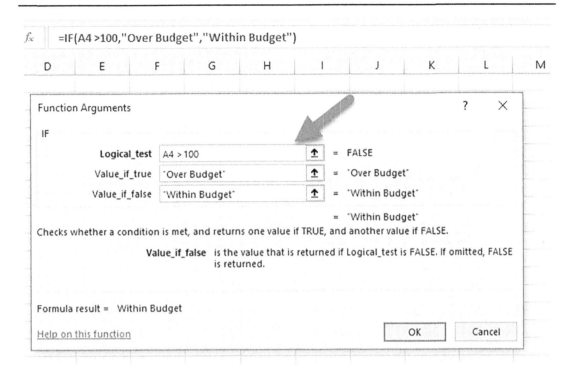

fx =IF(A4 >100,"Over Budget","Within Budget")

After entering the arguments, click **OK** and the formula will be inserted in the formula bar.

Chapter 2: Lookup and Reference Functions

The Lookup and Reference functions can be found by clicking on the **Lookup & Reference** command button on the Formulas tab on the Ribbon. Excel provides many functions to enable you to look up one piece of data using another. Reference functions allow you to search for specific information or return certain information about your worksheet.

In this chapter, we'll cover functions that enable you to:

- Lookup data in a list, table, or range based on a lookup value.
- Transpose a column or row of data.
- Choose a value from a list, table, or range based on a search index.
- Return the address of a cell in your worksheet.
- Display the formula of a cell (rather than the return value).
- Return the number of rows or columns in a range.

Find Data with XLOOKUP

XLOOKUP is a new function recently introduced as a replacement for the VLOOKUP function. Just like its predecessor, XLOOKUP searches a range or an array and returns a value corresponding to the first match it finds on the same row in another range.

For instance, you can look up the *Price* of a product in a data list using the *product ID* or *Name*. Similarly, you can return the name of an employee using their employee ID. If XLOOKUP does not find a match, you can tell it to return the closest (approximate) match.

Unlike VLOOKUP, which only allows you to return values from a column to the right of the lookup range, XLOOKUP can return values from columns to the left or the right of the lookup range. XLOOKUP also returns exact matches by default, which makes it easier and more convenient to use than its predecessor.

Note The XLOOKUP function is only available to Microsoft 365 subscribers. If you are using a 'one-time purchase' version of Excel 2019 or Excel 2016, XLOOKUP will not be available. If you are a Microsoft 365 subscriber and you cannot find this function in Excel, update your Microsoft 365 installation and this function should become available.

Syntax:

=XLOOKUP(lookup_value, lookup_array, return_array, [if_not_found], [match_mode], [search_mode])

Arguments and Descriptions

Argument	Description
lookup_value	Required. What value are you searching for? Excel will look for a match for this value in the *lookup_array*. You can provide a value here or a cell reference containing the value you want to find.
lookup_array	Required. Where do you want to search? This is the lookup range containing the columns you want to include in your search, for example, A2:D10.
return_array	Required. Which range contains the values you want to return? This is the return range. The return range can have one or more columns as XLOOKUP can return more than one value.
[if_not_found]	Optional. This optional argument enables you to enter a piece of text to return if a valid match is not found. If this argument is omitted and a valid match is not found, XLOOKUP will return the #N/A error.
[match_mode]	Optional. This optional argument enables you to specify a match mode from four options: 0 (or omitted) = Exact match. If no match is found an error will be returned (#N/A). This is the default if you omit this argument. -1 - Exact match or the next smallest item, if an exact match is not found.

	1 - Exact match or the next largest item, if an exact match is not found.
	2 - Performs a wildcard match where you can use the characters *, ?, and ~ for wildcard searches.
[search_mode]	Optional. This optional argument enables you to specify the order in which you want to perform the search:
	1 (or omitted) - Search first to last. This is the default if this argument is omitted.
	-1 - Perform the search in reverse order - last to first.
	2 - Perform a binary search for data sorted in ascending order. If lookup_array is not sorted in ascending order, invalid results will be returned.
	-2 - Perform a binary search for data sorted in descending order. If lookup_array is not sorted in descending order, invalid results will be returned.

-⊙-Tip
Regarding the *search_mode* argument, in earlier versions of Excel, performing binary searches on sorted lists produced quicker results, but in Microsoft 365, non-binary searches are equally fast. Hence, it is no longer beneficial to use binary search options for sorted lists. Use 1 or -1 for the *search_mode* argument as it means you don't require a sorted table.

Vertical Lookup

In this example, we are using XLOOKUP to return the reorder level of the product entered in cell F1. The formula is in cell F2.

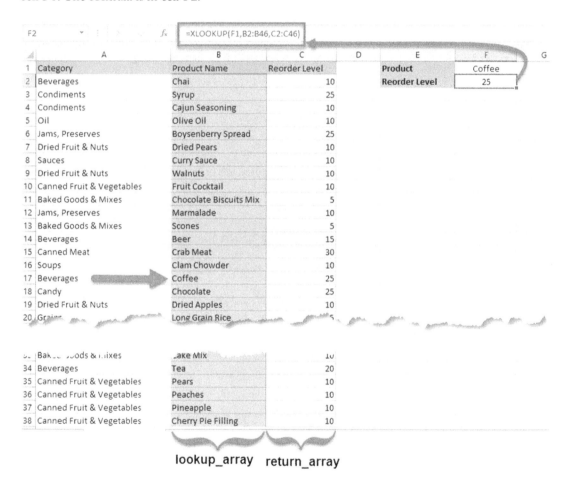

Formula explanation:

=XLOOKUP(F1,B2:B46,C2:C46)

The formula says, in range B2:B46, find the value in cell F1 (which in this case is "Coffee") and return the value on the same row in range C2:C46.

The *if_not_found* argument has not been provided here so if a match is not found it will return an error which is the default behaviour.

The VLOOKUP equivalent of this formula would look like this:

=VLOOKUP(F1,B2:C46,2,0)

One benefit of using the XLOOKUP equivalent over this formula is that if we decide at some point to insert a column between columns B and C, it will not break the formula.

The lookup_array does not need to be sorted because XLOOKUP will return an exact match by default.

Horizontal Lookup

XLOOKUP can perform both vertical and horizontal lookups. Thus, you can also use it in place of the HLOOKUP function.

In the example below, we can retrieve the value associated with a month using the name of the month.

=XLOOKUP(B7,A3:L3,A4:L4)

The formula uses only the first 3 arguments of the XLOOKUP function. B7 is the lookup_value, A3:L3 is the lookup_array, and A4:L4 is the return_array.

Note that a horizontal lookup_array must contain the same number of columns as the return_array.

Simultaneous Vertical and Horizontal Lookup

In this example, we will use two XLOOKUP functions to perform both a vertical and horizontal match. Here, our formula will first look for the Salesperson named "Mark" in range A4:A15, then look for "Q3" in the top row of the table (range B3:E3) and return the value at the intersection of the two. Previously, you would need to use the INDEX/MATCH/MATCH combination to achieve the same result.

I4				f_x	=XLOOKUP(G4,A4:A15,XLOOKUP(H4,B3:E3,B4:E15))				
	A	B	C	D	E	F	G	H	I	J
1	**Sales data**									
2										
3	**Salesperson**	**Q1**	**Q2**	**Q3**	**Q4**					
4	Penny	17,526	23,972	**61,066**	22,596		Mark	Q3	19,062	
5	Leslie	49,405	36,646	**21,899**	62,629					
6	Sally	78,658	16,529	**14,976**	68,184					
7	Shaun	80,176	84,918	**66,561**	65,326					
8	Julie	86,988	29,692	**30,197**	80,960					
9	Velma	94,514	13,333	**78,000**	59,718					
10	Ian	23,183	21,547	**40,408**	57,767					
11	Cassandra	70,597	19,615	**54,664**	68,175					
12	Mark	16,832	91,907	**19,062**	22,167					
13	Kathy	45,446	14,638	**52,312**	92,069					
14	Renee	34,583	78,213	**21,295**	26,964					
15	Judith	18,689	91,081	**66,795**	96,860					

Formula explanation:

=XLOOKUP(G4,A4:A15,XLOOKUP(H4,B3:E3,B4:E15))

The first XLOOKUP function has the following arguments:

lookup_value = G4

lookup_array = A4:A15

return_array = XLOOKUP(H4,B3:E3,B4:E15)

The second XLOOKUP, which is executed first, performs a horizontal search on B3:E3, using the value in cell H4 (which is "Q3") as the lookup_value, then returns the range **D4:D15**. Notice that the second XLOOKUP returns a range rather than a value. This range is what is used as the return_array argument for the first XLOOKUP.

So, after the second XLOOKUP has been executed, the first XLOOKUP will look like this:

=XLOOKUP(G4,A4:A15,D4:D15)

To examine how the formula performs the task, you can use the **Evaluate Formula** dialog box in Excel to see how each part of the formula is evaluated.

Follow the steps below to open the Evaluate Formula dialog box:

1. Select the cell with the formula you want to evaluate. In this case, it is cell **I4**.

2. On the **Formulas** tab, in the **Formula Auditing** group, click the **Evaluate Formula** command button.

3. In the Evaluate Formula dialog box, continue clicking the **Evaluate** button until the second XLOOKUP function has been evaluated and its result displayed as an argument to the first XLOOKUP function. For our example, you will need to click the Evaluate button three times.

You will notice that the second XLOOKUP performs a search using the lookup_value, "Q3", and then returns the range **D4:D15** (displayed as an absolute reference $D$4:D15). We can use XLOOKUP here as the *return_array* argument of the first XLOOKUP function because XLOOKUP can return a range as well as a value.

Next, the main XLOOKUP then performs a lookup using the value in cell G4, "Mark" as the lookup_value, cells A4:A15 as the lookup_array, and cells D4:D15 as the return_array to return the final result.

Return Multiple Values with Horizontal Spill

In this example, we want to be able to enter the name of a sales rep and return the number of orders and sales associated with them. This means the function will return more than one value. XLOOKUP is also an array function because it can return an array of values from the return_array.

In the formula below, the lookup_value is in cell G2, the lookup_array argument is range A2:A12 and the return_array argument is range C2:D12.

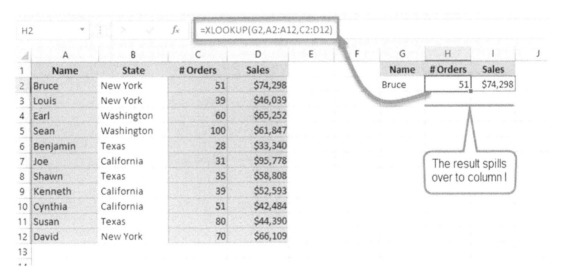

Formula explanation:

=XLOOKUP(G2,A2:A12,C2:D12)

As you can see from the formula, the return_array contains columns C and D. Thus, when we enter the name "Bruce" in cell G2, XLOOKUP returns the values in columns C and D from the same row. As the function returns more than one value, the result spills into cell I2.

The range containing the spilled result has a blue border around it indicating that the result has spilled into other cells. This is known as the **spill range**.

Return Multiple Values with Vertical Spill

To get the formula to spill vertically, we can use another example where we need to return the sales for more than one person on our list.

In this example, we first use the FILTER function to generate a filtered list of *Names* based in the *State* "New York". The function returns an array of names that spill vertically in the range G2:G4.

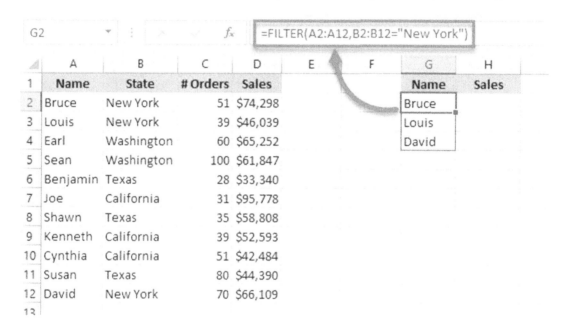

Note
     FILTER is a relatively new dynamic array function in Excel that will become fully available to all Microsoft 365 users from July 2020 (if you do not already have it).

Next, we want to get the *Sales* associated to the names on our filtered list and insert them in column H. To do this, we use XLOOKUP in cell H2 and select cells G2:G4 for our lookup_value argument.

When you select your lookup_value on the worksheet (G2:G4), XLOOKUP will recognise the range as the return value of a dynamic array and will indicate that in the formula with a hash (#).

| H2 | ▼ | ⋮ | ✕ | ✓ | *fx* | =XLOOKUP(G2#,A2:A12,D2:D12) |

◢	A	B	C	D	E	F	G	H	I
1	**Name**	**State**	**# Orders**	**Sales**			**Name**	**Sales**	
2	Bruce	New York	51	$74,298			Bruce	$74,298	
3	Louis	New York	39	$46,039			Louis	$46,039	
4	Earl	Washington	60	$65,252			David	$66,109	
5	Sean	Washington	100	$61,847					
6	Benjamin	Texas	28	$33,340					
7	Joe	California	31	$95,778					
8	Shawn	Texas	35	$58,808					
9	Kenneth	California	39	$52,593					
10	Cynthia	California	51	$42,484					
11	Susan	Texas	80	$44,390					
12	David	New York	70	$66,109					

Formula explanation:

=XLOOKUP(G2#,A2:A12,D2:D12)

The lookup_value argument in the formula is **G2#**.

G2# (note the hash) designates the entire range of the spill data. It tells us that G2 is the starting point of the array of values returned from a dynamic array formula.

The lookup_array is the Name column (A2:A12), and the return_array is the Sales column (D2:D12).

When you type in the formula in cell H2 and press Enter, XLOOKUP will return all the sales associated with the names in the dynamic array in column G. As we have more than one value, it will spill down vertically in column H2.

One benefit of using XLOOKUP like this is that the formula will dynamically adjust to the dynamic array in column G. For example, if the filter is changed and there are more names on the list, the formula in cell H2 will still work in returning the corresponding sale values. We don't have to worry about copying the formula down to additional cells.

Common XLOOKUP Errors and Solutions

- **#N/A error**

  If an exact match is not found, and the *if_not_found* and *match_mode* arguments are omitted, then XLOOKUP will return an #N/A error.

  There may be scenarios where you will not know if your formula will generate this error, for example, when it is filled down to multiple cells in a column. If you want to replace the #N/A error with a meaningful message, then specify it in the if_not_found argument.

  For example:
  =XLOOKUP(F2,B2:B12,D2:D12,"Item not found")

- **#VALUE! error**

  This error is often generated because the lookup array and return array are not the same length. When you get this error, check that these ranges are the same length. If you are performing a vertical lookup, they should have the same number of rows. If you are carrying out a horizontal lookup, they should have the same number of columns.

- **#NAME? in cell**

  The #NAME? error value usually means that there is something wrong with the cell references. A typo in the cell reference or omitting the colon can generate this error. When you get this error, check your cell references. To help avoid errors and typos in cell references, select them on the worksheet with your mouse rather than typing them in the formula.

- **#REF! error**

  If XLOOKUP is referencing another workbook that is closed, you will get a #REF! error. To avoid this error, ensure all workbooks referenced in your formula are open.

- **#SPILL! Error**

  When returning multiple values, if there is already data in the spill range, a #SPILL! error will be returned. To avoid this error, ensure there is no data in the range that will contain the returned results.

Note   To learn more about XLOOKUP and other exciting dynamic array functions introduced recently, see my book **Excel XLOOKUP and Other Lookup Functions**. It goes into greater depth, covering the advanced features of XLOOKUP and several other dynamic array functions. For more information, go to:

https://www.excelbytes.com/excel-books

Find Data with VLOOKUP

With the introduction of XLOOKUP, the VLOOKUP function (and the less popular HLOOKUP) are now legacy functions in Excel. XLOOKUP should be your go-to function for any task for which you would have previously used VLOOKUP. XLOOKUP is easier to use, more intuitive, and richer in terms of functionality. But as mentioned earlier in this chapter, XLOOKUP is only available to Microsoft 365 subscribers.

Here are a couple of reasons why VLOOKUP will still be relevant for some time:

- If you have a perpetual license version of Excel 2016 or Excel 2019, you will not have access to XLOOKUP. VLOOKUP will still be what you would use for lookups until the next version of Excel.

- If you intend to send your worksheet to someone with a perpetual license version of Excel, you may want to use VLOOKUP for any lookup tasks because formulas with XLOOKUP will not work when they open your worksheet.

- In an organization, you may encounter VLOOKUP in formulas while maintaining existing worksheets.

The VLOOKUP function (vertical lookup) is one of the most commonly used lookup functions in Excel. VLOOKUP is an updated version of the legacy LOOKUP function, which is still available in Excel (for backward compatibility).

VLOOKUP enables you to find one piece of information in a workbook based on another piece of information. For example, if you have a *Products* table, you can find and return the *Product Code* by providing the *Product Name* to the VLOOKUP function.

Syntax and Arguments

Syntax

= VLOOKUP (lookup_value, table_array, col_index_num, [range_lookup])

Arguments

Argument	Description
lookup_value	Required. What value are you searching for? This is the lookup value. Excel will look for a match for this value in the leftmost column of your chosen range. You can provide a value here or a cell reference.
table_array	Required. What columns do you want to search? This is the lookup table containing the columns you want to include in your search e.g. A2:D10.
col_index_num	Required. Which column contains the search result? In table_array, starting from 1, count from the first column to determine what this number should be.
range_lookup	Optional. If you want an exact match, enter FALSE or 0 here. However, if an approximate match is OK, then enter TRUE or 1. For TRUE, you would need to sort the leftmost column in ascending order for correct results. This is an optional argument and if omitted the default will be TRUE.

Standard VLOOKUP Example

In the example below, we use VLOOKUP to find the *Price* and *Reorder Level* of a product by entering the product name in cell G2. The formula is in cell G3, and as you can see from the image below, it searches the table for *Dried Pears* and returns the price from the second column in our table array (B2:D46).

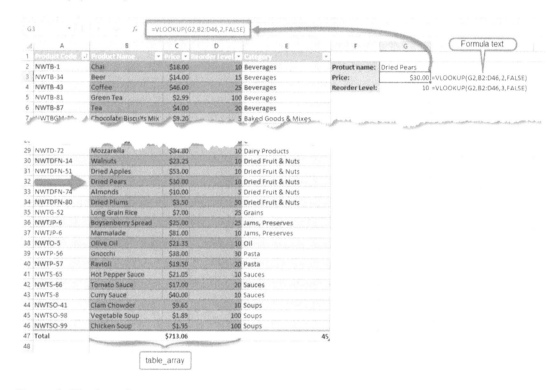

Formula Explanation:

To look up the **Price** for "Dried Pears" the formula is:

=VLOOKUP(G2, B2:D46, 2, FALSE)

The formula uses a lookup value in cell G2 to search a table array which is B2:D46.

The col_index_num argument is **2**, meaning we want VLOOKUP to search the first column, and once a match is found, return the value on the same row in the second column of table_array, which is the **Price** column.

The range_lookup is **FALSE**, which tells VLOOKUP that we want an exact match.

To look up the **Reorder Level** for Dried Pears we use the same formula and just change the col_index_num argument to 3, meaning we want to return values from the third column in table_array, which is the Reorder Level column.

=VLOOKUP(G2, B2:D46, **3**, FALSE)

Here, the VLOOKUP search for Dried Pears returns a Reorder Level of **10**.

Finding an Approximate Match with VLOOKUP

In the following example, we want to calculate the commission each Sales Rep is entitled to, based on their sales. We have a Commission table to the right of the Sales report with a graduated scale of rates against sales.

We want to ensure that if an exact match is not found on the commission table that an approximate match is applied for the sales rep. $5,000 or more in sales is 2% commission, $10,000 or more is 5%, $20,000 or more is 10%, and so on.

C3			f_x	=VLOOKUP(B3,table_array,2,TRUE)		
	A	B	C	D	E	F
1	Sales				Commission table	
2	Sales Rep	Sales	Commisson		Sales	Rate
3	Berna Alger	$7,372	2%		$0	0%
4	Rich Donaldson	$23,895	10%		$5,000	2%
5	Erwin Wofford	$31,323	15%		$10,000	5%
6	Arvilla Leon	$3,024	0%		$20,000	10%
7	Simone Sharkey	$73,033	25%		$30,000	15%
8	Guillermina Canales	$7,735	2%		$40,000	20%
9	Stacey Lovett	$22,417	10%		$50,000	25%
10	Jaunita Headrick	$1,483	0%			
11	Romaine Ashford	$9,028	2%			
12	Juliann Keane	$26,980	10%			
13						

Formula Explanation:

=VLOOKUP(B3,table_array,2,TRUE)

The *lookup_value* is cell B3 which is the value for which we want an approximate match in the lookup range (cells E3:F9).

Note that the lookup range (E3:F9) is named **table_array**. This is known as a named range. The benefit of using named ranges in formulas you want to fill down is that a named range is an absolute reference. This ensures the cell references you want to remain the same will not change as you fill down the formula.

The *col_index_num* is set to 2. This means we want to return values from the second column in table_array.

The optional *range_lookup* argument is set to TRUE which tells Excel to return an approximate match if an exact match is not found. The default for the *range_lookup* argument is TRUE if omitted so you do not need to set this argument explicitly to TRUE. I have entered it here for demonstration purposes only.

Using VLOOKUP and the CHOOSE Function for Left Lookups

In this example, we want to add the product code to the list of orders on the left of the worksheet below. The product codes can be found in the *Product list* to the right of the *Orders*.

	A	B	C	D	E	F	G
1	**Orders**				**Product list**		
2	Order Date	Product Name	Product Code		Product Code	Product Name	Price
3	01/02/2016	Boysenberry Spread			NWTB-1	Chai	18.00
4	01/05/2016	Dried Pears			NWTCO-3	Syrup	10.00
5	04/07/2016	Granola			NWTCO-4	Cajun Seasoning	22.00
6	04/23/2016	Walnuts			NWTO-5	Olive Oil	21.35
7	04/28/2016	Gnocchi			NWTJP-6	Boysenberry Spread	25.00
8	05/13/2016	Ravioli			NWTDFN-7	Dried Pears	30.00
9	06/20/2016	Long Grain Rice			NWTS-8	Curry Sauce	40.00
10	06/22/2016	Tomato Sauce			NWTDFN-14	Walnuts	23.25
11	06/26/2016	Mozzarella			NWTCFV-17	Fruit Cocktail	39.00
36	04/20/201.	Chicken Soup			NWT... ...8		1.
37	04/27/2017	Brownie Mix			NWTCFV-89	Peaches	1.5
38	05/11/2017	Cake Mix			NWTCFV-90	Pineapple	1.8
39	05/15/2017	Tea			NWTCFV-91	Cherry Pie Filling	2
40	08/15/2017	Mustard			NWTCFV-92	Green Beans	1.2
41	08/22/2017	Dried Plums			NWTCFV-93	Corn	1.2
42	09/16/2017	Green Tea			NWTCFV-94	Peas	1.5
43	09/24/2017	Tomato Sauce			NWTCM-95	Tuna Fish	2
44					NWTCM-96	Smoked Salmon	4
45					NWTC-82	Hot Cereal	5
46					NWTSO-98	Vegetable Soup	1.89
47					NWTSO-99	Chicken Soup	1.95

One limitation of VLOOKUP is that we can only return values in a column to the right of the lookup range. Our lookup range, in this case, is F3:F47 and the return range is E3:E47. The return values are in a column to the left of the lookup column.

To solve this problem, we can use the CHOOSE function to rearrange the columns for the table_array argument of VLOOKUP.

When we apply the CHOOSE function to our formula, we get the following:

=VLOOKUP(B3,CHOOSE({1,2},$F$3:$F$47,$E$3:$E$47),2,FALSE)

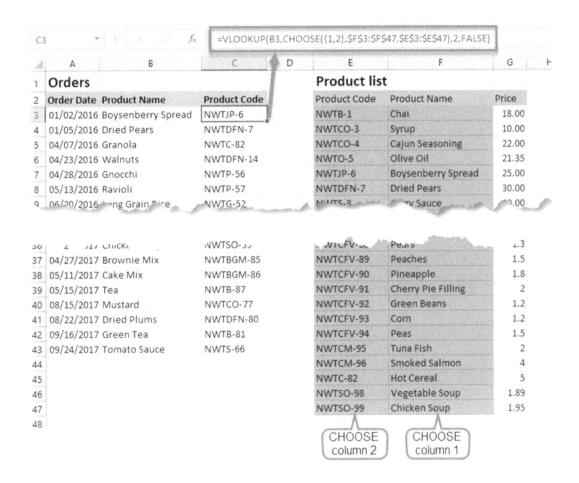

Formula explanation:

=VLOOKUP(B3,CHOOSE({1,2},$F$3:$F$47,$E$3:$E$47),2,FALSE)

Our table_array is E3:F47 and we want to return values in column E. We want a method in our formula that reverses the order of the columns, that is, put column E to the right of column F. The CHOOSE formula can do this:

CHOOSE({1,2},$F$3:$F$47,$E$3:$E$47)

This formula has F3:F47 as the *value1* argument and E3:E47 as the *value2* argument. Both ranges have been converted to absolute references.

The *index_num* argument of our CHOOSE function is {1,2}, which tells the function to return the data in the order *value1* and *value2*, that is, column F before column E.

With the range (E3:E47) as the second column in table_array, VLOOKUP can now lookup values in the first column (F3:F47), and return values from the second column E3:E47.

To populate the other cells in column C, we can fill down the formula. The absolute references we have used means the lookup and return ranges remain the same.

-Ò-**Tip**
We can make this formula a little easier to understand by using full column references as long as there will be no other data in the columns apart from the data being used by the formula.

With full column references, the formula would look like this:

=VLOOKUP(B3,CHOOSE({1,2},F:F,E:E),2,FALSE)

VLOOKUP and Error Handling

When using the VLOOKUP formula in Excel, sometimes you may encounter the #N/A error, which happens when the formula cannot find the lookup value.

When handling errors caused by VLOOKUP, you want to make sure you are using the right formula for your scenario. In this example, we will cover how to use the IFERROR function or the IFNA function with VLOOKUP to show something meaningful in place of an error.

In the example below, we use both IFERROR and IFNA to trap the same error.

 Note

For the syntax and arguments of IFERROR, see chapter 3 in Book 3.

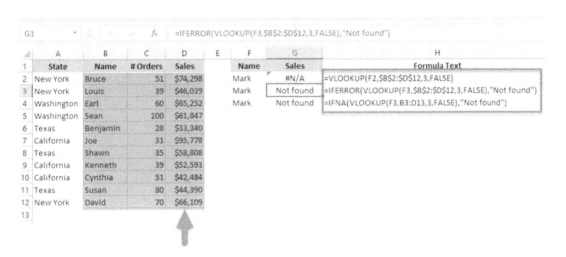

Formula explanation:

=VLOOKUP(F2,$B$2:$D$12,3,FALSE)

The formula is using the lookup value in cell F2 to search the table array (B2:D12) and return the *Sales* on the same row on column D. The lookup value we have used, "Mark", is not on the list of names in column B so the formula generates an #N/A error in cell G3.

=IFERROR(VLOOKUP(F3,$B$2:$D$12,3,FALSE),"Not found")

This formula is performing the same task as the first formula, but this time it is wrapped in an IFERROR function. IFERROR traps the #N/A error and returns "Not found" which is the value we have specified in the *value_if_error* argument.

=IFNA(VLOOKUP(F3,B3:D13,3,FALSE),"Not found")

The above VLOOKUP formula is nested in an IFNA function which traps the #N/A error and returns our specified value, "Not found".

VLOOKUP and Wildcards

VLOOKUP supports using wildcards for partial matches, but you need to use ampersands to concatenate an asterisk before and after the lookup_value argument.

		G2			f_x	=VLOOKUP("*"&F2&"*",Furniture,3,FALSE)		
	A	B		C	D	E	F	G
1	Order Date	Product		No. of Items	Sales		Find product	Sales
2	01/02/2016	New Paolo Manual Recliner Chair		19	$14,782.00		Verona	$2,256.00
3	01/05/2016	Collection Bradley Riser Recline Fabric Chair		5	$1,405.00			
4	...6	Verona 1 Shelf Telephone Table		8	$2,256.00			
5	04/23/2016	Fabric Chair in a Box - Denim Blue		14	$8,876.00			
6	04/28/2016	Habitat Oken Console Table		28	$1,008.00			
7	05/13/2016	Lukah Leather Chair		9	$3,105.00			
8	06/20/2016	Collection New Bradley Manual Recliner Chair		23	$3,726.00			
9	06/22/2016	Floral Fabric Tub Chair		10	$7,800.00			
	...2016	...ric Chair		11	...00			
24	04/27/2017	Windsor 2 Seater Cuddle Chair			$2,416.00			
25	05/11/2017	Tessa Fabric Chair		5	$2,360.00			
26	05/15/2017	Fabric Wingback Chair		30	$12,150.00			
27	08/15/2017	Harley Fabric Cuddle Chair		18	$4,446.00			
28	08/22/2017	Fabric Wingback Chair		19	$7,695.00			
29	09/16/2017	Tessa Fabric Chair		30	$7,560.00			
30	09/24/2017	Collection Martha Fabric Wingback Chair		15	$2,055.00			

Return range

Formula explanation:

=VLOOKUP("*"&F2&"*",Furniture,3,FALSE)

Our lookup_value is "*"&F2&"*". The expression concatenates an asterisk to either side of the cell with the search term. So, the search term in this example will evaluate to *Verona*. This tells the formula to find the first item on the list with "Verona" anywhere within the string.

The table_array argument is a range named Furniture, which is range B2:D30.
Our col_index_num (the return range) is 3. This is column D which is the third column in table_array.

A wildcard search requires you to set the range_lookup argument to FALSE, i.e. an exact match. This means if your search term is not found anywhere in your list, VLOOKUP will return an error.

Best Practices for VLOOKUP

- **Use absolute references for the table array**.

  Using absolute references allows you to fill-down a formula without having the cell references change. An absolute reference ensures VLOOKUP always looks at the same table array even when the formula is filled to other cells.

- **Do not store a number or date as a text value.**

  When searching for numbers or dates, ensure the data in the first column of the table array is not stored as text. Otherwise, the formula might return an incorrect or unexpected value. Number and date values are right-aligned while text values are left-aligned by default. Therefore, if your numbers or dates are left-aligned in the cell, you need to check that they are using the right cell format.

- **Sort the first column.**

  If you want VLOOKUP to find the next best match, that is, the range_lookup argument is TRUE, then make sure the first column in table_array is sorted.

- **Use wildcard characters.**

  You can use a wildcard in lookup_value if range_lookup is FALSE and lookup_value is text. A question mark (?) matches any single character, and an asterisk (*) matches any sequence of characters. If you want to find an actual question mark or asterisk as part of the text in table_array, type a tilde (~) in front of the character.

  For example, =VLOOKUP("Dried*",B2:D46,2,FALSE) will find the first item starting with "Dried" in the first column of table_array.

- **Make sure your data does not contain erroneous characters.**

  If you are searching for text values in the first column of the table array, ensure the data in the first column does not have leading or trailing spaces, non-printable characters, and inconsistent use of straight and curly quotation marks. In cases like these, the formula might return an unexpected value.

  To clean up your data you can use the TRIM function to remove any extra spaces or the CLEAN function to removes all nonprintable characters.

Common VLOOKUP Errors and Solutions

- **Wrong value returned**

  If you omit the range_lookup argument or set it to TRUE (that is, for an approximate match), you need to sort the first column of table_array alphabetically or numerically. If the first column is not sorted, the return value might be something unexpected. So, either use FALSE for an exact match or sort the first column of the table array if you want an approximate match.

- **#N/A error in cell**

  If the range_lookup argument is FALSE, and an exact match is not found you will get an #N/A error. You will also get an #N/A error if range_lookup is TRUE, and the lookup_value is smaller than the smallest value in the first column of table_array.

- **#REF! in cell**

  You will get the #REF error if the col_index_num argument is greater than the number of columns in the table array.

- **#VALUE! in cell**

  You will encounter a #VALUE! error if lookup_value argument is over 255 characters. Use wildcards for partial matches if the values in the lookup range are over 255 characters.

  The #VALUE! error will also be generated if the col_index_num argument contains text or is less than 1. Ensure col_index_num is not less than 1.

- **#NAME? in cell**

  The #NAME? error value usually means that the formula is missing quotes. If you enter a text value directly in your formula (instead of a cell reference) make sure you enclose the value in quotes. For example, =VLOOKUP("Dried Pears", B2:D46, 2, FALSE). You will also get this error if you make a mistake when typing in the cell reference. To avoid cell reference typos, select cell references on the worksheet with your mouse rather than typing them in the formula.

Find Data with HLOOKUP

The HLOOKUP function (horizontal lookup) searches for a value in the top row of a range or table and then returns a value in the same column from a row you specify in the range or table. The function carries out a horizontal search on the first column of the specified range for the lookup value (criteria). Then it uses the criteria to return another value from the same column but on a row below.

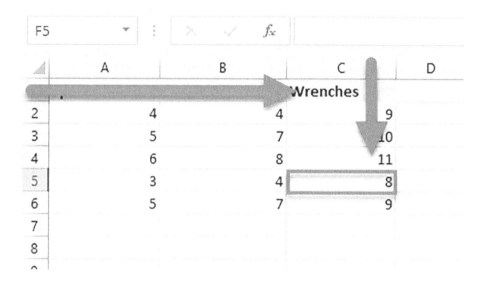

Use HLOOKUP when your lookup values are in a row at the top of a range or table, and you want to look down a specified number of rows. VLOOKUP, on the other hand, is suitable when your lookup values are in a column to the left of the data you want to search for.

Syntax

HLOOKUP(lookup_value, table_array, row_index_num, [range_lookup])

Arguments

Argument	Description
Lookup_value	Required. This is the value to be used as the lookup value and it should be in the first row of table_array. Lookup_value can be text, a value, or a reference.
Table_array	Required. This is a range, or table which contains the data being looked up. You can use cell references or a named range.
Row_index_num	Required. This is the row number from which you want the value returned counting from 1 from the first row of the range.
Range_lookup	Optional. This argument is to specify whether HLOOKUP should find an exact match or an approximate match. TRUE is for an approximate match while FALSE is for an exact match. If this argument is omitted, it'll default to TRUE.

Example

▲	A	B	C
1	Spanners	Bolts	Wrenches
2	4	4	9
3	5	7	10
4	6	8	11
5	3	4	8
6	5	7	9
7			

Using the data above, we get the following results using HLOOKUP to query the range:

=HLOOKUP("Bolts",A1:C6,6,FALSE)

349

Answer: 7

This is using "Bolts" as the lookup value to return a value on row 6 from the same column.

****

=HLOOKUP("Spanners",A1:C6,3,FALSE)

Answer: 5

This is using "Spanners" as the lookup value to return a value on row 3 from the same column.

****

=HLOOKUP("Wrenches",A1:C6,3)

Answer: 10

This is using "Wrenches" as the lookup value to return a value on row 3 from the same column.

MATCH Function

The MATCH function searches for a given item in a list and then returns the relative position of the item in the list. That means, MATCH tells you where in your list you can locate your value after you provide search parameters.

If MATCH cannot find an exact match, it will find the closest item to the lookup value. This can be useful in situations where you want to identify the cut-off point in a list of values.

For example, if the range A1:A5 has the values 10, 30, 26, 44, and 100, the formula =MATCH(44,A1:A5,0) will return 4, because 44 is the fourth item in the range.

MATCH is most useful when used as an argument in another function where you need to return the position of a specific item in your data as one of the arguments of the other function.

Syntax

MATCH(lookup_value, lookup_array, [match_type])

Arguments

Argument	Description
lookup_value	Required. This is the value that you want to match in your list. This argument can be a number, cell reference, text, or logical value.
lookup_array	Required. This is the list or range of cells to be searched.
match_type	Optional. This argument specifies how the function will behave. You have three options for this argument -1, 0, or 1. The default is 1 if the argument is omitted. **1 (or omitted)** = MATCH finds the largest value that is less than or equal to the lookup value. The values in the list must be in ascending order. **0** = MATCH finds the first value that's exactly equal to lookup_value. The values in the range can be in any order. **-1** = MATCH finds the smallest value that is greater than or equal to lookup_value. The values in the list must be in descending order.

Example 1

In the example below, we provide MATCH with a lookup_value of 21 (in cell B11), the lookup_array is B2:B9 and the match_type is set to 1.

=MATCH(B11, B2:B9, 1)

This means the function will return the row with the highest value that is *less than or equal to* 21. In this case, the value is 20 and the row is 5, so MATCH returns 5.

Example 2

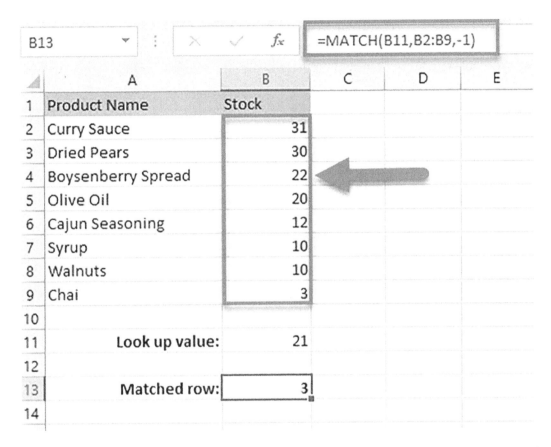

In this example, we provide the MATCH function with a lookup_value of **21**, the lookup_array is **B2:B9** and the match_type is set to **-1**.

=MATCH(B11, B2:B9, -1)

Result: 3

To use a match_type of -1, the range needs to be sorted in descending order. In this case, the function will return the row with the lowest value that is *greater than or equal to* 21. The value is 22 and the row is 3, so MATCH returns 3.

Example 3

If we use a match_type of 0 for both examples above, we'll get an error (#N/A) as MATCH will not be able to find an exact match in lookup_array.

If we use a lookup_value of 22 instead for the example:

=MATCH(22, B2:B9, 0)

MATCH will return 3 as 22 is in the third row of the range.

Product Name	Stock
Curry Sauce	31
Dried Pears	30
Boysenberry Spread	22
Olive Oil	20
Cajun Seasoning	12
Syrup	10
Walnuts	10
Chai	3

CHOOSE Function

The CHOOSE function allows you to use an index number to return a value from a list of arguments. You can use CHOOSE to select one out of a maximum of 254 values based on the index number.

Syntax

CHOOSE(index_num, value1, [value2], ...)

Arguments

Argument	Description
Index_num	Required. This argument specifies the value to be selected from the list. The Index_num argument must be a number between 1 and 254, or a formula, or cell reference that contains a number between 1 and 254.
Value1	Required. The first value is required. Values can be numbers, cell references, ranges, formulas, functions, or text.
[value2], ...	Optional. You can have up to 253 additional optional values.

Remarks

If the index_num argument is less than 1 or greater than the number of the last value in the list, CHOOSE returns an error (#VALUE!). If index_num is a fraction, it will be truncated to the lowest integer before it is used.

Example 1

Let's say we have the days of the week in a list and we want to return the day of the week for number 4.

=CHOOSE(4, Mon, Tue, Wed, Thu, Fri, Sat, Sun)

It will return "Thu", as this is the 4th item on the list.

Example 2

The CHOOSE function is most useful when used in combination with another function. For example, we can nest the CHOOSE function within the SUM function.

Let's say we want the SUM function to calculate a specific range on our worksheet from several ranges based on a number we provide. In the example below, we provide 4 to represent quarter four (QTR4) on the worksheet. The number is entered in cell B20.

C20				f_x	=SUM(CHOOSE(B20,B3:B17,C3:C17,D3:D17,E3:E17))		

	A	B	C	D	E	F	G	H
1	Sales by Quarter							
2	Product	QTR1	QTR2	QTR3	QTR4			
3	Chai	300	300	200	400			
4	Beer	300	200	400	300			
5	Coffee	350	400	500	500			
6	Green Tea	250	150	100	300			
7	Tea	100	400	100	500			
8	Chocolate Biscuits Mix	320	200	100	300			
9	Scones	250	500	200	100			
10	Brownie Mix	350	400	550	200			
11	Cake Mix	200	370	300	200			
12	Granola	250	100	200	400			
13	Hot Cereal	350	500	300	200			
14	Chocolate	350	200	500	500			
15	Fruit Cocktail	200	230	250	200			
16	Pears	100	200	300	450			
17	Peaches	200	300	200	600			
18								
19								
20	CHOOSE QTR	4	5150					
21								

Formula explanation

The following formula is entered in cell C20:

=SUM(CHOOSE(B20,B3:B17,C3:C17,D3:D17,E3:E17))

Result: 5150

The CHOOSE function is first evaluated and it returns the range E3:E17. The SUM function then sums up E3:E17 to provide the total for that quarter.

Of course, looking at the example above, it may appear that it would be easier to just sum up each quarter separately. However, there may be situations when we want to do this, for example, as part of a summary report in another worksheet.

-☼-Tip

The CHOOSE function is useful for specific types of problems. For most lookup tasks in Excel, the VLOOKUP would suffice so I would recommend experimenting with VLOOKUP first to see if it would solve the problem before using CHOOSE.

TRANSPOSE Function

The TRANSPOSE function enables you to transpose data in your worksheet. If you want to rotate data on your worksheet you can use the Transpose option on the paste command. TRANSPOSE provides a way to carry out the same task without having to manually copy and paste the data. This can come in handy when you want to copy and transpose data from several ranges across different worksheets.

Syntax

TRANSPOSE(array)

Argument

The *Array* argument is required. This is a range of cells that you want to transpose.

Example:

In this example, we want to transpose the data in cells A1:B4 in the table below.

To get TRANSPOSE to work, ensure:

1. You select a destination range where the number of columns matches the number of rows in the source. For example, if the source has 4 rows then you must select 4 columns for the destination.

2. The number of rows in the destination should match the number of columns in the source.

3. You must also press CTRL+SHIFT+ENTER to enter the formula as it is an array function.

Note With the introduction of dynamic array support for formulas in Microsoft 365, you can now just select the first cell of the destination range, type in the formula, and press **ENTER**. Excel will spill the result across the required destination cells. If you are using a version of Excel that comes with Microsoft 365, you no longer need to use CTRL+SHIFT+ENTER to confirm your result. **If you are using a perpetual-license version of Excel, you'll still need to use CTRL+SHIFT+ENTER to confirm your result**.

A7	▼	⋮	×	✓	ƒ𝑥	{=TRANSPOSE(A1:B4)}

	A	B	C	D	E	F
1	QTR1	$2,000.00				
2	QTR2	$3,000.00				
3	QTR3	$1,400.00				
4	QTR4	$5,000.00				
5						
6						
7	QTR1	QTR2	QTR3	QTR4		
8	2000	3000	1400	5000		
9						
10						

Steps to using TRANSPOSE:

1. Select the destination range.

2. In the formula bar, type **=TRANSPOSE(**

3. Enter the range, for example, A1:B4. You can manually enter this or select it on the worksheet by clicking and dragging from the beginning of the range to the end.

4. Type in the closing bracket but don't press Enter.

5. Press CTRL+SHIFT+ENTER

   This will enclose the formula in curly brackets {}, indicating it is an array formula and the return values are across several cells.

ADDRESS function

You can use the ADDRESS function to return the address of a cell in a worksheet when you provide the row and column numbers as arguments. For example, =ADDRESS(4,6) returns $F$4.

Syntax

ADDRESS(row_num, column_num, [abs_num], [a1], [sheet_text])

Arguments

Argument	Description
row_num	Required. A number that specifies the row number to use in the cell reference.
column_num	Required. A number that specifies the column number to use in the cell reference.
abs_num	Optional. A number that specifies the type of reference to return, e.g. absolute, relative, or mixed references. The default is Absolute reference, and this will be used if abs_num is omitted. Argument values 1 (or omitted) = Absolute reference 2 = Mixed reference. Absolute row, relative column 3 = Mixed reference. Relative row, absolute column 4 = Relative reference
A1	Optional. This is a logical value that specifies whether to use the A1 or R1C1 style of reference. TRUE is A1 and FALSE is R1C1. If omitted, A1 is used.
sheet_text	Optional. This is a text value specifying the name of the worksheet to get the cell reference from. To be used when connecting to an external sheet. If this argument is omitted the current sheet is used.

Note   In Excel, A1 referencing means columns are labelled alphabetically and rows numerically. R1C1 referencing means both columns and rows are labelled numerically. The A1 reference style is the default and the recommendation for most occasions. However, if you need to change the reference style, click **File** > **Options** > **Formulas**. Under **Working with formulas**, check or uncheck the **R1C1 reference style** checkbox. The default reference style is A1 so R1C1 should be unchecked by default.

Examples

Example 1	
Formula:	=ADDRESS(2,4)
Description:	Absolute reference in the current sheet.
Result:	$D$2

Example 2	
Formula:	=ADDRESS(2,4,2)
Description:	Mixed reference. Absolute row; relative column.
Result:	D$2

Example 3	
Formula:	=ADDRESS(2,4,2,FALSE)
Description:	Mixed reference. Absolute row; relative column using the R1C1 reference style.
Result:	R2C[4]

Example 4	
Formula:	=ADDRESS(2,4,1,FALSE,"[Book2]Sheet1")
Description:	An absolute reference to another workbook (Book2) and worksheet.
Result:	[Book2]Sheet1!R2C4

Example 5	
Formula:	=ADDRESS(2,4,1,FALSE,"Accounts sheet")
Description:	An absolute reference to another worksheet.
Result:	'Accounts sheet'!R2C4

FORMULATEXT Function

The FORMULATEXT function enables you to display the formula from one cell in another cell in your worksheet. This is useful when you're trying to identify errors in your syntax or compare different formulas side by side. Instead of being able to only check your formulas one at a time by clicking on each cell, you can use the FORMULATEXT function to reveal the formulas in several cells at the same time.

Syntax

FORMULATEXT(reference)

Argument	Description
reference	Required. This can be a reference to a cell in the current workbook or another open workbook.

FORMULATEXT will return an #N/A error if:

- The cell used as the *Reference* argument does not contain a formula.

- *Reference* is in an external workbook that is not open.

- The formula can't be displayed due to worksheet protection.

If the Reference argument points to more than one cell, for example, a range, FORMULATEXT will return the value in the upper leftmost cell in the range.

Example

In this example, we have some values in column A. In column B we have several formulas used to aggregate the values from column A. To display the formulas on the sheet we use FORMULATEXT in column C.

C2		⋮	✕ ✓	fx	=FORMULATEXT(B2)	

	A	B	C	[
1	Values	Aggregate results	Formula text	
2	$18.00	$126.35	=SUM(A2:A9)	
3	$10.00	$21.06	=AVERAGE(A2:A9)	
4	$22.00	6	=COUNT(A2:A9)	
5	$21.35	$30.00	=MAX(A2:A9)	
6	$25.00	$10.00	=MIN(A2:A9)	
7	$30.00	$21.68	=MEDIAN(A2:A9)	
8				

COLUMNS Function

The COLUMNS function returns the number of columns in an array or range. This function is mostly used as an argument in other functions. For example, in situations where you need to return the number of columns in a specified range as an argument of another function.

Syntax

COLUMNS(array)

Argument	Description
array	Required. This can be an array or a reference to a range of cells for which you want to count the number of columns.

Example

In this example, we want to count the number of columns in a dataset in cells A1:J5.

The formula used to get the count is:

=COLUMNS(A1:J5)

Result: 10.

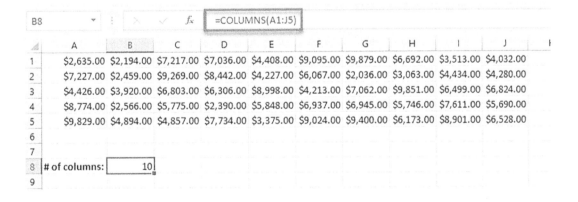

ROWS Function

The ROWS function returns the number of rows in an array or range. Like the COLUMNS function, the ROWS function is mostly useful as an argument within another function. For example, on occasions when you need to return the number of rows in a specified range as one of the arguments of another function.

Syntax

ROWS(array)

Argument	Description
array	Required. This can be an array or a reference to a range of cells for which you want to count the number of rows.

Example

In this example, we use ROWS to count the number of rows in a dataset in cells A1:E23.

Formula: =ROWS(A1:E23)

Result: 23

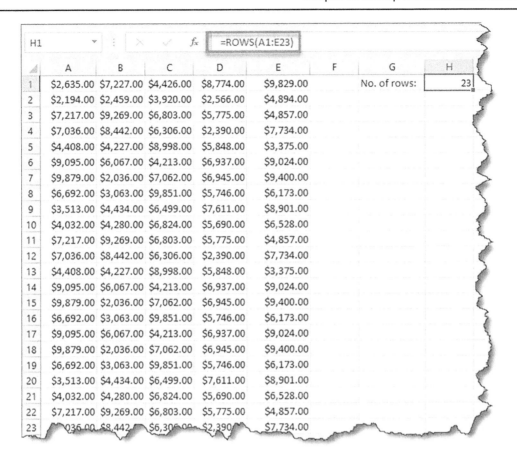

INDEX Function

The INDEX function enables you to return a value or a series of values from a range.

There are two forms of the INDEX function:

1. Array form
2. Reference form

INDEX Function - Array Form

The array form of this function can return a single value, an entire row, or an entire column from a chosen range.

Syntax

INDEX(array, [row_num], [column_num])

Arguments

Argument	Description
Array	Required. The *array* argument is a range of cells or an array constant. If the range contains only one row or column, the corresponding row_num or col_num is optional.
Row_num	If Row_num is omitted, Column_num is required. Selects the row in the *array* argument from which to return a value.
Column_num	If Column_num is omitted, Row_num is required. Selects the column in the *array* argument from which to return a value.

Remarks

- If the *array* argument has more than one row and more than one column, and only Row_num or Column_num is used, INDEX returns an array of the entire row or column in the *array* argument.

- INDEX returns a single value (at the intersection of Row_num and Column_num) if both arguments are used.

- INDEX returns an array of values, i.e. the entire column or row if you set Row_num or Column_num to 0 (zero).

- To return an entire row or column, you'll need to select the number of cells for the result (destination) that is equal to the number of cells of the source. For example, if the source *row* has 4 cells, you must select 4 cells horizontally for the result. Alternatively, if the source *column* has 4 cells, you must select 4 cells vertically for the result.

- You must press **CTRL+SHIFT+ENTER** to return the entire row or column. If you just press enter, it will not work as expected.

Example 1

In this example, we return the value in Q3 for Toronto with the following formula:

=INDEX(B7:E10,3,4)

B7:E10 is the array, 3 is the row number, and 4 is the column number.

E2		▾	⋮	✕	✓	*fx*	=INDEX(B7:E10,3,4)

◢	A	B	C	D	E	F
1	Quaterly Data					
2					$6,306.00	
3						
4						
5		**2015**				
6		**London**	**Paris**	**New York**	**Toronto**	
7	Q1	$2,635.00	$2,194.00	$7,217.00	$7,036.00	
8	Q2	$7,227.00	$2,459.00	$9,269.00	$8,442.00	
9	Q3	$4,426.00	$3,920.00	$6,803.00	$6,306.00	
10	Q4	$8,774.00	$2,566.00	$5,775.00	$2,390.00	
11						

Example 2

In this example, we can return the sum of the entire row for Q1 by combining the INDEX function with the SUM function.

We make the row_num argument 1 and the column_num argument 0 (zero), specifying that we want to return all the cells in row one from the range.

=SUM(INDEX(B7:E10,1,0))

| E2 | ▾ | : | ✕ | ✓ | *fx* | =SUM(INDEX(B7:E10,1,0)) |

◢	A	B	C	D	E	F
1	Quaterly Data					
2					$19,082.00	
3						
4						
5		**2015**				
6		London	Paris	New York	Toronto	
7	Q1	$2,635.00	$2,194.00	$7,217.00	$7,036.00	
8	Q2	$7,227.00	$2,459.00	$9,269.00	$8,442.00	
9	Q3	$4,426.00	$3,920.00	$6,803.00	$6,306.00	
10	Q4	$8,774.00	$2,566.00	$5,775.00	$2,390.00	
11						

INDEX Function - Reference form

The reference form of the INDEX function returns the value of the cell at the intersection of a row and column. The reference argument can be made up of non-contiguous ranges and you can pick which range to search using the area_num argument.

Syntax

INDEX(reference,[row_num],[col_num],[area_num])

Arguments

Argument	Description
Reference	Required. A reference to one or more cell ranges. If you are entering more than one range for the reference, enclose this argument in parentheses. For example, INDEX((A1:B10,D1:D10),3,4)
Row_num	Required. Selects the row in the *array* argument from which to return a value. If Row_num is omitted, Column_num is required.
Column_num	Optional. Selects the column in the *array* argument from which to return a value. If Column_num is omitted, Row_num is required.
Area_num	Optional. Selects a range in *reference* from which the intersection of *Row_num* and *Column_num* will be returned. The first area is numbered 1, the second is 2, the third 3, and so on. If *Area_num* is left out of the formula, the default, area 1, will be used. The areas need to be on the same worksheet.

Remarks

- If you specify areas in *reference* that are not on the same worksheet as each other, the function will return an error (#VALUE!). If you need to use ranges that are on different worksheets, it's recommended that you use the array form of INDEX and use another function to generate the range that makes up the array. You could use the CHOOSE function, for example, to calculate which range will be used.

- If each area in reference contains only one row or column, the Row_num or Column_num argument, respectively, is optional. For example, for a single row reference, use INDEX(reference, column_num).

- Row_num and Column_num must point to a cell within *array* or the function will return an error (#REF!).

Example

In this example we have four ranges making up the *reference* argument:

1. 2015 = B7:E10
2. 2016 = H7:K10
3. 2017 = B14:E17
4. 2018 = H14:K17

To return a value from one of these ranges, we specify the range with *Area_num*. The ranges are numbered by the order of entry, starting from 1.

B7:E10 = 1; H7:K10 = 2; B14:E17 = 3; H14:K17 = 4

In this case, we've used a cell reference, J2, to enter the *Area_num* so that the value can be easily changed on the worksheet to point to a different range if needed.

=INDEX((B7:E10,H7:K10,B14:E17,H14:K17),3,4,J2)

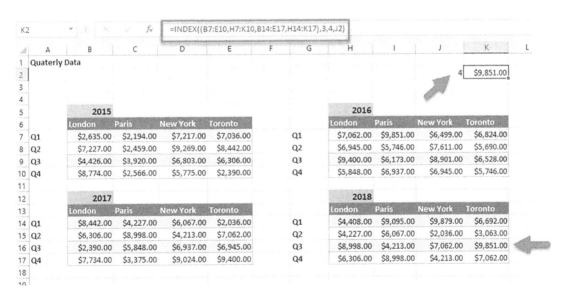

The formula returns **$9,851.00** from the third row and fourth column in the fourth range.

Chapter 3: Logical Functions

The logical functions in Excel can be found by clicking the Logical command button on the Formulas tab of the Ribbon. A logical function requires a logical test before carrying out one evaluation from several options. If the test evaluates to TRUE it executes one statement, and if the test is FALSE, it executes a different statement. A statement can be a calculation, a value, a string, or even another function. Logical functions can be nested, enabling you to carry out multiple logical tests before executing the statement.

In this chapter, we'll cover functions that enable you to:

- Select which statement to execute based on the result of a logical test.
- Check that multiple conditions are met with nested functions before executing a statement.
- Check that at least one of several conditions is met before executing a statement.
- Identify values in a list and provide replacement values.
- Trap errors in formulas and return a meaningful message.

IF Function

The IF function is one of the popular functions in Excel used to create conditional formulas. The IF function allows you to carry out a logical test (using comparison operators) that evaluates to TRUE or FALSE. The function executes one statement if the test is TRUE and another statement if the test is FALSE.

Syntax:

IF(logical_test, value_if_true, [value_if_false])

Arguments

Argument	Description
logical_test	Required. This is a value or expression that can be evaluated to TRUE or FALSE.
value_if_true	Required. This is the value that's returned if the logical test is true.
value_if_false	Optional. This is the value that's returned if the logical test is false. If the logical test is FALSE and this argument is omitted, nothing happens.

In its simplest form this is what the function says:

IF (something is TRUE, then do A, otherwise do B)

Therefore, the IF function will return a different result for TRUE and FALSE.

Example 1

A common way the IF function is used is to determine if a referenced cell has any value or not. If the result is 0 then it returns a blank cell.

In the example below, the formula for the total for *Jan* was entered in cell **I2** and we want to drag the formula down to populate the totals for *Feb* to *Dec.* Without the IF function, it would display $0 for the unpopulated months, however, we want the totals for the unpopulated months to be blank instead of $0 even with the formula in place.

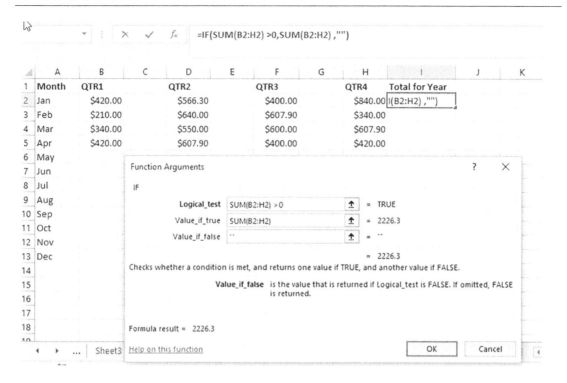

Thus, the formula for Jan in cell **I2** is:

=IF(SUM(B2:H2) >0,SUM(B2:H2) ,"")

The IF function in this example checks to see if the sum of Jan is greater than zero. If true it returns the sum. If it is false, then it returns a blank string.

When we populate the other fields with the formula, we get the following.

| | | | | fx | =IF(SUM(B2:H2) > 0,SUM(B2:H2),"") | | | | |

	A	B	C	D	E	F	G	H	I	J
	Month	QTR1		QTR2		QTR3		QTR4	Total for Year	
	Jan	$420.00		$566.30		$400.00		$840.00	2226.3	
	Feb	$210.00		$640.00		$607.90		$340.00	1797.9	
	Mar	$340.00		$550.00		$600.00		$607.90	2097.9	
	Apr	$420.00		$607.90		$400.00		$420.00	1847.9	
	May									
	Jun									
	Jul									
	Aug									
	Sep									
	Oct									
	Nov									
	Dec									

Example 2

In another example, we could use the results of an evaluation to return different values in our worksheet.

Let's say we have a budgeting sheet and want to use a "Status" column to report on how the **Actual** figure compares to the **Budgeted** figure. In this case, we can use the IF statement to test whether the actual figure is greater than the budgeted figure. If **Actual** is greater than **Budgeted**, the formula would enter "Over Budget", otherwise it would enter "Within Budget".

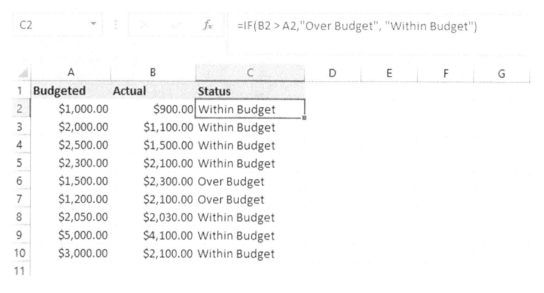

=IF(B2 > A2,"Over Budget", "Within Budget")

The IF function checks to see if the value in B2 is greater than the value in A2. If it is, it returns "Over Budget" otherwise it returns "Within Budget".

Example 3

In another example, say we have products for sale. When **10 or more** items are purchased, we apply a **10%** promotional discount.

E2	▼	⋮	✕	✓	*fx*	=IF(C2>=10,D2 - (D2 * 0.1),D2)

⬔	A	B	C	D	E
1	Product	Cost	Quantity	Sub-Total	Total (with discount)
2	Chai	$1.80	10	$18.00	$16.20
3	Beer	$1.50	15	$22.50	$20.25
4	Coffee	$2.00	25	$50.00	$45.00
5	Green Tea	$2.00	50	$100.00	$90.00
6	Tea	$1.30	20	$26.00	$23.40
7	Chocolate Biscuits Mix	$5.20	5	$26.00	$26.00
8	Scones	$4.90	5	$24.50	$24.50
9	Brownie Mix	$4.20	10	$42.00	$37.80
10	Cake Mix	$4.80	10	$48.00	$43.20
11					

Formula explanation

=IF(C2>=10,D2 - (D2 * 0.1),D2)

The logical test checks if C2 is greater than or equal to 10.

If true it returns the sub-total minus 10%.

If false it returns the sub-total.

The AutoFill handle was used to populate the other cells in the range E2:E10 with the formula.

-�Oʹ-Tip   The AutoFill handle appears as a plus sign (+) when you place the mouse pointer on the lower-right corner of the active cell.

Nested IF Functions

You can also use an IF function as an argument within an IF function. This is called a nested IF statement. You can nest up to seven IF statements. A nested IF statement might be required if you need to carry out more than one logical test in your function.

In the example below, we use a nested IF statement to test for 3 possible values and return a different result for each one.

We have a spreadsheet to record the score of exams and we want to mark everything under 40 as FAIL, between 40 and 69 as CREDIT, and 70 or more as MERIT.

The formula would look like this:

=IF(A2 < 40, "FAIL",IF(A2 < 70,"CREDIT","MERIT"))

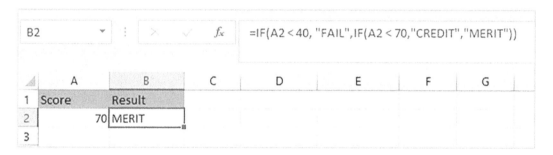

Formula explanation

=IF(A2 < 40, "FAIL",IF(A2 < 70,"CREDIT","MERIT"))

The first IF statement checks if A2 is less than 40. If it is TRUE, it returns "FAIL" and ends the evaluation there. If A2 < 40 is FALSE, the second IF test is executed.

The second IF function checks if A2 is less than 70. If true it returns "CREDIT", and if false, it returns "MERIT".

🔅-**Tip**   The IFS function was introduced in Excel 2016 as a better way of addressing multiple logical tests in one formula. As much as possible, use IFS in place of multiple nested IF statements. It is much easier to read when you have multiple tests.

Advanced IF Functions

An advanced IF function is a hybrid of a logical function and a statistics or mathematics function. Advanced IF functions are covered in more detail in this book in the chapters for Maths Functions and Statistical Functions. In this section, we briefly examine some of the important advanced IF functions you can use as one solution instead of combining two functions.

AVERAGEIF

Syntax:

=AVERAGEIF(range, criteria, [average_range])

This function returns the average (arithmetic mean) of data that meets the value you've entered as criteria. The optional *average_range* argument allows you to specify another range for the values if it is separate from the one with the criteria.

Example:

=AVERAGEIF(A2:A20,"<2000")

This means, return the average of all the values in cells A2 to A20 that are greater than 2000.

AVERAGEIFS

Syntax:

=AVERAGEIFS(average_range, criteria_range1, criteria1, [criteria_range2, criteria2], ...)

This function is similar to AVERAGEIF, however, it allows you to specify multiple ranges and multiple criteria in the arguments. You can specify up to 127 ranges and criteria.

COUNTIF

This function returns the count of the values in a range that meets the specified criteria.

Syntax:

=COUNTIF(range, criteria)

In its simplest form this function says:

=COUNTIF(Where do you want to look?, What do you want to look for?)

Example:

=COUNTIF(A2:A10,"New York")

This will return the count of the number of cells in A2:A10 with the value "New York".

COUNTIFS

COUNTIFS(criteria_range1, criteria1, [criteria_range2, criteria2]…)

This function is like the COUNTIF function in that it returns a count based on a condition you specify. However, you can specify multiple ranges and criteria. You can specify up to 127 range/criteria pairs.

SUMIF

This function returns the sum of values in a range that match a given criterion.

Example:

=SUMIF(A2:A10, ">10")

This means, return the sum of all the values in cells A2 to A10 that are greater than 10.

SUMIFS

Syntax:

SUMIFS(sum_range, criteria_range1, criteria1, [criteria_range2, criteria2], ...)

This function returns the sum of values that meet several criteria. You can specify up to 127 range/criteria pairs.

Note All advanced IF functions briefly touched on above are covered in more detail elsewhere in this book. Check the table of contents for which chapter a function has been covered.

IFS Function

The IFS function enables you to carry out multiple logical tests and execute a statement that corresponds to the first test that is TRUE. The tests need to be entered in the order in which you want the statements executed so that the right result is returned as soon as a test is passed. IFS was created as a better approach to nested IF statements which can quickly become too complex.

Note The IFS function was introduced in Excel 2016. If you're subscribed to Microsoft 365, ensure you have the latest version of Office installed.

Syntax

IFS(logical_test1, value_if_true1, [logical_test2, value_if_true2], [logical_test3, value_if_true3],…)

Arguments

Argument	Description
logical_test1	Required. This is the condition that is being tested. It can evaluate to TRUE or FALSE.
value_if_true1	Required. The result to be returned if logical_test1 evaluates to TRUE.
logical_test2… logical_test127	Optional. A condition that evaluates to TRUE or FALSE. You can have up to 127 tests in total.
value_if_true2… value_if_true127	Optional. The results to be returned if logical_test2…logical_test127 evaluates to TRUE.

Remarks

The IFS function allows you to test up to 127 different tests. However, it is generally advised not to use too many tests with IF or IFS statements. This is because multiple tests need to be entered in the right order and it can become too complex to update or maintain.

Tip As much as possible, use IFS in place of multiple nested IF statements. It is much easier to read when you have multiple conditions.

Example 1

In the example below, we use the IFS function to solve a problem we addressed earlier with nested IF statements.

In this problem, we want to assign grades to different ranges of exam scores.

Score and Grades

1. 70 or above = MERIT
2. 50 to 69 = CREDIT
3. 40 to 49 = PASS
4. less than 40 = FAIL

We derive the following formula to achieve our aim:

=IFS(A2>=70,"MERIT",A2>=50,"CREDIT", A2>=40,"PASS", A2<40,"FAIL")

Formula explanation

=IFS(A2>=70,"MERIT",A2>=50,"CREDIT", A2>=40,"PASS", A2<40,"FAIL")

The IFS function as been used to create four logical tests in sequential order:

A2>=70,"MERIT"
A2>=50,"CREDIT"
A2>=40,"PASS"
A2<40,"FAIL"

A2 is a reference to the score. As you can see, each score is tested against each condition in sequential order. As soon as a test is passed the corresponding grade is returned and no further testing is carried out.

Example 2

In this example, we want to set different priority levels for reordering items depending on the number of items in stock.

Priority Level:

1. 5 or less = 1
2. 10 or less = 2
3. Less than 20 = 3

The formula we use to accomplish this task is:

=IFS(A2>20,"N/A",A2<=5,1, A2<=10,2, A2<20,3)

B2			f_x	=IFS(A2>20,"N/A",A2<=5,1, A2<=10,2, A2<20,3)				
	A	B	C	D	E	F	G
1	**In stock**	**Priority Level**					
2	10	2					
3	25	N/A					
4	9	2					
5	10	2					
6	4	1					
7	10	2					
8	15	3					
9	10	2					
10	10	2					
11	5	1					
12	10	2					
13	5	1					
14	15	3					
15							

Formula explanation

=IFS(A2>20,"N/A",A2<=5,1, A2<=10,2, A2<20,3)

First, we insert a test to mark the Priority Level for any products greater than 20 as "N/A" (not applicable) as those have no re-order priority yet. Then we carry out the tests in sequential order from the smallest value to the largest to ensure that the right corresponding value is returned as soon as a test is passed.

You can also apply conditional formatting to the results column to highlight the records with the highest priority. In this case, 1 is the highest priority.

For steps on how to apply conditional formatting to cells, see **chapter 5 in Book 1: Excel Basics.**

SWITCH Function

The SWITCH function evaluates an expression against a list of values and returns the value that corresponds to the first match. If no match is found, an optional default value may be returned.

Note The SWITCH function was introduced in Excel 2016 so will not be available in an earlier version of Excel. If you're subscribed to Microsoft 365, ensure that you have the latest version of Office.

Syntax

SWITCH(expression, value1, result1, [default or value2, result2],…[default or value3, result3])

Arguments

Argument	Description
expression	Required. The expression argument is the value that will be compared against the list of values in value1…value126. *Expression* can be a number, date or some text.
value1…value126	The value argument is a value that will be compared with the expression argument. You can have up to 126 values.
result1…result126	This is the value to be returned when the corresponding argument matches the *expression* argument. A *result* must be supplied for each corresponding *value* argument. You can have up to 126 results to match each value argument.
default	Optional. Default is the value to be returned if no match is found. *Default* must be the last argument in the function, and it is identified by not having a corresponding result value.

Excel functions are limited to 254 arguments, so you can only use up to 126 pairs of *value* and *result* arguments.

Example

In the following example, we have a column of numbers and we would like to switch the numbers to text descriptions that describe the numbers in a more meaningful way.

List of values we want to switch:

    1 = Quarter 1
    2 = Quarter 2
    3 = Quarter 3
    3 = Quarter 4

Formula:

=SWITCH(A2,1,"Quarter 1",2,"Quarter 2",3,"Quarter 3",4,"Quarter 4","No match")

B2				fx	=SWITCH(A2,1,"Quarter 1",2,"Quarter 2",3,"Quarter 3",4,"Quarter 4","No match")

	A	B	C	D	E	F	G	H	I
1	Value	Quarter							
2	2	Quarter 2							
3	6	No match							
4	4	Quarter 4							
5	7	No match							
6	1	Quarter 1							
7									

On the occasions when no match is found like in 6 and 7, the default value, "No Match", is returned.

-☼-Tip

    The *result* arguments have been entered directly in the formula here for demonstration purposes only. In a production worksheet, it would be better to enter the values in a lookup range in your worksheet and then use cell references in your formula. That way it is easier to maintain.

IFERROR Function

This function is used to trap errors in Excel formulas and return a meaningful message. It is like how errors are trapped and handled in computer code. IFERROR can trap the following error types: #VALUE!, #N/A, #DIV/0!, #REF!, #NAME?, #NUM!, or #NULL!.

Syntax

IFERROR(value, value_if_error)

Arguments

Argument	Description
Value	Required. This is the argument that is checked for an error. This can be a cell reference or a formula.
Value_if_error	Required. This is the value that is returned if the formula evaluates to an error.

Remarks

- If either *value* or *value_if_error* points to an empty cell, IFERROR treats it as an empty string value (""").

- If *value* is an array formula, IFERROR returns an array of results, one for each cell in the results range.

Example

In the following example, we use the IFERROR formula to trap any errors in our formula in column C and return a text message "Calculation error".

For the purpose of this exercise, the FORMULATEXT function has been used in D2:D5 to reveal the formulas in columns C2:C5.

| C2 | ▼ | : | × | ✓ | *fx* | =IFERROR(B2/A2,"Calculation error") |

◢	A	B	C	D	E
1	Target	Actual Units Sold	Percentage		
2	200	35	18%	=IFERROR(B2/A2,"Calculation error")	
3	10	0	0%	=IFERROR(B3/A3,"Calculation error")	
4	120	50	42%	=IFERROR(B4/A4,"Calculation error")	
5		5	Calculation error	=IFERROR(B5/A5,"Calculation error")	
6					
7					
8					
9					

AND Function

The AND function is used to determine if all conditions in a test are TRUE. This is useful for problems where you want to carry out more than one logical test and you want to check that they all evaluate to TRUE. This function is useful for situations where you want to check that several prerequisites are met before a condition is applied.

Syntax

AND(logical1, [logical2], ...)

Arguments

Argument	Description
Logical1	Required. This is the first condition that you want to test that can either evaluate to TRUE or FALSE.
Logical2, ...	Optional. You can have up to 254 additional conditions you want to test that can evaluate to either TRUE or FALSE.

Remarks

- The arguments must evaluate to logical values (i.e. TRUE or FALSE) or must be references to cells that contain logical values.

- If an argument contains an array or reference that points to text or empty cells, those values will be ignored.

- If the specified range contains no logical values, the #VALUE! error is returned by the AND function.

Example

In this example, we want to apply a discount for order items that meet a certain criterion.

We want a formula that:
1. Checks that a product is on promotion.
2. Checks that the number of units ordered is 3 or more.
3. Apply a discount if the item is on promotion and 3 or more have been ordered.

	A	B	C
1	**Product Name**	**On Promotion**	**Units Ordered**
2	Chai	Yes	3
3	Syrup	Yes	1
4	Cajun Seasoning	Yes	6
5	Olive Oil	No	7
6	Boysenberry Spread	Yes	1
7	Dried Pears	No	1
8	Curry Sauce	Yes	2
9	Walnuts	Yes	3
10	Fruit Cocktail	No	4
11	Chocolate Biscuits Mix	Yes	2
12	Marmalade	Yes	3
13	Scones	Yes	5
14	Beer	Yes	10
15	Crab Meat	No	7

The AND formula we use to carry out both tests is:

AND(B2="yes",C2>=3)

Next, we use the AND function as an argument inside an IF function. The IF statement returns "Apply discount" if our AND statement returns TRUE, and "No discount" if our AND statement returns FALSE.

The final formula looks like this:

=IF(AND(B2="yes",C2>=3)=TRUE,"Apply discount","No discount")

| D2 | ▼ | : | × | ✓ | *fx* | =IF(AND(B2="yes",C2>=3)=TRUE,"Apply discount","No discount") |

◢	A	B	C	D	E	F
1	**Product Name**	**On Promotion**	**Units Ordered**	**Discount status**		
2	Chai	Yes	3	Apply discount		
3	Syrup	Yes	1	No discount		
4	Cajun Seasoning	Yes	6	Apply discount		
5	Olive Oil	No	7	No discount		
6	Boysenberry Spread	Yes	1	No discount		
7	Dried Pears	No	1	No discount		
8	Curry Sauce	Yes	2	No discount		
9	Walnuts	Yes	3	Apply discount		
10	Fruit Cocktail	No	4	No discount		
11	Chocolate Biscuits Mix	Yes	2	No discount		
12	Marmalade	Yes	3	Apply discount		
13	Scones	Yes	5	Apply discount		
14	Beer	Yes	10	Apply discount		
15	Crab Meat	No	7	No discount		
16						

The AND function has been combined with the IF function to make it more robust. Using AND as an argument in IF enabled us to carry out two logical tests within its *logical_test* argument and return one logical value.

OR Function

The OR function is used to determine if any conditions in a test are TRUE. This is useful for problems where you want to carry out more than one logical test and you want to return a value if at least one of them evaluates to TRUE.

This function is best used in conjunction with other logical functions for more complex test scenarios involving multiple logical tests. For example, the IF function requires you to test a condition to determine which return statement to execute. If you combine IF and OR, it enables you to test multiple conditions instead of just one.

Syntax

OR(logical1, [logical2], ...)

Arguments

Argument	Description
Logical1	Required. This is the first condition that you want to test that can either evaluate to TRUE or FALSE.
Logical2, ...	Optional. You can have up to 254 additional conditions you want to test that can evaluate to either TRUE or FALSE.

Remarks

- The maximum number of arguments you can have for the OR functions is 255.

- The arguments must evaluate to logical values (i.e. TRUE or FALSE) or must be references to cells that contain logical values.

- If an argument contains references that point to text or empty cells, those values will be ignored.

- If the specified range contains no logical values, the #VALUE! error is returned by the AND function.

Example

In this example, we need to determine which sales staff qualify for a sales commission based on the sales they've generated.

The sales figures are in the table below. Under the main table, we have a lookup table for the Amount per Criteria. These are the goals to be referenced in our formula to calculate the **Commission** for each salesperson.

The IF function can be used in combination with OR to achieve our aim.

The following formula is entered in cell D2 and copied down to the other cells in column D using the Fill Handle.

=IF(OR(B2>=$B$15,C2>=$B$16),B2*$B$17,0)

D2				fx	=IF(OR(B2>=$B$15,C2>=$B$16),B2*$B$17,0)	

	A	B	C	D	E
1	**Name**	**Sales**	**Signups**	**Commission**	**Bonus**
2	Nancy Freehafer	$12,500	20	$250	$188
3	Andrew Cencini	$14,300	25	$286	$215
4	Jan Kotas	$9,000	10	$180	$0
5	Mariya Sergienko	$8,050	5	$161	$0
6	Steven Thorpe	$5,000	7	$0	$0
7	Michael Neipper	$8,900	10	$178	$0
8	Robert Zare	$7,900	10	$0	$0
9	Laura Giussani	$6,000	17	$120	$0
10	Anne Hellung-Larsen	$11,000	18	$220	$0
11					
12					
13					
14	**Criteria**	**Amount**			
15	Sales Goal	$8,000			
16	Signup Goal	15			
17	Commission	2.0%			
18	Bonus Goal	$12,000			
19	Bonus %	1.5%			
20					
21					
22					

- Sales people need to exceed Sales Goal OR Signup Goal to earn a **Commission**.

- Sales people need to exceed Sales Goal AND Signup Goal to earn a **Bonus**.

Formula explanation

=IF(OR(B2>=$B$15,C2>=$B$16),B2*$B$17,0)

The formula says:

IF **Sales** are greater than or equal to (>=) the **Sales Goal**, OR **Signups** are greater than or equal to (>=) the **Signup Goal**, then multiply Sales by the Commission (2.0%), otherwise, return 0.

Chapter 4: Math Functions

The mathematics functions in Excel can be found by clicking the Math & Trig command button on the Formulas tab of the Ribbon. The drop-down menu lists all the Math & Trig functions. This category of functions in Excel ranges from common arithmetic functions to complex functions used by mathematicians and engineers.

Our focus here will be on the arithmetic functions as many of the trigonometric functions are applicable to mathematics problems requiring specialist knowledge that's outside the scope of this book.

In this chapter, we'll cover functions that enable you to:

- Sum up data in contiguous or non-contiguous ranges.
- Sum up data based on certain criteria using a single function.
- Use multiple criteria to determine which data to add up.
- Automatically generate random numbers between two given numbers.
- Automatically round up or round down numbers with a function.
- Calculate the square root of a number.

SUM Function

The SUM function enables you to add values on your spreadsheet. You can add individual values, cell references, ranges or a mix of all three. You can sum up contiguous cells or non-contiguous cells.

Syntax

SUM(number1,[number2],...)

Arguments

Argument	Description
Number1	Required. The first cell reference, range, or number for which you want to calculate the sum. The argument can be a number like 4, a cell reference like A10, or a range like A2:A10.
Number2, ...	Optional. Additional cell references, ranges or numbers for which you want to calculate the sum, up to a maximum of 255.

Example 1

In this example, we have values in cells B2 to B13 that you want to sum up.

We could either use the AutoSum command on the ribbon or enter the formula in the formula bar:

=SUM(B2:B13)

SUM ▼ ⋮ ✕ ✓ *fx* =SUM(B2:B13)

◢	A	B	C	D	E
1	**Month**	**Expenses**			
2	Jan	$400.00			
3	Feb	$640.00			
4	Mar	$550.00			
5	Apr	$420.00			
6	May	$310.50			
7	Jun	$566.30			
8	Jul	$607.90			
9	Aug	$300.80			
10	Sep	$500.50			
11	Oct	$700.00			
12	Nov	$840.00			
13	Dec	$900.00			
14	**Sum**	=SUM(B2:B13)			
15		SUM(**number1**, [number2], ...)			
16					

Example 2

To sum up data in different ranges, i.e. non-contiguous data, you can enter the ranges as different arguments in the SUM function.

=SUM(B2:B13,D2:D13,F2:F13,H2:H13)

| H2 | ▼ | : | ✕ | ✓ | fx | =SUM(B2:B13,D2:D13,F2:F13,H2:H13) |

◢	A	B	C	D	E	F	G	H	I
1	Month	Year 1		Year 2		Year 3		Year 4	
2	Jan	$420.00		$566.30		$400.00		$840.00	
3	Feb	$210.00		$640.00		$607.90		$340.00	
4	Mar	$340.00		$550.00		$600.00		$607.90	
5	Apr	$420.00		$607.90		$400.00		$420.00	
6	May	$310.50		$500.00		$210.00		$400.00	
7	Jun	$500.00		$566.30		$420.00		$607.90	
8	Jul	$300.00		$607.90		$505.00		$790.00	
9	Aug	$700.00		$400.00		$500.00		$733.00	
10	Sep	$410.00		$500.50		$900.00		$500.50	
11	Oct	$800.00		$607.90		$700.00		$600.00	
12	Nov	$840.00		$840.00		$840.00		$300.00	
13	Dec	$900.00		$1,100.00		$1,200.00		$1,000.00	
14									
15	Total							3,H2:H13)	

SUMIF Function

The SUMIF function is the combination of a math function and a logical function. It allows you to sum up data in a range of cells based on a certain criterion.

Syntax

SUMIF(range, criteria, [sum_range])

Arguments

Argument	Description
range	Required. This is the range of cells that you want to evaluate based on the condition in *criteria*.
criteria	Required. This is the condition (or logical test) that is used to determine which cells are summed up in *range*. This can be an expression, cell reference, text, or function. **Note**: If this argument is text or includes logical or mathematical symbols like greater than (>), for example, it must be enclosed in double-quotes (""). If *criteria* is numeric, quotation marks are not required.
sum_range	Optional. You use this argument if you want to add up values in a different range from those specified in the range argument. If this argument is omitted, then the cells specified in *range* are used.

Remarks

- Cells in the range argument must be numbers, names (for example, named ranges or tables), arrays, or references that contain numbers. Text values and blanks are ignored.

- You can use wildcard characters (like a question mark "?" or an asterisk "*") as the criteria argument. A question mark matches any single character while an asterisk matches any sequence of characters. Type a tilde (~) before the character if you want to find an actual question mark or asterisk.

Example 1

In this example, we're using SUMIF to sum up all Sales over $5,000.

The formula used is:

=SUMIF(A2:A11,">5000")

A14		fx	=SUMIF(A2:A11,">5000")

	A	B	C	D	E
1	Sales	Commission			
2	$2,635	$132			
3	$7,227	$361			
4	$4,426	$221			
5	$4,774	$239			
6	$9,829	$491			
7	$20,000	$1,000			
8	$2,459	$123			
9	$11,300	$565			
10	$2,566	$128			
11	$10,894	$545			
12					
13	**Report**				
14	$59,250	⬅	Sum of sales over $5,000		
15	$2,963		Commission for sales over $5,000		
16					

The formula is using the criteria argument of ">5000" to filter which values will be added to the sum from the range A2:A11.

Example 2

In this example, we're using SUMIF to sum up all Commissions for sales over $5,000. We'll be using the *sum_range* argument to specify the cells we want to sum up as they are different from the cells specified in the *range* argument.

The formula we use is:

=SUMIF(A2:A11,">5000", B2:B11)

	A	B	C	D
A15		fx	=SUMIF(A2:A11,">5000", B2:B11)	
	Sales	Commission		
1	**Sales**	**Commission**		
2	$2,635	$132		
3	$7,227	$361		
4	$4,426	$221		
5	$4,774	$239		
6	$9,829	$491		
7	$20,000	$1,000		
8	$2,459	$123		
9	$11,300	$565		
10	$2,566	$128		
11	$10,894	$545		
12				
13	**Report**			
14	$59,250		Sum of sales over $5,000	
15	$2,963		Commission for sales over $5,000	
16				
17				

Formula explanation

=SUMIF(A2:A11,">5000", B2:B11)

The formula is using the criteria argument ">5000" to select the values in column A (Sales) for which the corresponding values in column B (Commission) will be added to the sum. So, even though we applied the criteria to column A, the values summed up come from Column B.

SUMIFS Function

The SUMIFS function is like the SUMIF function however you can use multiple criteria to determine which cells in a range are included in the sum. SUMIFS enables you to have up to a total of 127 range/criteria pairs.

Syntax

SUMIFS(sum_range, criteria_range1, criteria1, [criteria_range2, criteria2], ...)

Arguments

Argument	Description
Sum_range	Required. This is the range of cells you want to sum up.
Criteria_range1	Required. The range that is tested using *Criteria1*.
	Criteria_range1 and *Criteria1* are a pair where *Criteria1* is used to search *Criteria_range1* for matching values. Once items in the range are found, their corresponding values in *Sum_range* are added.
Criteria1	Required. This is the criteria used to apply the filter on criteria1_range that selects the data subset. For example, criteria can be entered as 40, ">40", C6, "bolts", or "125".
Criteria_range2, criteria2, ...	Optional. You can have additional range/criteria pairs up to a maximum of 127 pairs in total.

Remarks

- If you are testing for text values, make sure the criterion is in quotation marks.

- You can use wildcard characters like the question mark (?) and asterisk (*) in your criteria to enable you to find matches that are not exact but similar. The question mark matches any single character and the asterisk matches a sequence of characters. To find a character like a question mark or asterisk, type a tilde sign (~) in front of the character.

- The *Criteria_range* argument must reference a range that has the same number of rows and columns as the *Sum_range* argument.

Example

In the following example, we want to sum up Sales totals using 2 criteria.
1. State name
2. Orders that are greater than or equal to 40 (>=40)

Formula

=SUMIFS($D$2:$D$12,$B$2:$B$12,F2,$C$2:$C$12,G2)

H2				fx	=SUMIFS($D$2:$D$12,$B$2:$B$12,F2,$C$2:$C$12,G2)			
	A	B	C	D	E	F	G	H
1	Name	States	No. Orders	Sales		States	Orders	Total Sales for matching orders
2	Bruce	New York	51	$74,298		New York	>=40	$140,407
3	Louis	New York	39	$46,039		Texas	>=40	$44,390
4	Earl	Washington	60	$65,252		California	>=40	$42,484
5	Sean	Washington	100	$61,847		Washington	>=40	$127,099
6	Benjamin	Texas	28	$33,340				
7	Joe	California	31	$95,778				
8	Shawn	Texas	35	$58,808				
9	Kenneth	California	39	$52,593				
10	Cynthia	California	51	$42,484				
11	Susan	Texas	80	$44,390				
12	Dav	New York	70	$66,109				
13								
14								

Formula explanation

=SUMIFS($D$2:$D$12,$B$2:$B$12,F2,$C$2:$C$12,G2)

- The *Sum_range* argument references the Sales column **D2:D12** (an absolute reference has been used - **$D$2:$D$12**).

Tip To convert *Sum_range* to an absolute reference, you can add the dollar signs manually in the formula bar or click on the reference within the formula (i.e. D2:D12) and press the F4 key. This ensures that the reference will not change when the formula is copied to other cells.

- The *Criteria_range1* is **B2:B12** (an absolute reference has also been used here - **$B$2:$B$12**)

Press F4, with the argument selected, to make this an absolute reference.

- The Criteria1 argument is **F2**. This is a reference to the States we want to use as our criteria. A cell reference has been used for this argument to make it easier to change. This has been left as a relative reference because we want it to change relatively as we copy the formula to other cells.

- The *Criteria_range2* is **$C$2:$C$12** (in absolute reference form).

- The *Criteria2* argument is **G2** (>=40). A cell reference has been used for this argument to make it easier to change.

We enter the formula in cell **H2** and then copy it down the column to sum up the **Total Sales** for orders that match the criteria for each state.

AGGREGATE Function

The AGGREGATE function returns an aggregate in a list or database. This function brings together all the aggregate functions into one. Instead of using individual aggregate functions, like SUM, AVG, MAX etc. you simply enter a number in one of its arguments to specify the type of aggregate you want to execute. You can also set the option to ignore hidden rows and error values.

There are two forms of the AGGREGATE function:

1. Reference form
2. Array form

Syntax

Reference form

> AGGREGATE(function_num, options, ref1, [ref2], …)

Array form

> AGGREGATE(function_num, options, array, [k])

Arguments

Function_num: Required. The *function_num* argument is a number between 1 to 19. This is the number that specifies which aggregate function to use. See the list below.

1=AVERAGE	2=COUNT	3=COUNTA
4=MAX	5=MIN	6=PRODUCT
7=STDEV.S	8=STDEV.P	9=SUM
10=VAR.S	11=VAR.P	12=MEDIAN
13=MODE.SNGL	14=LARGE	15=SMALL
16=PERCENTILE.INC	17=QUARTILE.INC	18=PERCENTILE.EXC
19=QUARTILE.EXC		

Options: Required. This argument is a numerical value from 1 to 7 that determines which values to ignore in the range we want to evaluate.

Options and behaviour:

- 0 or omitted=Ignore nested AGGREGATE and SUBTOTAL functions

- 1=Ignore hidden rows, nested AGGREGATE and SUBTOTAL functions

- 2=Ignore error values, nested AGGREGATE and SUBTOTAL functions

- 3=Ignore hidden rows, error values, nested AGGREGATE and SUBTOTAL functions

- 4=Ignore nothing

- 5=Ignore hidden rows

- 6=Ignore error values

- 7=Ignore hidden rows and error values

Ref1: Required. This is the first numeric argument for functions that take multiple numeric arguments for ranges that you want to aggregate. Ref1 can be a range, an array (for functions that take an array), or a formula.

Ref2,... Optional. This is for additional numeric arguments. You can have up to 253 arguments in total for which you want the aggregate value.

For the functions that take an array argument, ref1 will be an array, an array formula, or a reference to the range we want to aggregate. Ref2 is a second argument that is required for some functions. The functions listed below require a ref2 argument:

- LARGE(array,k)
- SMALL(array,k)
- PERCENTILE.INC(array,k)
- QUARTILE.INC(array,quart)
- PERCENTILE.EXC(array,k)
- QUARTILE.EXC(array,quart)

Remarks

- As soon as you type **=AGGREGATE(** in the formula bar you'll see a drop-down list of all functions that you can use as arguments for *function_num*. For the *options* argument, you'll also get a dropdown list for the values you can enter.

- AGGREGATE will return a #VALUE! error if a second ref argument is required but not provided.

- The AGGREGATE function is designed for columns of data i.e. ranges that are vertical. It is not designed for rows of data i.e. ranges that are horizontal.

Examples

In the following example, we'll use different instances of the AGGREGATE function to evaluate the data in the range below.

	A	B	C
1	#DIV/0!	56	
2	90	81	
3	31	95	
4	#NUM!	49	
5	41	34	
6	150	92	
7	34	58	
8	87	93	
9	33	120	
10	53	89	
11	74	92	
12			
13			

Example 1 - MAX	
Formula	=AGGREGATE(4, 6, A1:A11)
Result	150
Description	Returns the maximum value in range A1:A11 while ignoring error values in the range.

Example 2 - LARGE	
Formula	=AGGREGATE(14, 6, A1:A11, 3)
Result	87
Description	Returns the third largest value in range A1:A11 while ignoring error values in the range.

Example 3 - SMALL	
Formula	=AGGREGATE(15, 6, A1:A11)
Result	#VALUE!
Description	Returns a #VALUE! error because AGGREGATE is expecting a second ref argument here. The function referenced (SMALL) requires one.

Example 4 - MEDIAN	
Formula	=AGGREGATE(12, 6, A1:A11, B1:B11)
Result	77.5
Description	Returns the median from both columns while ignoring error values in the range.

Example 5	
Formula	=MAX(A1:A2)
Result	#DIV/0!
Description	Returns an error value since there are error values in the referenced range.

Tip

The AGGREGATE function will be overkill for the common aggregate tasks in Excel like sum, average, count etc. Only use this function if you're calculating one of the more complex aggregate types like STDEV.S, QUARTILE.INC, PERCENTILE.INC etc. For everyday aggregate tasks, use the standard functions like SUM, AVG, MIN and MAX.

MOD Function

The MOD function is useful for calculations where you want to return the remainder of a division between two numbers. The result has the same sign as the divisor.

Syntax

MOD(number, divisor)

Arguments

Argument	Description
Number	Required. The number being divided for which you want to find the remainder.
Divisor	Required. The number being used for the division. MOD will return the #DIV/0! error value if the divisor is 0.

Example

Formula	Result	Description
=MOD(4, 3)	1	Reminder 4/3
=MOD(-4, 3)	1	Reminder -4/3 **Note**: MOD returns a result with the same sign as the divisor.
=MOD(4, -3)	-1	Reminder 4/-3
=MOD(-4, -3)	-1	Reminder -4/-3

RANDBETWEEN Function

The RANDBETWEEN function returns a random integer between two numbers you specify. This function comes in handy when you want to generate sample data between two numbers. For example, if you want to generate some sample data between 1 and 100 in several cells, you could use RANDBETWEEN to generate a random number in one cell and copy the formula over the required range.

Syntax

RANDBETWEEN(bottom, top)

Arguments

Argument	Description
Bottom	Required. The smallest integer to be returned.
Top	Required. The largest integer to be returned.

The random values are regenerated each time the worksheet is recalculated. Hence, if you generate random values that you don't want to change each time the worksheet is recalculated, you need to copy only the values to another range without the formulas.

Example

In this example, we will use the RANDBETWEEN function to generate sample data for student scores between 0 and 100.

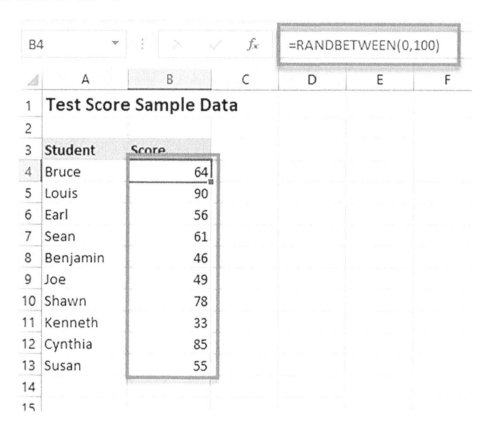

| B4 | | | | f_x | =RANDBETWEEN(0,100) | |

	A	B	C	D	E	F
1	Test Score Sample Data					
2						
3	Student	Score				
4	Bruce	64				
5	Louis	90				
6	Earl	56				
7	Sean	61				
8	Benjamin	46				
9	Joe	49				
10	Shawn	78				
11	Kenneth	33				
12	Cynthia	85				
13	Susan	55				
14						
15						

-Tip To keep only the generated values without the formula, generate the sample data in a different part of your worksheet and then copy and paste only the values into your target range. For example, if you wanted random values in cells B2:B10, generate the values using RANDBETWEEN in cells F2:F10 and then copy and paste only the values in B2:B10, then delete the values in F2:F10.

ROUND Function

The ROUND function rounds a number to a specified number of digits. For example, if you have 25.4568 in cell A1 and you want to round the figure to two decimal places, you can use the following formula:

=ROUND(A1, 2)

The function will return: 25.46

Syntax

ROUND(number, num_digits)

Arguments

Argument	Description
number	Required. This argument is the number that you want to round.
num_digits	Required. This is the number of decimal places to which you want to round the number.

Remarks

• The number is rounded to the specified number of decimal places if num_digits is greater than 0 (zero).

• The number is rounded to the nearest integer if num_digits is 0.

• The number is rounded to the left of the decimal point if num_digits is less than 0.

• Use the ROUNDUP function if you want to always round up (away from zero).

• Use the ROUNDDOWN function if you want to always round down (toward zero).

Examples

In the following examples, the ROUND function is applied to several values. The table displays the formula, the result, and a description of the outcome.

Formula	Result	Description
=ROUND(3.15, 1)	3.2	Rounds 3.15 to one decimal place.
=ROUND(4.149, 1)	4.1	Rounds 4.149 to one decimal place.
=ROUND(-2.475, 2)	-2.48	Rounds -2.475 to two decimal places.
=ROUND(57.5, -1)	60	Rounds 57.5 to one decimal place to the left of the decimal point.
=ROUND(671.3,-3)	1000	Rounds 671.3 to the nearest multiple of 1000.
=ROUND(1.78,-1)	0	Rounds 1.78 to the nearest multiple of 10.
=ROUND(-70.45,-2)	-100	Rounds -70.45 to the nearest multiple of 100.

ROUNDUP Function

The ROUNDUP function rounds a number up, away from 0 (zero).

Syntax

ROUNDUP(number, num_digits)

Arguments

Argument	Description
Number	Required. This argument is for the number that you want to round up.
Num_digits	Required. The number of decimal places to which you want to round up the number.

Remarks

- ROUNDUP is like ROUND, except that it always rounds a number up.

- *Number* is rounded up to the specified number of decimal places if num_digits is greater than 0 (zero).

- *Number* is rounded up to the nearest integer if num_digits is 0.

- *Number* is rounded up to the left of the decimal point if num_digits is less than 0.

Examples

In the following examples, ROUNDUP is applied to several values. The table displays the formula, the result, and a description of the outcome.

Formula	Result	Description
=ROUNDUP(3.15, 1)	3.2	Rounds 3.15 up to one decimal place.
=ROUNDUP(4.149, 1)	5	Rounds 4.149 up to zero decimal places.
=ROUNDUP(-2.475, 2)	-2.48	Rounds -2.475 to two decimal places.
=ROUNDUP(57.5, -1)	60	Rounds 57.5 to one decimal place to the left of the decimal point.
=ROUNDUP(671.3,-2)	700	Rounds 671.3 to two decimal places to the left of the decimal point.
=ROUNDUP(1.78,0)	2	Rounds 1.78 up to zero decimal places.
=ROUND(-70.45,-2)	-100	Rounds -70.45 to the nearest multiple of 100.

ROUNDDOWN Function

The ROUNDOWN function rounds a number down, towards zero.

Syntax

ROUNDDOWN(number, num_digits)

Arguments

Argument	Description
Number	Required. This argument is for the number that you want to round down.
Num_digits	Required. The number of decimal places you want to round the number down to.

Remarks

- ROUNDOWN works like ROUND except that it always rounds a number down.

- *Number* is rounded down to the specified number of decimal places if num_digits is greater than 0 (zero).

- *Number* is rounded down to the nearest integer if num_digits is 0.

- *Number* is rounded down to the left of the decimal point if num_digits is less than 0.

Examples

In the following examples, ROUNDOWN is applied to several values. The table displays the formula, the result, and a description of the outcome.

Formula	Result	Description
=ROUNDOWN(3.15, 1)	3.1	Rounds 3.15 down to one decimal place.
=ROUNDOWN(4.149, 0)	4	Rounds 4.149 down to zero decimal places.
=ROUNDOWN(-2.475, 2)	-2.47	Rounds -2.475 down to two decimal places.
=ROUNDOWN(57.5, -1)	50	Rounds 57.5 down to one decimal place to the left of the decimal point.
=ROUNDOWN(671.3,-2)	600	Rounds 671.3 down to the nearest multiple of 100.
=ROUNDOWN(1.78,0)	1	Rounds 1.78 down to zero decimal places.
=ROUNDOWN(-71.45,-1)	-70	Rounds -71.45 down to the nearest multiple of 10.

SQRT Function

This function returns a positive square root of any number.

Syntax

SQRT(number)

Argument	Description
Number	Required. This is the number for which you want to calculate the square root. If *number* is negative, the function returns an error value (#NUM!).

Example

The SQRT function has been applied to the following numbers.

B2				f_x	=SQRT(A2)	
	A	B		C	D	
1	Number	Square root				
2	16	4				
3	6602	81.25269226				
4	4414	66.43794097				
5	5788	76.07890641				
6	1216	34.87119155				
7	0	0				
8	1	1				
9	820	28.63564213				
10	852	29.18903904				
11	6358	79.73706792				
12	924	30.39736831				
13	8689	93.21480569				
14	6614	81.32650245				
15	-10	#NUM!				
16	4163	64.52131431				
17	8942	94.56214888				
18	2628	51.26402247				
19	4010	63.3245608				
20	9465	97.28823156				
21						

Chapter 5: Statistical Functions

You can access the statistical functions in Excel by clicking on the More Functions button on the Formulas tab. On the drop-down menu, highlight the Statistical option to display a list of all the statistical functions in alphabetical order. The statistical functions in Excel range from everyday statistical functions like AVERAGE, MIN, MAX etc. to more specialized functions used by statisticians.

In this chapter, we'll cover functions that enable you to:

- Calculate the average, min, max and median of values in a range.
- Use a specific criterion to determine which values to aggregate.
- Use multiple criteria to determine which values to aggregate.
- Count the number of values in a range of cells that meet a certain condition.
- Count the number of values in a range that meet multiple criteria.
- Count the number of cells that contain numbers in a range or table.
- Count the number of empty cells in a range or table.

COUNT Function

The COUNT function will count the number of cells that contain numbers in a range, or a list of numbers provided as arguments. The COUNT function only counts populated cells. For example, if you have a range with 20 cells, and only 5 of the cells have numbers, the count function will return 5.

Syntax

COUNT(value1, [value2], ...)

Arguments

Argument	Description
Value1	Required. The first range within which you want to count numbers.
Value2	Optional. Additional cell references or ranges in which you want to count numbers. You can have a maximum of 255 arguments for this function.

Remarks

- You can have a maximum of 255 arguments for this function. Each argument could be a number, a cell reference, or a range.

- The COUNT function counts numbers, dates, or text representations of numbers (i.e. a number enclosed in quotation marks, like "1").

- Error values or text that cannot be translated into numbers are not counted.

- Use the COUNTA function if you want to count text, logical values or error values.

- Use the COUNTIF function or the COUNTIFS function if you want to count only numbers that meet a specific condition.

Example

In this example, we use the COUNT function to count the values in two ranges.

The formula is:

=COUNT(A3:D20,F3:I20)

	A	B	C	D	E	F	G	H	I	J	K	L
L2						fx	=COUNT(A3:D20,F3:I20)					
1		2018					2019					
2	QTR1	QTR2	QTR3	QTR4		QTR1	QTR2	QTR3	QTR4		Count	131
3	70	83	16	37		26	56	47	17			
4	73	71	88	52		87	57	36	87			
5	38	65		19		38	50	51	68			
6	87	56	91	55		62	40	26	77			
7	18	97	39	82			98	98	25			
8	86	15		85		47	59	60	61			
9	28		98	86		41	19	10	11			
10	45	80	43	73			92	95	59			
11	60	92	98	34		51	38	13	91			
12	51	64	25	50		81	84		60			
13	79	29	69	27		62	69	17	65			
14	65	54	95	22		73	53	40	67			
15	91		10	91		66		83	74			
16	88	97	91	89		48	58	78	25			
17	40	88		15		66	12	55	85			
18	12	54	22	87		59	10	66	20			
19	42	17	51	33			67		26			
20	78			32		52	32	62	61			
21												

This is a simple formula with two arguments to represent the two ranges in which we want to count values: A3:D20 and F3:I20. Note that the blank cells are not counted.

COUNTIF Function

The COUNTIF function is a combination of a statistical function and a logical function. It allows you to count the number of cells that meet a criterion. For example, you can count only the values in a list of orders that exceed $1,000.

Syntax

COUNTIF(range, criteria)

Arguments

Argument	Description
range	Required. This is the group of cells that you want to count. This argument can contain numbers, a named range, or references that contain numbers.
criteria	Required. This is the condition that is used to determine which cells will be counted. This can be a cell reference, text, expression, or function. For example, you can use a number like 40, a logical comparison like ">=40", a cell reference like D10, or a word like "bolts".

Remarks

- If *criteria* is text or includes logical or mathematical symbols, for example, greater than (>), it must be enclosed in double-quotes ("). If *criteria* is a numeric value, quotation marks are not required.

Example

In this example, we're using COUNTIF to count all Sales over $5,000.

The formula we use is:

=COUNTIF(B2:B11,">5000")

	C14					f_x	=COUNTIF(B2:B11,">5000")

	A	B	C	D	E
1	Salesperson	Sales	Commission		
2	Bruce	$2,635	$132		
3	Louis	$7,227	$361		
4	Earl	$4,426	$221		
5	Sean	$4,774	$239		
6	Benjamin	$9,829	$491		
7	Joe	$20,000	$1,000		
8	Shawn	$2,459	$123		
9	Kenneth	$11,300	$565		
10	Cynthia	$2,566	$128		
11	Susan	$10,894	$545		
12					
13	Report				
14	Count of sales over $5,000		5		
15	Count of commissions over $200		7		
16					

The first argument is the range we want to count - **B2:B11**.

The second argument is the criteria - greater than $5,000 (">£5000").

Note that the criteria is included in quotes because it includes a logical symbol.

Other examples

In the following examples, we have a table of data which we query with different COUNTIF formulas. The formulas, results and descriptions are shown below.

| A2 | ▼ | : | ✕ | ✓ | f_x | Tea |

◢	A	B	C
1	**Product**	**Orders**	
2	Tea	9	
3	Pears	20	
4	Peaches	21	
5	Pineapple	30	
6	Cherry Pie Filling	6	
7	Green Beans	10	
8	Corn	5	
9	Peas	10	
10	Tuna Fish	12	
11	Tea	5	
12	Tea	12	
13	Peaches	10	
14	Peas	2	

Formula 1	
Formula	=COUNTIF(A2:A14,"Tea")
Result	3
Description	Counts number of cells with tea.

Formula 2	
Formula	=COUNTIF(A2:A14,A4)
Result	2
Description	Counts the number of cells with peaches (the value in A4).

Formula 3	
Formula	=COUNTIF(A2:A14,A2)+COUNTIF(A2:A14,A3)
Result	4
Description	Counts the number of teas and pears in A2:A14.

Formula 4	
Formula	=COUNTIF(B2:B14,">20")
Result	2
Description	Counts the number of values in cells B2:B14 greater than 20.

Formula 5	
Formula	=COUNTIF(B2:B14,"<>"&B7)
Result	10
Description	Counts the number of cells with a value not equal to 10 in cells B2:B14. The ampersand (&) is used for concatenation.

Formula 6	
Formula	=COUNTIF(A2:A14,"T*")
Result	4
Description	Counts the number of items starting with T in cells A2:A14.

COUNTIFS Function

The COUNTIFS function enables you to count values in multiple ranges using multiple criteria to determine what values to count.

Syntax

COUNTIFS(criteria_range1, criteria1, [criteria_range2, criteria2]…)

Arguments

Argument	Description
criteria_range1	Required. The first range you want to evaluate using the associated criteria, which is criteria1.
criteria1	Required. This is the first criteria and it pairs with criteria_range1. It could be a number, cell reference, expression, or text that define which cells will be counted. For example, criteria can be expressed as 40, ">=40", D10, "bolts", or "40".
criteria_range2, criteria2, ...	Optional. Additional ranges and criteria pairs. You can have a total of 127 range/criteria pairs.

Remarks

- Each additional range must have the same number of rows and columns as criteria_range1. The ranges do not have to be adjacent to each other.

- If the criteria argument points to an empty cell, the COUNTIFS function treats the empty cell as a 0 value.

- If you are testing for text values, for example, "apples", make sure the criterion is in quotation marks.

- You can use wildcard characters like the question mark (?) and asterisk (*) in your criteria to enable you to find matches that are similar but not the same. The question mark matches any single character and the asterisk matches a sequence of characters. To find a character like a question mark or asterisk, type a tilde sign (~) in front of the character.

Example

In the following example, we want to count the number of people for each state with 40 or more orders. This problem requires us to use two criteria to evaluate two columns. We will be using the state name and ">=40" to determine which records meet our criteria.

We apply the following formula to solve the problem:

=COUNTIFS($B$2:$B$12,F2,$C$2:$C$12,G2)

	A	B	C	D	E	F	G	H
	H2			f_x	=COUNTIFS($B$2:$B$12,F2,$C$2:$C$12,G2)			
1	Name	State	No. Orders	Sales		States	Orders	# People
2	Bruce	New York	51	$74,298		New York	>=40	2
3	Louis	New York	39	$46,039		Texas	>=40	1
4	Earl	Washington	60	$65,252		California	>=40	1
5	Sean	Washington	100	$61,847		Washington	>=40	2
6	Benjamin	Texas	28	$33,340				
7	Joe	California	31	$95,778				
8	Shawn	Texas	35	$58,808				
9	Kenneth	California	39	$52,593				
10	Cynthia	California	51	$42,484				
11	Susan	Texas	80	$44,390				
12	Dav	New York	70	$66,109				
13								

Formula explanation:

=COUNTIFS($B$2:$B$12,F2,$C$2:$C$12,G2)

- The Criteria_range1 argument references the State column **B2:B12** (an absolute reference has been used - $B$2:$B$12).

-⎯Tip
    To convert a cell reference to an absolute reference, select the reference in the formula bar and press the F4 key. You can also type in the dollar signs manually, but it is faster and less error-prone to use F4. An absolute reference ensures the referenced cells do not change relatively when the formula is copied to other cells.

- The Criteria1 argument is **F2**. This is a reference to the State we want to use as our criteria. A cell reference has been used for this argument to make it easier to change.

Also, this argument has been entered as a relative reference because we want it to change relatively as we copy the formula to other cells.

- The *Criteria_range2* is the *No. Orders* column (**$C$2:$C$12**). We will be using our second criteria to evaluate this column. Again, use the F4 key to make it an absolute reference.

- The *Criteria2* argument is **G2** (>=40). A cell reference has been used for this argument to make it easier to change.

We enter the formula in cell **H2** and then copy it down the column to count the number of people with orders that match the criteria for each state.

COUNTA Function

The COUNTA function counts the number of cells that are not empty in a group of cells or range. The difference between the COUNTA and COUNT is that COUNTA counts all cells containing an entry, including empty text ("") and even error values. COUNT, on the other hand, only counts cells that contain numeric values.

Syntax

COUNTA(value1, [value2], ...)

Arguments

Argument	Description
value1	Required. The first argument represents the range in which you want to count cells with an entry.
value2, ...	Optional. You can have additional value arguments up to a maximum of 255 arguments in total.

Remarks

- If you want to count only cells that contain numeric values use the COUNT function.

- Use the COUNTIF function or the COUNTIFS function if you only want to count cells that meet a certain criterion.

Example

In the following example, we use the COUNTA function to count cells with entries in our range of cells. The group of cells containing our data, **A14:D14**, is a named range called *Orders_Range*.

The COUNTA function is demonstrated next to other functions like COUNT and COUNTBLANK to show the difference in the results.

Formula: =COUNTA(Orders_Range)

Result: 37

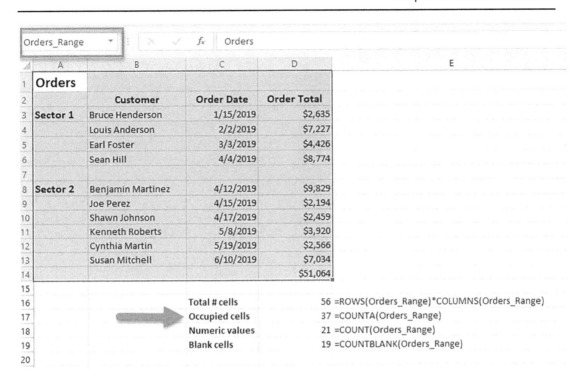

Orders_Range		f_x	Orders	

	A	B	C	D	E
1	**Orders**				
2		**Customer**	**Order Date**	**Order Total**	
3	**Sector 1**	Bruce Henderson	1/15/2019	$2,635	
4		Louis Anderson	2/2/2019	$7,227	
5		Earl Foster	3/3/2019	$4,426	
6		Sean Hill	4/4/2019	$8,774	
7					
8	**Sector 2**	Benjamin Martinez	4/12/2019	$9,829	
9		Joe Perez	4/15/2019	$2,194	
10		Shawn Johnson	4/17/2019	$2,459	
11		Kenneth Roberts	5/8/2019	$3,920	
12		Cynthia Martin	5/19/2019	$2,566	
13		Susan Mitchell	6/10/2019	$7,034	
14				$51,064	
15					
16			Total # cells	56 =ROWS(Orders_Range)*COLUMNS(Orders_Range)	
17			Occupied cells	37 =COUNTA(Orders_Range)	
18			Numeric values	21 =COUNT(Orders_Range)	
19			Blank cells	19 =COUNTBLANK(Orders_Range)	
20					

COUNTBLANK Function

The COUNTBLANK function is used to count the number of empty cells in a range.

Syntax

COUNTBLANK(range)

Argument	Description
range	Required. The first argument represents the range in which you want to count the blank cells.

Cells with formulas that return an empty string ("") are also counted. Cells with 0 (zero) are not counted.

Example

In the following example, we use the COUNTBLANK function to count the blank cells in the range **A14:D14** named *Orders_Range*.

Formula: =COUNTBLANK(Orders_Range)
Result: 19

Orders_Range	▼	:	×	✓	f_x	Orders	

	A	B	C	D	E
1	**Orders**				
2		**Customer**	**Order Date**	**Order Total**	
3	**Sector 1**	Bruce Henderson	1/15/2019	$2,635	
4		Louis Anderson	2/2/2019	$7,227	
5		Earl Foster	3/3/2019	$4,426	
6		Sean Hill	4/4/2019	$8,774	
7					
8	**Sector 2**	Benjamin Martinez	4/12/2019	$9,829	
9		Joe Perez	4/15/2019	$2,194	
10		Shawn Johnson	4/17/2019	$2,459	
11		Kenneth Roberts	5/8/2019	$3,920	
12		Cynthia Martin	5/19/2019	$2,566	
13		Susan Mitchell	6/10/2019	$7,034	
14				$51,064	
15					
16			Total # cells	56	=ROWS(Orders_Range)*COLUMNS(Orders_Range)
17			Occupied cells	37	=COUNTA(Orders_Range)
18			Numeric values	21	=COUNT(Orders_Range)
19			Blank cells	19	=COUNTBLANK(Orders_Range)
20					

AVERAGE Function

The AVERAGE function is one of the widely used aggregate functions in Excel. It returns the average of the arguments. The average is the arithmetic mean of a series of numbers and is calculated by adding up the numbers and then dividing by the count of those numbers.

Syntax

AVERAGE(number1, [number2], ...)

Arguments

Argument	Description
Number1	Required. The first cell reference, range or number for which you want to calculate an average.
Number2, ...	Optional. Additional cell references, ranges or numbers for which you want to calculate an average, up to a maximum of 255.

Remarks

- Arguments can be numbers, named ranges, or cell references that contain numbers.

- If any of the cells referenced in the arguments contain an error value, AVERAGE returns an error.

- Text, logical values, and empty cells are ignored, however, cells with the value zero (0) are included.

- Use the AVERAGEA function if you want to include logical values and text representations of numbers as part of the calculation.

- Use AVERAGEIF and AVERAGEIFS if you want to calculate the average of only the values that meets some criteria you've set.

Example

In the example below, we use the AVERAGE function to calculate the average of the scores in range B2:C19.

Formula: =AVERAGE(B2:C19)

	F1		▼	⋮	✕	✓	f_x	=AVERAGE(B2:C19)	
◢	A	B	C		D		E		F
1		Subject 1	Subject 2				Average score		51.86
2	Bruce	0	55						
3	Louis	57	61						
4	Earl	51	47						
5	Sean	74	74						
6	Benjamin	50	50						
7	Joe	30	52						
8	Shawn	95	N/A						
9	Kenneth	8	70						
10	Cynthia	30	45						
11	Susan	57	40						
12	John	67	76						

AVERAGEIF Function

The AVERAGEIF function is a combination of a statistical function and a logical function. AVERAGEIF returns the average (or arithmetic mean) of all the cells in a range that meet a specified condition.

Syntax

AVERAGEIF(range, criteria, [average_range])

Arguments

Argument	Description
Range	Required. A reference to one or more cells to average. This argument can include numbers, cell references, or named ranges.
Criteria	Required. This is a logical test that determines which cells are included in the average.
Average_range	Optional. The actual set of cells to average if not the cells in the *range* argument. If this argument is omitted, *range* is used.

Remarks

- Cells in range that contain logical values like TRUE or FALSE are ignored.

- AVERAGEIF will return an error (#DIV0!) if *range* is a blank or text value.

- If a cell in criteria is empty it is treated as a zero (0) value.

- AVERAGEIF returns the #DIV/0! error value if no cells in the range meet the criteria.

- You can use wildcard characters like the question mark (?) and asterisk (*) in your criteria to enable you to find matches that are similar but not the same. A question mark matches any single character while an asterisk matches a sequence of characters. To find a character like a question mark or asterisk, type a tilde sign (~) in front of the character.

- *Average_range* does not necessarily need to be the same number of rows and columns as *range*. The cells that are averaged are determined by using the top-left cell in *average_range* as the first cell, and then including cells that match the same number of rows and columns in *range*. See the examples below:

- If the *range* is A1:A10 and *average_range* is B1:B10, then the actual cells evaluated would be B1:B10.
- If range is A1:A10 and *average_range* is B1:B5, then the actual cells evaluated would be B1:B10.
- If range is A1:B5 and *average_range* is C1:C3, then the actual cells evaluated would be C1:D5.

Example

In the following example, we use the AVERAGEIF function to calculate the average exam scores for students per subject. We want to group the data by *Subject* (for example, Biology, Chemistry, Maths etc.) and average each group by *Score*.

The range we will be using to select the data - B2:B16, is different from the range we want to actually average - C2:C16.

	A	B	C	D	E	F
F2					=AVERAGEIF($B$2:$B$16,E2,$C$2:$C$16)	
1	Student	Subject	Score		Average per subject	
2	Bruce	Maths	55		Maths	56.2
3	Louis	Chemistry	61		Chemistry	50.0
4	Earl	Biology	47		English	68.0
5	Sean	English	74		Biology	43.5
6	Benjamin	Maths	50			
7	Joe	Chemistry	52			
8	Shawn	Biology	40			
9	Kenneth	English	70			
10	Cynthia	Maths	45			
11	Susan	Chemistry	40			
12	John	Maths	76			
13	Bruce	English	60			
14	Louis	Maths	61			
15	Earl	Chemistry	47			
16	Kenneth	Maths	50			
17						

Formula explanation:

=AVERAGEIF($B$2:$B$16,E2,$C$2:$C$16)

- The **Range** argument references the Subject column B2:B16 (this has been set to absolute reference - **$B$2:$B$16**).

  Tip

  To convert a cell reference to an absolute reference, select the reference in the formula bar and press the F4 key. You can also type in the dollar signs manually, but it is faster and less error-prone to use F4. An absolute reference ensures the referenced cells do not change relatively when the formula is copied to other cells.

- The **Criteria** argument is **E2**. This is a reference to the subjects we want to use as our criteria. Instead of directly entering this value into the formula, a cell reference has been used to make it easier to change. This argument is a relative reference (the default) because we want the cell to change relatively as we copy the formula to other cells.

- The **Average_range** is C2:C16 (which is **$C$2:$C$16** as an absolute reference). This is the range for which we want to calculate the average of values that meet our criteria. Use the F4 key to make it an absolute reference.

  We enter the formula in cell F2 to return the Maths average. Then the Fill Handle of the cell was used to copy the formula to cells F3:F5 which displays the average for the other subjects

AVERAGEIFS Function

The AVERAGEIFS function returns the average (arithmetic mean) of all cells that meet specific criteria you specify. This function allows you to specify several pairs of criteria to select the data that is included in the average. An IFS function enables you to create several range/criteria pairs used to select the data that meet the criteria.

Once items that meet the criteria have been identified, the average of the corresponding values in the main range is calculated. You can have up to a maximum of 127 range/criteria pairs as you can only have 255 arguments in an Excel function.

Syntax

AVERAGEIFS(average_range, criteria_range1, criteria1, [criteria_range2, criteria2], ...)

Arguments

Argument	Description
Average_range	Required. This is the range of cells for which you want the average calculated.
Criteria_range1	Required. The range that is evaluated using *Criteria1*. This is part of the first range/criteria pair.
Criteria1	Required. This is the criteria used to evaluate *criteria1_range* to select matching data. For example, criteria can be entered as 40, ">40", C6, "bolts", or "125".
Criteria_range2, criteria2, ...	Optional. You can have additional range/criteria pairs, up to a maximum of 127 total pairs.

Example

In this example, we have a list of orders from different sales reps for several states. We want to find the average sales per state for entries that are greater than or equal to 10 orders (>=10).

We apply the following formula to solve the problem:

=AVERAGEIFS($D$2:$D$12,$B$2:$B$12,F2,$C$2:$C$12,G2)

441

H2				f_x	=AVERAGEIFS($D$2:$D$12,$B$2:$B$12,F2,$C$2:$C$12,G2)			

	A	B	C	D	E	F	G	H
1	Name	State	# of Orders	Sales		States	Orders	Average Sales on 10 or more orders
2	Bruce	New York	12	$74,298		New York	>=10	$70,204
3	Louis	New York	5	$46,039		Texas	>=10	$58,808
4	Earl	Washington	15	$65,252		California	>=10	$52,593
5	Sean	Washington	11	$61,847		Washington	>=10	$63,550
6	Benjamin	Texas	9	$33,340				
7	Joe	California	3	$30,000				
8	Shawn	Texas	20	$58,808				
9	Kenneth	California	12	$52,593				
10	Cynthia	California	8	$42,484				
11	Susan	Texas	2	$20,000				
12	Dav	New York	10	$66,109				

Formula explanation:

=AVERAGEIFS($D$2:$D$12,$B$2:$B$12,F2,$C$2:$C$12,G2)

- The *Average_range* argument references the Sales column D2:D12 (an absolute reference has been used - **$D$2:$D$12**). This is the column for which we want to calculate the average.

-☼-Tip

To convert a cell reference to an absolute reference, select the reference in the formula bar and press the F4 key. You can also type in the dollar signs manually, but it is faster and less error-prone to use F4. An absolute reference ensures the referenced cells do not change relatively when the formula is copied to other cells.

- The *Criteria_range1* is B2:B12 (an absolute reference has been used - **$B$2:$B$12**).

- The *Criteria1* argument is **F2**. This is a reference to the state we want to use as our criteria. A cell reference has been used for this argument to make it easier to change.

  This has been left as a relative reference (default) because we want it to change as we copy the formula to other cells.

- The *Criteria_range2* argument is the **# of Orders** column, C2:C12. We will be using *Criteria2* to select the orders that meet the criteria from this range. An absolute reference has been used - **$C$2:$C$12**.

- The *Criteria2* argument is cell **G2** which represents our criteria (>=10). This argument is a matching pair for *Criteria_range2*. A cell reference has been used to make it easier to update with different criteria values.

The formula is entered in cell **H2** and then the Fill Handle of the cell is used to copy the formula to H3:H5. This calculates the average for the other states.

MAX, MIN, MEDIAN Functions

The MAX, MIN and MEDIAN functions are some of the most commonly used functions in Excel and are very similar in their arguments and how they're used. MAX returns the largest number in a specified set of values. MIN returns the smallest number in a set of values. MEDIAN returns the median which is the number in the middle of a set of numbers.

Syntax

Max function: MAX(number1, [number2], ...)

Min function: MIN(number1, [number2], ...)

Median function: MEDIAN(number1, [number2], ...)

Arguments – similar for all three functions

Argument	Description
Number1	Required. The first argument is required and can be a number, range, array, or reference that contain numbers.
number2, ...	Optional. You can have additional numbers, cell references, or ranges up to a maximum of 255 arguments which you want to evaluate.

Remarks

- The functions will return 0 (zero) if the arguments contain no numbers.

- If an argument is a reference or an array, only numbers in that reference or array are used. Logical values, text values, empty cells in the reference or array are ignored.

- The functions will return an error if arguments contain error values or text that cannot be translated into numbers.

- Text representations of numbers and logical values that you directly type into the arguments list are counted.

- For the MEDIAN function, if there is an even number of numeric values in the set, it calculates the average of the two numbers in the middle.

- Use the MAXA and MINA functions if you want to include logical values and text representations of numbers as part of the result for MAX and MIN. You can search for the MAXA or MINA via the **Insert Function** command on the Formulas tab on the Excel ribbon.

Example

In the example below, we want to show the maximum, minimum, and median values for the Sales column (D2:D12) in our table.

The following formulas return the desired results:

- MAX(D2:D12)

- MIN(D2:D12)

- MEDIAN(D2:D12)

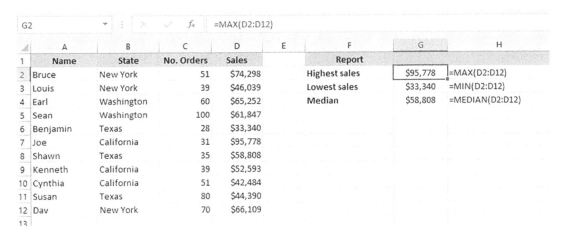

To add more cell references or ranges to the arguments you simply separate them with a comma, for example, MAX(C1:C5, G1:G5).

MAXIFS, MINIFS Functions

The MAXIFS and MINIFS functions are an extension of the MAX and MIN functions to include a conditional component in their functionality. MAXIFS returns the maximum value of all cells that meet the specified criteria. MINIFS returns the minimum value of all cells that meet the specified criteria. You can specify more than one set of criteria to determine which data is selected to be part of the evaluation.

An IFS function enables you to create several range/criteria pairs used to narrow down the data to only those that meet the criteria. Once items that meet the criteria have been identified, the minimum or maximum of the corresponding values in the main range is calculated.

You can have up to a maximum of 127 range/criteria pairs as you can only have 255 arguments in an Excel function.

Note These functions are new in Excel 2019 so will not be available in older versions of Excel. If you are subscribed to Microsoft 365, make sure you have the latest version of Excel installed.

Syntax

MAXIFS

MAXIFS(max_range, criteria_range1, criteria1, [criteria_range2, criteria2], ...)

MINIFS

MINIFS(min_range, criteria_range1, criteria1, [criteria_range2, criteria2], ...)

Arguments – similar for both functions

Argument	Description
max_range (MAX function) min_range (MIN function)	Required. The actual range of cells for which we want the maximum or minimum value determined.
criteria_range1	Required. The range that is evaluated using *criteria1*. This is part of the first range/criteria pair.

criteria1	Required. This is the criteria used to determine which cells in *criteria_range1* will be part of the calculation. This can be a number, expression, or text. For example, criteria can be entered as 40, ">40", C6, "bolts", or "125".
criteria_range2, criteria2, ...	Optional. You can have additional range/criteria pairs, up to a maximum of 127 total pairs.

Remarks

- The max_range (or min_range) and criteria_range arguments must have the same number of rows and columns, otherwise, these functions return the #VALUE! error.

- The range we use to filter the data does not necessarily have to be the same range that we want to generate the max or min value from.

Example

In this example, we want to produce reports that show the minimum and maximums sales per state. However, we only want to evaluate entries with 10 or more orders (>=10). So, we have two criteria that we want to use to determine the data to be evaluated.

Formulas

We use the following formulas to return the desired results.

Maximum:
=MAXIFS($D$2:$D$12,$B$2:$B$12,F3,$C$2:$C$12,G3)

Minimum:
=MINIFS($D$2:$D$12,$B$2:$B$12,F10,$C$2:$C$12,G10)

	A	B	C	D	E	F	G	H	I
1	Name	State	# of Orders	Sales		Maximum Sales			
2	Bruce	New York	12	$74,298		States	Orders	Maximum Sales	Formula Text
3	Louis	New York	5	$46,039		New York	>=10	$74,298	=MAXIFS($D$2:$D$12,$B$2:$B$12,F3,$C$2:$C$12,G3)
4	Earl	Washington	15	$65,252		Texas	>=10	$58,808	=MAXIFS($D$2:$D$12,$B$2:$B$12,F4,$C$2:$C$12,G4)
5	Sean	Washington	11	$61,847		California	>=10	$52,593	=MAXIFS($D$2:$D$12,$B$2:$B$12,F5,$C$2:$C$12,G5)
6	Benjamin	Texas	10	$33,340		Washington	>=10	$65,252	=MAXIFS($D$2:$D$12,$B$2:$B$12,F6,$C$2:$C$12,G6)
7	Joe	California	3	$30,000					
8	Shawn	Texas	20	$58,808		Minimum Sales			
9	Kenneth	California	12	$52,593		States	Orders	Minimum sales	Formula Text
10	Cynthia	California	8	$42,484		New York	>=10	$66,109	=MINIFS($D$2:$D$12,$B$2:$B$12,F10,$C$2:$C$12,G10)
11	Susan	Texas	2	$20,000		Texas	>=10	$33,340	=MINIFS($D$2:$D$12,$B$2:$B$12,F11,$C$2:$C$12,G11)
12	Dav	New York	10	$66,109		California	>=10	$52,593	=MINIFS($D$2:$D$12,$B$2:$B$12,F12,$C$2:$C$12,G12)
13						Washington	>=10	$61,847	=MINIFS($D$2:$D$12,$B$2:$B$12,F13,$C$2:$C$12,G13)
14									
15									

Formula explanation

We have used identical cell references and criteria arguments for both functions, so they can be described together.

MAXIFS($D$2:$D$12,$B$2:$B$12,F3,$C$2:$C$12,G3)

- The first argument for both functions is a reference to the Sales column, D2:D12. This is the actual range we want to evaluate for the minimum and maximum values. An absolute reference has been used - **$D$2:$D$12**.

-ᗧ-Tip
To convert a cell reference in the formula bar to an absolute reference, select the reference in the formula bar and press the F4 key. You can also enter the dollar signs manually, but it is faster and less error-prone to use F4. An absolute reference ensures the referenced cells do not change relatively when the formula is copied to other cells.

- The *Criteria_range1* argument is the **State** column B2:B12. This is part of the first range/criteria pair we'll use to establish our first condition. An absolute cell reference has been used - **$B$2:$B$12**.

- The *Criteria1* argument is **F2**. This is a cell reference to our first criteria, the name of the state which is "New York" in the case of cell F2. A cell reference has been used to hold the value to make it easier to change in future if we so desire.

  This has been left as a relative reference (default) because we want it to change as we copy the formula to other cells.

- The *Criteria_range2* argument is the **# of Orders** column, C2:C12. This is part of the second range/criteria pair. An absolute reference has been used - **$C$2:$C$12**.

- The *Criteria2* argument is cell **G2** which represents the criteria ">=10". This is part of the second range/criteria pair used to filter the data to be evaluated. A cell reference has been used to make it easier to update with different criteria values.

To display the results, we enter the MAXIFS formula in cell **H2** and use the Fill Handle of the cell to copy the formula down to **H5**. This calculates the maximum sales for the other states.

For the minimum values, we enter the MINIFS formula in cell **H10** and use the Fill Handle to copy the formula down to **H13** to calculate the minimum sales for the other states.

Chapter 6: Date and Time Functions

The date and time functions can be found in Excel by clicking the Date & Time command button on the Formulas tab on the Ribbon. The drop-down menu lists all the date and time functions in Excel.

Excel stores dates and times as serial numbers internally, for example, 43454.83583. The numbers to the left of the decimal point represent the date, and numbers to the right of the decimal point represent the time. This is what is used to carry out date and time calculations behind the scenes. Any entry that is formatted as a date/time is automatically converted internally into a serial number. For example, by default, January 1, 1900, is serial number 1, and January 1, 2019 is serial number 43466 because January 1, 2019 is 43466 days after January 1, 1900.

In this chapter, we'll cover functions that enable you to:

- Return the day, month or year from a given date.
- Add or subtract days, months, and years from dates.
- Combine different values into a single date.
- Return the number of days, months, or years between two dates.
- Convert date values entered as text into recognized Excel dates, for example, in the case of imported data.
- Return the number of whole working days between two dates.
- Return the current date or the date and time.
- Return the decimal number for a given time.

Date Formats

Before delving into the date functions, we need to look at date formats in Excel and how to set cells to different date formats. The default date and time formats used by Excel will be the ones you have set in your regional settings in Windows (or macOS for Macs).

The short date format used in Europe is Day/Month/Year (i.e. dd/MM/yyyy) while in the United States the short date format is Month/Day/Year (i.e. M/d/yyyy).

You can change the way dates are displayed in your Excel worksheet regardless of your regional date settings in Windows or macOS.

To change the date format in Excel:

1. Select the cell(s) for which you want to change the date format.

2. Click the dialog box launcher on the Number group on the Home tab to launch the **Format Cells** window.

3. Under **Category**, select **Date**.

4. Under **Locale (location)**, select the locale you want, for example, English (United States).

5. Under **Type**, select the date format you want.

6. To select a different time format, select **Time** under Category and follow the same steps as above to choose a time format.

7. When done, click **OK**.

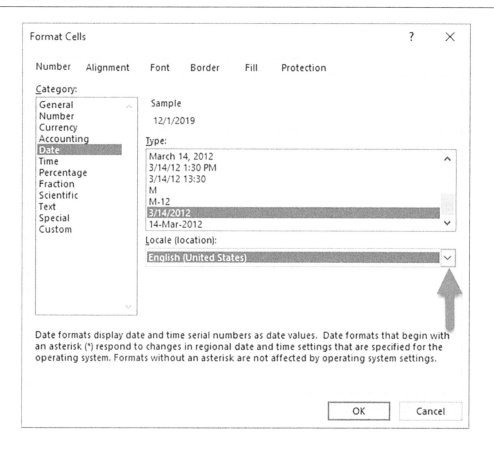

Note For the examples in this chapter, we will use the United States short date convention **M/d/yyyy**. If you're in a region using the dd/MM/yyyy convention, simply swap the month and day of the dates used in the examples.

DAY, MONTH, YEAR Functions

The DAY, MONTH, YEAR functions are very similar and are usually used together, so will be covered together in this chapter. They all take a single argument which is a serial number representing a date.

DAY returns the day (an integer between 1 to 31) corresponding to a date entered as its argument.

MONTH returns the month (an integer between 1 to 12, representing January to December) corresponding to a date entered as its argument.

YEAR returns the year (as an integer in the range 1900-9999) corresponding to a date entered as its argument.

Syntax

DAY(serial_number)

MONTH(serial_number)

YEAR(serial_number)

Argument	Description
Serial_number	Required. All three functions have the same kind of argument. This argument must be a recognised date. It is the date for the day, month, or year you want to return.
	You can use the DATE function in this argument to ensure a proper date is entered, for example, DATE(2019,4,28). Problems may occur if dates are entered as text.

Remarks

- Dates are stored in Excel as sequential serial numbers to enable calculations to be carried out. For example, by default, 1/1/1900 is serial number 1, and 1/1/2018 is serial number 43101 because 1/1/2018 is 43101 days after 1/1/1900.

- The values returned by the YEAR, MONTH and DAY functions are always Gregorian values regardless of the date format of the argument. For example, if the entered date is

Hijri (Islamic Calendar), the values returned by the DAY, MONTH and YEAR functions will be the equivalent in the Gregorian calendar.

Example 1

In this example, we use the DAY, MONTH and YEAR functions to extract the day, month and year from a given date in cell A1, **January 18, 2019**.

Formulas:
=DAY(A1)
=MONTH(A1)
=YEAR(A1)

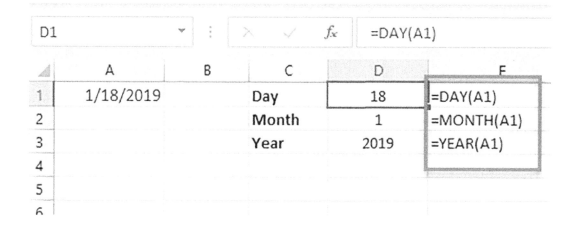

Example 2

In this example, we want to add 6 years to December 15, 2017. To calculate the date, we need to use the YEAR, MONTH, and DAY functions as arguments within the DATE function.

When we combine these functions with DATE, we get the following:

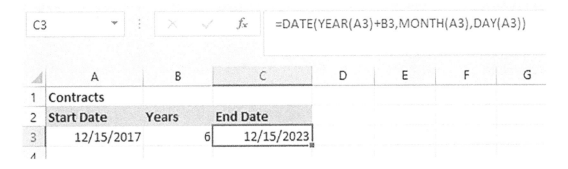

Formula Explanation

=DATE(YEAR(A3)+B3,MONTH(A3),DAY(A3))

The *year* argument of the DATE function has **YEAR(A3)+B3**. This will return 2023 (i.e. 2017 + 6). The other functions return the month and day respectively in the *month* and *day* arguments.

To subtract years, use the minus sign (−) in place of the plus sign (+) in the formula.

DATE Function

The DATE function enables you to combine different values into a single date.

Syntax

DATE (year, month, day)

Arguments

Argument	Description
Year	Required. This argument can have one to four digits. Excel uses the date system on your computer to interpret the year argument.
Month	Required. The month argument should be a positive or negative integer between 1 to 12, representing January to December. If the month argument is a negative number (-*n*) the function returns a date that is *n* months back from the last month of the previous year. For example, DATE(2019,-4,2) will return the serial number representing August 2, 2018.
Day	Required. This argument can be a positive or negative integer from 1 to 31, representing the day of the month.

Remarks

- Excel stores dates and times internally as sequential serial numbers to be used in calculations. For example, by default, 1/1/1900 is serial number 1, and 1/1/2018 is serial number 43101 because 1/1/2018 is 43101 days after 1/1/1900.

- If the month argument is greater than 12, the function adds that number of months to the last month of the specified year. For example, DATE(2018,14,4) will return the serial number representing February 4, 2019.

- If Day is greater than the number of days in the specified month, the function adds that number of days to the first day of the next month of the specified date. For, example, DATE(2019,1,36) returns the serial number representing February 5, 2019.

- If Day is less than 1, the function subtracts that number of days from the last day of the previous month of the specified date. For example, DATE(2018,2,-15) will return the serial number that represents January 16, 2018. 15 was subtracted from the 31 days in January which is the previous month to that specified in the function.

- Excel sometimes automatically detects a date entry and formats the cell accordingly. However, if you copied and pasted a date from another source, you may need to manually format the cell to a date to display the date properly.

💡-Tip   To prevent unwanted results, always use four digits for the year argument. For example, "04" could mean "1904" or "2004." Using four-digit years prevents any confusion.

Example 1

In this example, we want to combine values from different cells for the month, day, and year into a date value recognised in Excel.

- Month: 4
- Day: 14
- Year: 2018

When we use the DATE function to combine the values into a single date, we get the following:

=DATE(C2,A2,B2)

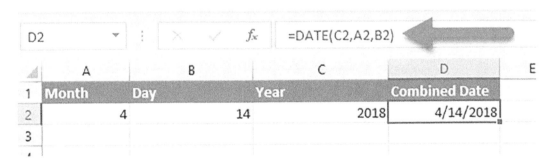

Example 2

This example was covered in a previous chapter but is also applicable here. In this example, we want to add 6 years to December 15, 2017.

To calculate the date, we combine the YEAR, MONTH, and DAY functions with the DATE function. These three functions have been covered in a previous section of this chapter.

- YEAR returns the year corresponding to a date entered as its argument.

- MONTH returns the month corresponding to a date entered as its argument.

- DAY returns the day corresponding to a date entered as its argument.

When we combine these functions with the DATE function, we get the following formula:

=DATE(YEAR(A3)+B3,MONTH(A3),DAY(A3))

Answer: 12/15/2023.

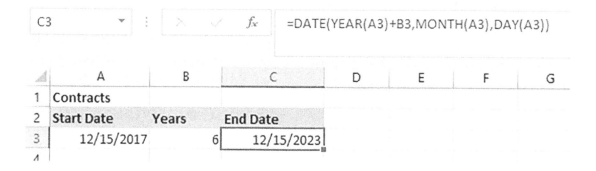

Formula Explanation

=DATE(YEAR(A3)+B3,MONTH(A3),DAY(A3))

The *year* argument of the DATE function has **YEAR(A3)+B3**. This will return 2023 (i.e. 2017 + 6). The other functions return the month and day respectively in the *month* and *day* arguments.

To subtract years, use the minus sign (−) in place of the plus sign (+) in the formula.

Example 3

In this example, we want to add 15 months to December 15, 2017.

Formula:

=DATE(YEAR(A3),MONTH(A3)+B3,DAY(A3))

Answer: 03/15/2019

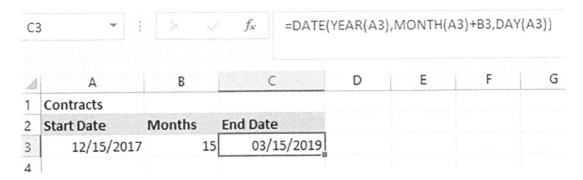

Formula Explanation

In the *month* argument of the DATE function, the syntax, **MONTH(A3)+B3** is what is used to add 15 months to the date. The DATE function will automatically calculate the date from the arguments provided.

To subtract months, use the − sign in place of the + sign in the formula.

Example 4

In this example, we want to add 20 days to December 15, 2017.

Formula:

=DATE(YEAR(A3),MONTH(A3),DAY(A3)+B3)

Answer: 1/4/2018

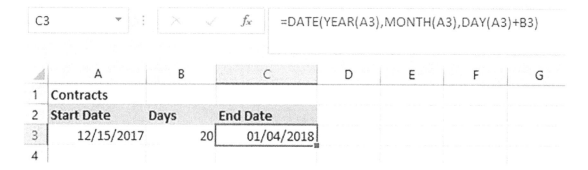

Formula Explanation

The 20 days were added to the DAY function in the *day* argument (i.e. DAY(A3)+B3) of the DATE function. The DATE function accurately returns the End Date based on the input we've provided.

To subtract days, use the minus sign (–) in place of the plus sign (+) in the formula.

To find the difference between two dates you can use the DATEDIF which is covered later in this chapter.

DATEDIF Function

The DATEDIF function calculates the difference between two dates. This function provides one of the easiest ways in Excel to calculate the difference between two dates. It can return the number of days, months, or years between two dates.

DATEDIF is a "hidden" function in Excel because you'll not find it on the list of date functions or when you search for it using the Insert Function dialog box. You must enter it manually any time you want to use it. It is a legacy function from Lotus 1-2-3 but operational on all versions of Excel.

Syntax

DATEDIF(start_date, end_date, unit)

Arguments

Argument	Description
start_date	Required. This argument represents the start date of the period.
end_date	Required. This argument represents the end date of the period.
unit	Required. This argument represents the unit of measurement you want to return - days, months, or years. It should be entered as a string.
	It can be one of Y, M, D, YM, or YD.
	"Y" = Calculates the number of years in the period.
	"M" = Calculates the number of months in the period.
	"D" = Calculates the number of days in the period.
	"YM" = Calculates the difference between the months in start_date and end_date. The days and years of the dates are ignored.
	"YD"= Calculates the difference between the days of start_date and end_date. The years of the dates are ignored.

Note There is also an "MD" argument that calculates the number of days while ignoring the month and years. However, Microsoft no longer recommends the use of the MD argument in this function because under some conditions it could return a negative number.

Example 1

In the example below, we want to calculate the age of someone born on December 1, 1980.

Formula:

=DATEDIF(A2,TODAY(),"Y")

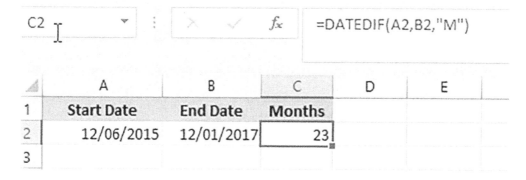

We combined the DATEDIF function with the TODAY function to get the desired result. The TODAY function returns today's date, so this formula will always use today's date to calculate the age. The "Y" argument returns the difference in years.

Example 2

To calculate the number of months between two dates we use the "M" argument of the function.

=DATEDIF(A2,B2,"M")

DAYS Function

The DAYS function returns the number of days between two dates.

Syntax

DAYS (end_date, start_date)

Arguments

Argument	Description
start_date	Required. This argument represents the start date of the period.
end_date	Required. This argument represents the end date of the period.

Example

In this example, we want to calculate the number of days between two dates, December 1, 2018, and December 1, 2019.

Formula:

=DAYS(B2, A2)

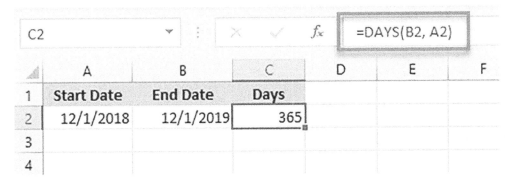

If you're entering the dates directly into the function, you need to enclose them in quotation marks.

For example:

DAYS ("12/01/18", "12/01/2019") will return 365 days.

EDATE Function

The EDATE function allows you to add or subtract months from a given date. EDATE is useful for calculating end dates that are the same day of the month as the start date.

Syntax

EDATE(start_date, months)

Arguments

Argument	Description
Start_date	Required. This argument should be a date representing the start date. It can be a cell reference or a value. Cell references should have the Date format. Use the DATE function for values directly entered. For example, use DATE(2019,1,25) for January 25, 2019. You may get inconsistent results if dates are entered as text.
Months	Required. An integer representing the number of months before or after start_date. A positive value for months returns a date in the future and a negative value returns a date in the past.

Remarks

- Dates are stored in Excel as sequential serial numbers as this is how calculations are carried out internally. For example, by default, 1/1/1900 is serial number 1, and 1/1/2018 is serial number 43101 because 1/1/2018 is 43101 days after 1/1/1900.

- If start_date is not a valid date, EDATE will return an error value (#VALUE!).

- If the months argument is not an integer, it is truncated.

Example

In the following example, we use the EDATE function to calculate the expiry dates for a series of lease contracts with different start dates (A3:A15) and a different lease length (B3:B15).

Formula:

=EDATE(A3,B3)

The formula was entered in cell A3 and copied to the other cells in the column with the Fill handle.

	A	B	C	D
	C3		=EDATE(A3,B3)	
1	**Property Lease**			
2	**Start Date**	**Length (Months)**	**Expiry Date**	
3	1/28/2018	24	1/28/2020	
4	4/4/2018	12	4/4/2019	
5	4/16/2018	12	4/16/2019	
6	5/21/2018	24	5/21/2020	
7	5/28/2018	36	5/28/2021	
8	10/27/2018	6	4/27/2019	
9	11/9/2018	24	11/9/2020	
10	12/7/2018	12	12/7/2019	
11	12/14/2018	24	12/14/2020	
12	2/21/2019	36	2/21/2022	
13	5/6/2019	6	11/6/2019	
14	7/25/2019	24	7/25/2021	
15	11/29/2019	12	11/29/2020	
16				

Note that the cells in A3:A15 and C3:C15 were set to the **Date** format so that the dates are displayed properly.

DATEVALUE Function

The DATEVALUE function converts a date that is entered as text to a serial number in Excel that is recognized as a date. The DATEVALUE function is useful in situations where a worksheet contains dates that were imported from another application and seen as text in Excel. You will need to convert the values to recognised dates in Excel to carry out date evaluations.

Once you've converted the values to Excel dates, you can then sort, filter, or add/subtract dates. DATEVALUE returns a serial number internally recognised as a date. To format this number as a date you must apply a **Date** format to the cell.

For example, the formula =DATEVALUE("1/1/2019") returns 43466, which is the serial number for the date, January 1, 2019.

Syntax

DATEVALUE(date_text)

Argument	Description
Date_text	Required. Text that represents a date in an Excel date format, or a reference to a cell that contains text that represents a date in an Excel date format. For example, "1/30/2008" or "30-Jan-2008" are text strings within quotation marks that represent dates.

Remarks

- The date_text argument must represent a date between January 1, 1900, and December 31, 9999. DATEVALUE will return an error if the date_text argument falls outside this range.

- If you omit the year part of the date in the date_text argument, the DATEVALUE function will use the current year from your computer's internal clock.

- Dates are stored in Excel as sequential serial numbers as this is how calculations are carried out internally. For example, by default, 1/1/1900 is serial number 1, and 1/1/2018 is serial number 43101 because 1/1/2018 is 43101 days after 1/1/1900.

- Most functions in Excel automatically convert date values to serial numbers.

Example

In the example below, we convert several date text values to serial numbers using the DATEVALUE function.

| B2 | ▼ | : | ⤫ | ✓ | f_x | =DATEVALUE(A2) |

	A	B	C	D
		General number		
1	**Date as Text**	**format**	**Date format (US)**	**Formula**
2	22 May 2011	40685	5/22/2011	=DATEVALUE(A2)
3	5 Jul	43286	7/5/2018	=DATEVALUE(A3)
4	01/01/2019	43466	1/1/2019	=DATEVALUE(A4)
5	April 2019	43556	4/1/2019	=DATEVALUE(A5)
6				
7				
8				

Formula Explanation

=DATEVALUE(A2)

- In the image above, the cells in column A have the text format, the cells in column B have the general number format, and the cells in column C have the date format.

- The DATEVALUE function has been used to convert the text values in A2:A5 to date values in B2:B5. The results are displayed as date serial numbers because the cells have the General number format.

- The DATEVALUE function has been used to convert the text values from A2:A5 to date values in C2:C5. However, in this case, the same results are shown as dates because the Date format has been applied to the range.

NETWORKDAYS Function

The NETWORKDAYS function returns the number of whole working days between two dates. Working days exclude weekends and any dates specified in the *holidays* argument. You can use NETWORKDAYS to calculate employee pay and other benefits based on the number of days worked in a specific period.

Syntax

NETWORKDAYS(start_date, end_date, [holidays])

Arguments

Argument	Description
Start_date	Required. A date that represents the start date.
End_date	Required. A date that represents the end date.
Holidays	Optional. A range, list, or table with one or more dates to be excluded from the working calendar, for example, state holidays, federal holidays, and floating holidays.

Remarks

- If you're entering a date directly as an argument, you should use the DATE function to ensure the argument is converted to a date. For example, use DATE(2019,5,23) instead of "May 23, 2019". Problems can occur if dates are entered as text. If you are referencing a date in a cell, ensure the date format is applied to the cell.

- Dates are stored in Excel as sequential serial numbers as this is how calculations are carried out internally. For example, by default, 1/1/1900 is serial number 1, and 1/1/2018 is serial number 43101 because 1/1/2018 is 43101 days after 1/1/1900.

Example

In the example below, we use the NETWORKDAYS function to calculate the number of workdays between the **Project start date** and **Project end date** of several projects. We also provide a range called **Holiday_range** as the optional *Holidays* argument. **Holiday_range** contains the holiday dates we want to exclude from the count of workdays.

Formula:

=NETWORKDAYS(A2,B2,Holidays_range)

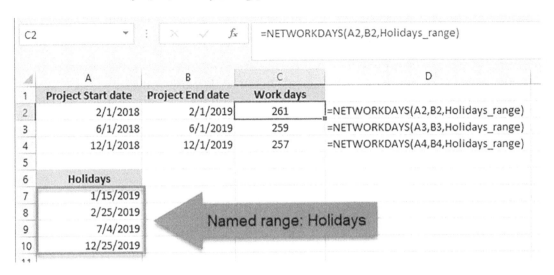

The answers are displayed in the **Work days** column.

Column D is used to display the formulas in column C2:C4 (Workdays).

Tip If you want to be able to specify weekend days that are different from the default Saturday and Sunday used in the Gregorian calendar, use the NETWORKDAYS.INTL function instead of NETWORKDAYS.

To access the NETWORKDAYS.INTL function, on the Excel ribbon, navigate to **Formulas > Date & Time > NETWORKDAYS.INTL**.

NOW Function

The NOW function returns the current date and time. It's a straightforward function with no arguments. The function displays the date in the cell using the date and time format of your regional settings. Check the **Date Formats** section of this book for how to change the date format of a cell.

You can use the NOW function in situations where you need to display the current date and time on a worksheet and have it updated every time you open the worksheet. You can also use the NOW function to calculate a date value if you want it to always be based on the current date and time.

Syntax

NOW()

Remarks

- The results of the NOW function are not continuously updated. It only updates when the worksheet is recalculated i.e. when new values or formulas are entered, or a macro that contains the function is run.

- If the cell containing the NOW function was changed to a General format, it would display the current date as a serial number, for example, 43454.83583. Numbers to the left of the decimal point represent the date, and numbers to the right represent the time. For example, the serial number 0.5 represents the time 12:00 noon.

- Excel stores dates and times as sequential serial numbers so that they can be used in calculations internally. For example, by default, 1/1/1900 is serial number 1, and 1/1/2018 is serial number 43101 because 1/1/2018 is 43101 days after 1/1/1900.

Example

In the example below, the NOW function is used in different formulas to display date calculations based on the current date and time.

Formulas:
    =NOW()
    =NOW()-10.5

=NOW()+10
=NOW()+2.25

| | C2 | | | | f_x | =NOW() |

	A	B	C
1	Formula	Description	Result
2	=NOW()	Returns the current date and time	12/20/2018 20:35
3	=NOW()-10.5	Returns the date and time 10 days and 12 hours ago (-10.5 days ago)	12/10/2018 08:35
4	=NOW()+10	Returns the date and time 10 days in the future	12/30/2018 20:35
5	=NOW()+2.25	Returns the date and time 2 days and 6 hours in the future (+2.25 days ago)	12/23/2018 02:35
6	=NOW()	Returns the current date and time (General Number cell format)	43454.85772
7			
8			
9			

TODAY Function

The TODAY function returns the serial number of the current date. Excel stores dates as serial numbers, however, when you enter this function, the cell is automatically changed to a date format to display the value as a date instead of a serial number. To see the date value as a serial number, you must change the cell format to General or Number.

The TODAY function is useful when you want to display the current date on your worksheet, regardless of when the workbook was opened.

It is also useful for calculating the difference between dates. For example, you can calculate the number of years between two dates by using the TODAY formula in combination with the YEAR function:

= YEAR(TODAY())-1979

The formula uses the TODAY function as an argument for the YEAR function to return the current year. The formula then subtracts 1979 from the current year to return the number of years between 1979 and now.

Syntax

TODAY()

Remarks

- Excel stores dates and times as sequential serial numbers so that they can be used in calculations internally. For example, by default, 1/1/1900 is serial number 1, and 1/1/2018 is serial number 43101 because 1/1/2018 is 43101 days after 1/1/1900.

- If the TODAY function does not update when you open the worksheet, you might need to change the settings in Excel Options that determine when the workbook recalculates.

  To change the Calculation options, navigate to:

  1. File > Options > Formulas.
  2. Under **Calculation options**, ensure **Automatic** is selected.

Example

In the example below, the TODAY function is used in different formulas to display the current date and to calculate other dates based on today's date.

Formulas:
    =TODAY()
    =TODAY()+10
    =DAY(TODAY())
    =MONTH(TODAY())
    =YEAR(TODAY())-1979

| C2 | | f_x | =TODAY() | |

	A	B	C	D
1	Formula	Description	Result	
2	=TODAY()	Returns the current date.	12/21/2018	
3	=TODAY()+10	Returns the current date plus 10 days.	12/31/2018	
4	=DAY(TODAY())	Returns the current day of the month (1 - 31).	21	
5	=MONTH(TODAY())	Returns the current month of the year (1 - 12).	12	
6	= YEAR(TODAY())-1979	TODAY is used as an argument in the YEAR function to return the number of years between 1979 and the current date.	39	
7				
8				

TIME Function

The TIME function returns the decimal number representing a specified time. Excel stores dates and times as serial numbers internally.

Example: 43454.83583

The numbers to the left of the decimal point represent the date and numbers to the right of the decimal point represent the time.

The TIME function will return a decimal number ranging from 0 (zero) to 0.99988426, representing the times from 0:00:00 (12:00:00 AM) to 23:59:59 (11:59:59 PM). If the cell has the General format before the function was entered, the result is formatted as a date to properly display the time instead of a decimal number.

Syntax

TIME(hour, minute, second)

Arguments

Arguments	Descriptions
Hour	Required. This argument can be a number from 0 (zero) to 32767 representing the hour. Any value larger than 23 will be divided by 24 and the remainder will then be treated as the hour value. For example, TIME(29,0,0) = TIME(5,0,0) = .20833 or 5:00 AM.
Minute	Required. This argument can be a number from 0 to 32767 representing the minute. Any value larger than 59 will be divided by 60 and converted to hours and minutes. For example, TIME(0,810,0) = TIME(13,30,0) = .5625 or 1:30 PM.
Second	Required. This argument can be a number from 0 to 32767 representing the second. Any value larger than 59 will be divided by 60 and converted to hours, minutes, and seconds. For example, TIME(0,0,2120) = TIME(0,35,22) = .02456 or 0:35:22 AM

Example

In this example, the range B2:C3 has values for Hour, Minute and Second that we want to use for our calculation. The report in columns E to H shows the results of using the TIME function to evaluate the values in range B2:C3.

Formulas:
=TIME(A2,B2,C2)
=TIME(A3,B3,C3)

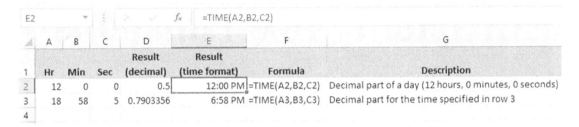

	E2				f_x	=TIME(A2,B2,C2)	
	A	B	C	D	E	F	G
1	Hr	Min	Sec	Result (decimal)	Result (time format)	Formula	Description
2	12	0	0	0.5	12:00 PM	=TIME(A2,B2,C2)	Decimal part of a day (12 hours, 0 minutes, 0 seconds)
3	18	58	5	0.7903356	6:58 PM	=TIME(A3,B3,C3)	Decimal part for the time specified in row 3
4							

Column G shows the results as decimal values because the cell Number format was set to General.

Column H shows the results as times because Excel automatically applies the Time format to a cell as it knows the TIME function returns a time.

Chapter 7: Text Functions

The text functions in Excel can be found in Excel by clicking the Text command button on the Formulas tab on the Ribbon. The drop-down menu lists all the text functions in Excel. If you work with Excel extensively, there are going to be occasions when you would need to use functions to manipulate text, especially when you work with data imported from other programs.

For example, when you import data into Excel from other applications, you may encounter irregular text spacing or data that's all uppercase. You may want to remove extra spaces from the data or convert uppercase text into proper casing (where only the first letter of each word is in uppercase).

In this chapter, we'll cover functions that enable you to:

- Find one text string within a second text string.
- Combine the text from multiple ranges or strings into one string.
- Specify a delimiter as a separator when combining text strings.
- Trim text by removing all extra spaces except single spaces between words.
- Convert text to uppercase or lowercase.
- Capitalize each word in a text string.
- Return the number of characters in a text string.
- Return a specified number of characters from the left, middle, or right of a string.
- Return a portion of a string based on a character or space within the string.

Tip The **Flash Fill** command on the Home tab now enables you to automatically perform many text-manipulation tasks for which you would previously use functions. To learn more about Flash Fill, see **chapter 2 in Book 1: Excel Basics**.

FIND Function

The FIND function is used to locate the starting position of one text string within another text string. It returns the position of the first character of the text your searching for within the second text. The search is case sensitive.

Syntax

FIND(find_text, within_text, [start_num])

Arguments

Argument	Description
Find_text	Required. This is the text you want to find.
Within_text	Required. This is the text containing the text you want to find.
Start_num	Optional. This argument specifies the point, in characters, from which you want to start the search in within_text. The first character in within_text is character number 1. If you omit this argument it will start from the first character in within_text.

Example 1

In this example, we use the FIND function to return the position of different characters in the string "United States". As you can see from the results, the FIND function is case sensitive.

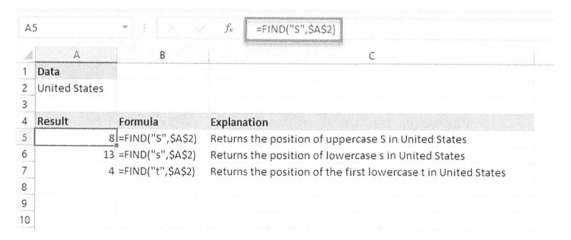

Example 2

The FIND function is most useful when used with another string function in Excel. For example, let's say we want to extract the first part of a reference number like NWTBGM-21. We can use FIND to locate the position of the divider and use the LEFT function to extract the part of the reference we want.

=LEFT(A2,1,FIND("-",A2,1)-1)

FIND returns the position of "-", which is 7 in this case. We need to subtract 1 from this number to remove the divider from the part of the string we're interested in. The LEFT function then uses 6 as the starting point to return the characters in the string starting from right to left. See the section **LEFT, RIGHT Functions** in this book for more on the LEFT function.

FINDB

The FIND function may not be available in all languages. There is an alternative version of this function called FINDB that is available for languages that support the double-byte character set (DBCS) The languages that support DBCS include Japanese, Korean, Chinese Simplified and Chinese Traditional.

FIND, on the other hand, is for computers with a default language that uses the single-byte character set (SBCS). These include English and most of the Western European languages.

Both functions do the same thing. If your system is set to English, you may only have FIND available.

CONCAT Function

The CONCAT function enables you to combine the text from multiple ranges or strings into one string. The function does not provide a delimiter, so you must add that manually in your formula. For example: =CONCAT("Hello"," ","world") will return *Hello world*.

Note
This function was introduced in Excel 2016 as a replacement for the CONCATENATE function. CONCATENATE is still available in Excel for backward compatibility but it is recommended that you use CONCAT going forward.

Syntax

CONCAT(text1, [text2],…)

Arguments

Argument	Description
text1	Required. This argument represents a text item to be joined. It could be a string or a range of cells with text.
[text2, ...]	Optional. Additional text to be joined. You can have up to a maximum of 253 arguments of text items to be joined. Each can be a string or a range of cells with text.

Remarks

- If the resulting string exceeds the cell limit which is 32767 characters, CONCAT returns the #VALUE! error.

- You can use the TEXTJOIN function if you want to include delimiters like spacing and/or commas between the texts you want to combine.

Example

In the example below, we used the CONCAT function in different ways to concatenate text from a range of cells.

D2			fx	=CONCAT(A2," ",B2)	

	A	B	C	D	E
1	First name	Lastname		Result	Formula text
2	Bruce	Henderson		Bruce Henderson	=CONCAT(A2," ",B2)
3	Louis	Anderson		Bruce & Louis	=CONCAT(A2, " & ", A3)
4	Earl	Foster		Bruce and Louis did a good job.	=CONCAT(A2, " and ", A3, " did a good job.")
5				Anderson, Louis	=CONCAT(B3,", ",A3)
6				Anderson, Louis	=B3 & ", " & A3
7					
8					
o					

Explanation of formulas

=CONCAT(A2," ",B2)

This formula concatenates the text in A2 and B2 with an empty string in-between represented by the empty string in the formula.

=CONCAT(A2, " & ", A3)

This formula concatenates the text in cells A2 and A3 with an ampersand sign (&) in the middle representing two first names.

=CONCAT(A2, " and ", A3, " did a good job.")

This formula uses the text in cells A2 and A3 to form part of a larger sentence.

=CONCAT(B3,", ",A3)

This formula concatenates the text in cells B3 and A3 with a comma in-between, representing the Last name and First name.

=B3 & ", " & A3

This formula does not use the CONCAT function but achieves the same goal of concatenating two text cells using ampersands.

TEXTJOIN Function

The TEXTJOIN function enables you to combine text values from multiple text strings into one string. The difference between the TEXTJOIN and the CONCAT function is that TEXTJOIN has extra arguments that allow you to specify a delimiter as a separator. It also has an argument you can set to ignore empty cells. If you enter an empty text string in the delimiter, this function will effectively concatenate the ranges.

Note This feature was introduced in Excel 2019. It should be available to you if you're a Microsoft 365 subscriber and you have the latest version of Office installed.

Syntax

TEXTJOIN(delimiter, ignore_empty, text1, [text2], ...)

Arguments

Argument	Description
delimiter	Required. This is the delimiter you want to use as a separator for text items in your string. This can be a string, one or more characters enclosed in double-quotes, or a cell reference containing a text string. If this argument is a number, it will be treated as text.
ignore_empty	Required. This should be either TRUE or FALSE. If TRUE it ignores empty cells.
text1	Required. This is the first text item to be joined. It can be a string, a cell reference or a range with several cells.
[text2, ...]	Optional. Additional optional text items to be joined. You can have a maximum of 252 arguments for the text items, including text1. Each can be a string, a cell reference or a range with several cells.

TEXTJOIN will return the #VALUE! error if the resulting string exceeds the cell limit which is 32767 characters.

Example

In the following example, we use TEXTJOIN in C2:C11 to combine the First name and Last name values from A2:A11 and B2:B11. The flexibility provided by TEXTJOIN enables us to swap the order of the names and separate them with a comma.

C2		f_x	=TEXTJOIN(", ", TRUE,B2,A2)	

	A	B	C	D
1	First name	Last name	Combined	Formula
2	Bruce	Henderson	Henderson, Bruce	=TEXTJOIN(", ", TRUE,B2,A2)
3	Louis	Anderson	Anderson, Louis	=TEXTJOIN(", ", TRUE,B3,A3)
4	Earl	Foster	Foster, Earl	=TEXTJOIN(", ", TRUE,B4,A4)
5	Sean	Hill	Hill, Sean	=TEXTJOIN(", ", TRUE,B5,A5)
6	Benjamin	Martinez	Martinez, Benjamin	=TEXTJOIN(", ", TRUE,B6,A6)
7	Joe	Perez	Perez, Joe	=TEXTJOIN(", ", TRUE,B7,A7)
8				
9	Name			
10	Bruce Henderson			
11	Louis Anderson			
12	Earl Foster			
13	Sean Hill			
14				
15	Combined			
16	Bruce Henderson, Louis Anderson, Earl Foster, Sean Hill			=TEXTJOIN(", ",TRUE,A10:A13)
17				

Explanation of formula

=TEXTJOIN(", ", TRUE,B2,A2)

The *delimiter* argument is a comma enclosed in quotes. The *ignore_empty* argument is TRUE because we want to ignore empty cells. The *text1* and *text2* arguments are the cell references B2 and A2, representing the First name and Last name. To populate the other results, we used the Fill Handle of cell C2 to copy the formula down the column.

-ݑ-Tip You can now use the **Flash Fill** command on the Excel Ribbon to achieve the same results as above. In certain situations, it would be faster to use Flash Fill for this than a formula. If you want to learn how to use Flash Fill, see **chapter 2 in Book 1: Excel Basics**.

=TEXTJOIN(", ",TRUE,A10:A13)

The second example uses the TEXTJOIN function to concatenate names in a range of cells (A10:A13) into a single string with a comma used as a separator.

TRIM Function

The TRIM function removes all spaces from a text string except single spaces between words. The aim of TRIM is to remove any extra spaces causing irregular spacing but not the natural spacing between words. The TRIM function is useful when you've imported data into Excel from another application and the text has irregular spacing.

Note The TRIM function does not remove the non-breaking space commonly used in HTML code or web pages - ** **. To remove this type of space you need to use the Find and Replace function in an HTML editor.

Syntax

TRIM(text)

Argument	Description
Text	Required. The single argument is the text you want to trim. This can be a text value or cell reference.

Example

In the following example, we use the TRIM function to remove all extra spaces from the text values in column A.

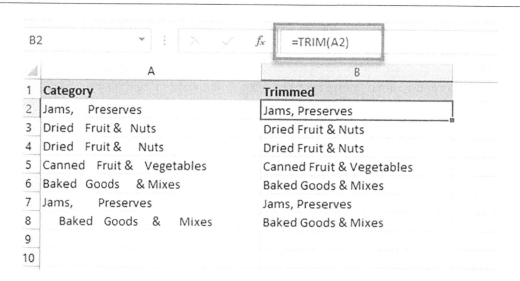

B2	f_x	=TRIM(A2)

	A	B
1	Category	Trimmed
2	Jams, Preserves	Jams, Preserves
3	Dried Fruit & Nuts	Dried Fruit & Nuts
4	Dried Fruit & Nuts	Dried Fruit & Nuts
5	Canned Fruit & Vegetables	Canned Fruit & Vegetables
6	Baked Goods & Mixes	Baked Goods & Mixes
7	Jams, Preserves	Jams, Preserves
8	Baked Goods & Mixes	Baked Goods & Mixes
9		
10		

UPPER, LOWER Functions

The UPPER and LOWER functions work in a similar way and take only one argument. UPPER converts text to uppercase while LOWER converts all uppercase text to lower case.

Syntax

UPPER(text)

LOWER(text)

Argument	Description
Text	Required. The text for which you want to change the case. This argument can be a cell reference or text string.

Example

In the example below, we use the UPPER and LOWER functions to change the case of the text values in column A.

B1		⋮	✕	✓	*fx*	=LOWER(A1)

	A	B	C
1	NWTB-1	nwtb-1	=LOWER(A1)
2	NWTCO-3	nwtco-3	=LOWER(A2)
3	Beverages	BEVERAGES	=UPPER(A3)
4	Condiments	CONDIMENTS	=UPPER(A4)
5	Oil	OIL	=UPPER(A5)
6	Jams, Preserves	JAMS, PRESERVES	=UPPER(A6)
7			
8			

LEN Function

The LEN function returns the number of characters in a text string. The LEN function is useful when used in conjunction with other Excel functions like MID where you can use LEN to return a value for one of its arguments.

Syntax

LEN(text)

Argument	Description
Text	Required. This is a text string or a cell reference containing the text for which you want to find the length. Spaces are counted as characters.

Example

In the following example, we use the LEN function to count the number of characters in an item code. The example also demonstrates how the LEN function can be used in combination with the MID function to return part of a string.

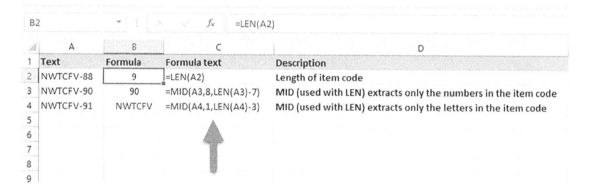

488

LENB

LENB is a variant of LEN for systems where the double-byte character set (DBCS) language is set as the default language. The languages that support DBCS include Japanese, Traditional Chinese, Simplified Chinese, and Korean. If your system is not set to the DBCS language set, LENB will just behave like LEN.

MID Function

The MID function enables you to extract a portion of a text string based on a starting position you specify and the number of characters you want to extract.

Syntax

MID(text, start_num, num_chars)

Arguments

Argument	Description
Text	Required. A text string or a cell reference containing the characters you want to extract.
Start_num	Required. This is a number representing the starting position of the first character you want to extract in *text*. The first character in *text* starts with 1, the second is 2 and so on.
Num_chars	Required. This is a number that specifies the number of characters you want to extract from *text*.

Remarks

- If the start_num argument is larger than the length of the string in our text argument, MID will return an empty text ("").

- MID will return the #VALUE! error if start_num is less than 1.

- MID returns the #VALUE! error if num_chars is a negative value.

Example

In the examples below, we use the MID function to extract characters from several text values.

B1				f_x	=MID(A1,4,3)	

▲	A	B	C	D
1	01-345-4000	345	=MID(A1,4,3)	Extract the 3 characters in the middle of the serial number
2	01-378-7890	378	=MID(A2,4,3)	
3	01-375-7891	375	=MID(A3,4,3)	
4	01-376-7892	376	=MID(A4,4,3)	
5				
6				
7	NWTCFV-88	88	=MID(A7,8,2)	Extract only the number portion of the item code
8	NWTCFV-89	89	=MID(A8,8,2)	
9	NWTCFV-90	90	=MID(A9,8,2)	
10	NWTCFV-91	91	=MID(A10,8,2)	
11				
12				

Formula description

=MID(A1,4,3)

For this formula, A1 is the cell reference containing the string we want to extract text from - "01-345-4000". The first character we want to extract is 3 which starts at position 4, so we have 4 as our *start_num*. We want to return 3 characters in total, so we have 3 as the *num_chars*.

=MID(A7,8,2)

This formula has A3 as the text argument and 8 as the *start_num* as this is the first character we want to return from the string which has 10 characters. The *num_chars* argument is 2 as this is the number of characters we want to return.

The benefit of using formulas like these is that you create them once and use the fill handle of the first cell to copy the formula to the other cells.

MIDB

MIDB is a variant of MID that counts each double-byte character as two. MIDB is for systems that support the double-byte character set (DBCS). The languages that support DBCS include Japanese, Traditional Chinese, Simplified Chinese, and Korean. If the default language on your computer supports DBCS, you would have MIDB instead of MID but both functions work in a similar way.

PROPER Function

The PROPER function capitalizes the first letter in a text string and converts all other letters in the string to lowercase letters. A text string is a continues stream of characters without spaces. Every letter after a space or punctuation character is capitalized.

Syntax

PROPER(text)

Argument	Description
Text	Required. This can be a string, a cell reference, or a formula that returns a text string that you want to partially capitalize.

Example

In the example below, we use the PROPER function to achieve the desired capitalization for a series of text strings.

=PROPER(A1)

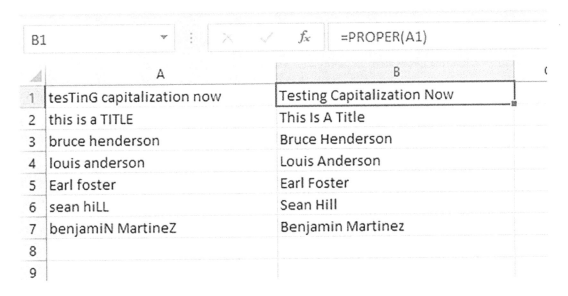

LEFT, RIGHT Functions

The LEFT function returns the leftmost characters in a text string based on the number of characters you specify in one of its arguments. The RIGHT function returns the rightmost characters in a text string based on a number you specify.

Syntax

LEFT(text, [num_chars])

RIGHT(text,[num_chars])

Arguments

Argument	Description
Text	Required. This argument represents the text string with the characters you want to extract.
Num_chars	Optional. This is a number that specifies the number of characters you want to extract from the left (for the LEFT function) or right (for the RIGHT function).

Remarks

- If *num_chars* is larger than the length of *text*, the functions will return all characters in *text*.

- If *num_chars* is omitted, the functions return only the first character for the LEFT function, and only the last character for the RIGHT function.

Example

In the example below, we use the LEFT and RIGHT functions to extract portions of text in different ways.

| B2 | ▼ | : | ✕ | ✓ | *fx* | =LEFT(A2) |

◢	A	B	C
1	Text	Result	Formula
2	Alabama - AL	A	=LEFT(A2)
3	Alaska - AK	K	=RIGHT(A3)
4	Arizona - AZ	Arizona	=LEFT(A4,7)
5	Arkansas - AR	AR	=RIGHT(A5,2)
6	California - CA	California	=LEFT(A6,FIND("-",A6)-1)
7	Colorado - CO	Colorado	=LEFT(A7,FIND("-",A7)-1)
8	Connecticut - CT	Connecticut	=LEFT(A8,FIND("-",A8)-1)
9	Delaware - DE	DE	=RIGHT(A9,LEN(A9)-(FIND("-",A9)+1))
10	Florida - FL	FL	=RIGHT(A10,LEN(A10)-(FIND("-",A10)+1))
11	Georgia - GA	GA	=RIGHT(A11,LEN(A11)-(FIND("-",A11)+1))
12			

Formula explanations

=LEFT(A2)

This formula takes in cell A2 as the text argument and ignores the optional Num_chars argument. This returns the first character on the left of the string.

=RIGHT(A3)

This formula takes in cell A3 as the text argument and ignores the optional Num_chars argument. Hence the result it returns is the last character in the string (or first from the right).

=LEFT(A4,7)

This formula takes in cell A4 as the text argument and has 7 as the Num_chars argument. It returns "Arizona" which is 7 characters from the left of the string.

=RIGHT(A5,2)

This formula takes in cell A4 as the text argument and has 7 as the Num_chars argument. It returns "AR" which is 2 characters from the right of the string.

=LEFT(A6,FIND("-",A6)-1)

This formula takes in cell A6 as the text argument. We calculate the Num_chars argument by using the FIND function to find and return the position of the dash character (-) in the text.

We then subtract 1 from the result to return the number of characters in the text before the dash. Hence **FIND("-",A6)-1** will return 10. The result is California. This formula will work for any piece of text separated by a dash for which we want to extract the left portion.

=RIGHT(A9,LEN(A9)-(FIND("-",A9)+1))

This formula takes in cell A9 as the text argument. We calculate the Num_chars argument by first using FIND to return the position of the dash character (-) in the text. We then add 1 to move to the position of the first character after the dash (on the right).

The LEN function is used to get the length of the string as we want to subtract the number of characters returned by FIND to give us the number of characters after the dash, which is 2 in this case. This formula will work for any piece of text separated by a dash for which we want to extract the right portion, regardless of the number of characters after the dash.

LEFTB, RIGHTB Functions

LEFTB and RIGHTB are variants of the LEFT and RIGHT functions that return characters in a text string based on the number of bytes you specify.

RIGHTB/LEFTB are for systems set to a default language that supports the double-byte character set (DBCS). The languages that support DBCS include Japanese, Traditional Chinese, Simplified Chinese, and Korean. If your system has a default language that supports DBCS then you would have LEFTB and RIGHTB in place of LEFT and RIGHT.

If your system has a default language that supports the single-byte character set (SBCS), LEFTB/RIGHTB will behave the same as LEFT/RIGHT, counting 1 byte per character.

Chapter 8: Financial Functions

The financial functions in Excel can be accessed by clicking the Financial button on the Formulas tab of the Ribbon. Most of the financial functions in Excel are specialized functions used for financial accounting so before we dive into these functions, we need to cover some financial definitions used in their arguments. Many terms like PV (Present Value), FV (Future Value), PMT (Payment), IPMT (interest payment) etc. come up numerous times in the different financial functions.

In this chapter, we'll cover functions that enable you to:

- Calculate the present value of an investment (or a loan).
- Calculate the future value of an investment.
- Calculate the net present value of an investment taking cash flows into account.
- Calculate the monthly payment for a loan over a given period.
- Calculate the straight-line depreciation of an asset over a given period.
- Calculate the sum-of-years' digits depreciation of an asset over a given period.
- Calculate the fixed-declining balance depreciation of an asset over a given period.
- Calculate the double-declining balance depreciation of an asset over a given period.

Definitions

Annuity
An annuity is a series of regular cash payments over a certain period. For example, a mortgage or a car loan is an annuity. An investment that pays you regular dividends is also an annuity. Most of the functions we will be covering in this chapter are known as annuity functions.

PV (Present Value)
This is the present value of an investment based on a constant growth rate. It is the lump-sum amount that a series of future payments is worth right now.

FV (Future Value)
This is the future value of an investment based on a constant rate of growth. For example, let's say you want to save $25,000 to pay for a project in 20 years, so, $25,000 is the future value. To calculate how much you need to save monthly, you'll also need to factor in an assumed interest rate over the period.

PMT (Payment)
This is the payment made for each period in the annuity. Usually, the payment includes the principal plus interest without any other fees, and it is set over the life of the annuity. For example, a $100,000 mortgage over 25 years at 3% interest would have monthly payments of $474. You would enter -474 into the formula as the *pmt*.

RATE
This is the interest rate per period. For example, if you get a loan at a 6% annual interest rate and make monthly payments, your interest rate per month would be 6%/12.

NPER (Number of periods)
This is the total number of payment periods in the life of the annuity i.e. the term. For example, if you get a 3-year loan and make monthly payments, your loan will have 3*12 periods. Hence, you would enter 3*12 into the formula for the *nper* argument.

Note The FA, PV, and PMT arguments can be positive or negative values depending on whether you are paying out money or receiving money. If you are paying out money, then the figures will be negative; if you are receiving money then the figures will be positive.

PV Function

The PV function calculates the present value of an investment (or a loan), assuming a constant interest rate. This is the amount that a series of future payments is currently worth. You can use PV with regular payments (such as a mortgage or other loan), periodic payments, or the future value of a lump sum paid now.

Syntax

PV(rate, nper, pmt, [fv], [type])

Arguments

Please see the Definitions chapter above for more a detailed description of these arguments.

Arguments	Description
Rate	Required. This is the interest rate per period.
Nper	Required. The total number of payment periods in an annuity i.e. the term.
Pmt	Required. This is the payment made for each period in the annuity.
	If you omit *pmt*, you must include the *fv* argument.
Fv	Optional. This is the future value of an investment based on an assumed rate of growth.
	If you omit fv, it is assumed to be 0 (zero), for example, the future value of a loan is 0. If you omit fv then you must include the pmt argument.
Type	Optional. This argument is 0 or 1 and indicates when payments are due.
	0 or omitted = at the end of the period.
	1 = at the beginning of the period.

Remarks

- You always need to express the rate argument in the same units as the nper argument. For example, say you have monthly payments on a three-year loan at 5% annual interest. If you use 5%/12 for *rate*, you must use 3*12 for *nper*. If the payments on the same loan are being made annually, then you would use 5% for rate and 3 for nper.

- In annuity functions, the cash paid out (like a payment to savings) is represented by a negative number. The cash you receive (like a dividend payment) is represented by a positive number. For example, a $500 deposit to the bank would be represented by the argument - 500 if you are the depositor, and by the argument 500 if you are the bank.

Example

In the example below, we use the PV formula to calculate:

1. The present value of a $500 monthly payment over 25 years at a rate of 1.5% interest.
2. The present value of the lump sum now needed to create $20,000 in 10 years at a rate of 3.5% interest.

E2				f_x	=PV(A2/12,B2*12,C2)	
	A	B	C	D	E	F
	Annual	Term		Future	Present	
1	Interest Rate	(years)	Payment	Value	Value	Formula
2	1.50%	25	($500.00)		$125,019.90	=PV(A2/12,B2*12,C2)
3	3.50%	10		$20,000.00	($14,100.94)	=PV(A3/12,B3*12,,D3)
4						
5						
6						

Explanation of Formulas:

=PV(A2/12,B2*12,C2)

As you've probably noticed, the units for *rate* and *nper* have been kept consistent by specifying them in monthly terms, A2/12 and B2*12. The payment (pmt) has been entered in the worksheet as a negative value as this is money being paid out.

=PV(A3/12,B3*12,,D3)

The present value is a negative number as it shows the amount of cash that needs to be invested today (paid out) to generate the future value of $20,000 in 10 years at a rate of 3.5% interest.

FV Function

The FV function calculates the future value (at a specified date in the future) of an investment based on a constant interest rate. You can use FV to calculate the future value of regular payments, periodic payments, or a single lump-sum payment.

Syntax

FV(rate,nper,pmt,[pv],[type])

Arguments

Please see the Definitions in this chapter for more a detailed description of these arguments.

Arguments	Description
Rate	Required. This is the interest rate per period.
Nper	Required. The total number of payment periods in an annuity i.e. the term.
Pmt	Required. This is the payment made for each period in the annuity. If you omit pmt, you must include pv.
Pv	Optional. This is the present value of an investment based on a constant growth rate. If you omit pv, it is assumed to be 0 (zero) and you must include pmt.
Type	Optional. The *type* is 0 or 1 and it indicates when payments are due. 0 (or omitted) = at the end of the period. 1 = at the beginning of the period.

Remarks

- You always need to express the rate argument in the same units as the nper argument. For example, say you have monthly payments on a three-year loan at 5% annual interest. If you use 5%/12 for *rate*, you must use 3*12 for *nper*. If the payments on the same loan are being made annually, then you would use 5% for rate and 3 for nper.

- In an annuity function, cash paid out (like a payment to savings) is represented by as a negative number. The cash you receive (like a dividend) is represented by a positive number. For example, a $500 deposit to the bank would be represented by the argument -500 if you are the depositor, and by the argument 500 if you are the bank.

Example

In the example below, we use the FV function to calculate:

1. The future value of a monthly payment of $200 over 10 months at an interest of 6% per annum.

2. The future value of a lump sum of $1,000 plus 12 monthly payments of $100, at an interest rate of 6%.

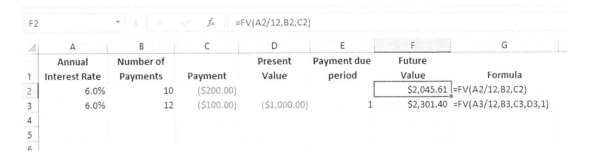

F2			f_x	=FV(A2/12,B2,C2)			
	A	B	C	D	E	F	G
	Annual	Number of		Present	Payment due	Future	
1	Interest Rate	Payments	Payment	Value	period	Value	Formula
2	6.0%	10	($200.00)			$2,045.61	=FV(A2/12,B2,C2)
3	6.0%	12	($100.00)	($1,000.00)	1	$2,301.40	=FV(A3/12,B3,C3,D3,1)
4							
5							
6							

Explanation of Formulas:

=FV(A2/12,B2,C2)

Note that the *rate* argument has been divided by 12 to represent monthly payments. The *pmt* argument is a negative value (C2) as this is money being paid out.

=FV(A3/12,B3,C3,D3,1)

This formula has the pmt argument as well as the optional pv argument which represents the present value of the investment. The payment due period is 1 which means the payment starts at the beginning of the period.

NPV Function

The NPV function calculates the net present value which is the present value of cash inflows and cash outflows over a period. It calculates the present value of an investment by applying a discount rate and a series of future payments that may be income (positive values) or payments/losses (negative values).

Syntax

NPV(rate,value1,[value2],...)

Arguments

Argument	Description
Rate	Required. This is the percentage rate of discount over the length of the investment.
Value1	Required. This represents either a payment/loss (negative value) or income (positive value).
value2, ...	Optional: You can have additional values representing payments and income up to a total of 254 value arguments.
	The length of time between these payments must be equally spaced and occur at the end of each period.

Remarks

- The rate argument in the function might represent the rate of inflation or the interest rate that you might get from an alternative form of investment, for example, a high-yield savings account.

- The value arguments represent the projected income (or loss) values over the period of the investment.

- Ensure you enter the payment and income values in the correct order because NPV uses the order of the value arguments to interpret the order of cash flows.

- The NPV investment begins one period before the date of the first cash flow (value1) and ends with the last cash flow (valueN) in the list of value arguments. If the first cash flow happens at the beginning of the period, you must add it to the result of the NPV function and not include it as one of its value arguments.

- The main difference between NPV and PV is that with PV, the cash flows can start at the beginning or end of the period while for NPV the cash flows start at the beginning of the period. Also, PV has the same cash flow amount throughout the investment while NPV can have different cash flow amounts.

- Arguments that are not numbers are ignored.

Example

In the example below, we are calculating the net present value of an initial investment of $50,000 over the course of five years, considering an annual discount rate of 2.5 percent.

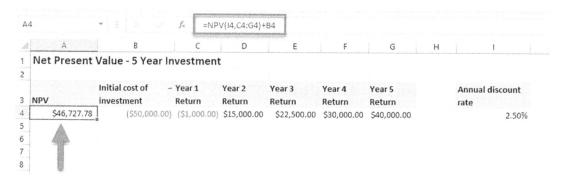

Formula explanation

=NPV(I4,C4:G4)+B4

In the figure above, Year 1 of the investment shows a loss of $1,000, hence, this has been entered as a negative value. The other years of the investment (years two to five) returned a profit, so these were entered as positive values.

The function uses two arguments, the *rate* and *value1*, which references cells C4:G4. The initial investment is added to the result returned by the function rather than being an argument in the function.

The result shows the net present value of the investment over five years is:

$46,727.78.

PMT Function

The PMT function calculates the payment for a loan on regular payments and a constant interest rate over a period. The PMT function is often used to calculate the repayment of a mortgage with a fixed interest rate.

Syntax

PMT(rate, nper, pv, [fv], [type])

Arguments

Arguments	Description
Rate	Required. This is the interest rate per period.
Nper	Required. This is the total number of payment periods in an annuity i.e. the term.
Pv	Required. This is the present value of a principal or a series of future payments.
Fv	Optional. This is the future value of an investment based on an assumed rate of growth. If you omit fv, it is assumed to be 0 (zero), i.e. the future value of a loan is 0.
Type	Optional. This argument is 0 or 1 and indicates when payments are due. 0 (or omitted) = at the end of the period. 1 = at the beginning of the period.

Remarks

- The payment returned by PMT is for the principal and interest. It does not include taxes, reserve payments, or other fees they may be associated with loans.

- You always need to express the *rate* argument in the same units as the *nper* argument. For example, say you have monthly payments on a three-year loan at 5% annual interest. If you use 5%/12 for *rate*, you must use 3*12 for *nper*. If the payments on the same loan are being made annually, then you would use 5% for rate and 3 for nper.

Tip
To calculate the total amount paid over the duration of the loan, simply multiply the value returned by PMT by the number of payments (nper).

Example

In the example below, we calculate the PMT for two loans:

1. A $10,000 loan over 12 payments at 8.0 percent interest.

2. A $10,000 loan over 60 payments at 4.9 percent interest.

| D2 | | | | | f_x | =PMT(A2/12,B2,C2) | |

	A	B	C	D	E	F
1	Annual Interest Rate	Number of payments	Amount of loan	PMT	Formula	
2	8.0%	12	$10,000.00	($869.88)	=PMT(A2/12,B2,C2)	
3	4.9%	60	$10,000.00	($188.25)	=PMT(A3/12,B3,C3)	
4						
5						

Formula explanation

=PMT(A2/12,B2,C2)

The rate argument is a reference to cell A2 divided by 12, to represent the interest rate in monthly terms as nper (cell B2) is also specified in monthly terms. The pv argument takes in C2, which is the present value of the loan $10,000.

Answer: ($869.88)

=PMT(A3/12,B3,C3)

This formula is also for a loan of $10,000, however, the nper is 60 and the rate is 4.9 percent.

Answer: ($188.25)

SLN Function

The SLN function is a depreciation function and calculates the straight-line depreciation of an asset over a period. It depreciates the asset by the same amount each year.

Syntax

SLN(cost, salvage, life)

Arguments

Argument	Description
Cost	Required. This is the initial cost of the asset you're depreciating.
Salvage	Required. This is the value at the end of the depreciation (also referred to as the salvage value of the asset).
Life	Required. This is the number of periods over which the asset is depreciating (also referred to as the useful life of the asset).

Example

In the example below, we have a report calculating the SLN depreciation of a couple of cars with a useful life of 10 years.

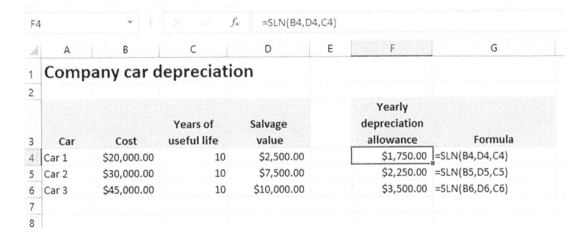

Formula explanation

=SLN(A4,C4,B4)

For Car 1, the *cost* references a cell B4 ($20,000), the *salvage* value references cell D4 ($2,500), and the life is C4 (10 years).

The formula returns $1,750, which is the yearly depreciation allowance to be made for the car. This value would be subtracted from the value of the car when listing this asset in the company's balance sheet.

The formula in F4 was copied down using the fill handle of the cell to calculate the SLN value of the other cars on the list.

SYD Function

The SYD function (sum of years' digits) is a depreciation function that returns the sum-of-years' digits depreciation of an asset over a specified period.

Syntax

SYD(cost, salvage, life, per)

Arguments

Argument	Description
Cost	Required. This is the initial cost of the asset you're depreciating.
Salvage	Required. This is the value at the end of the depreciation (also referred to as the salvage value of the asset).
Life	Required. This is the number of periods over which the asset is depreciating (also referred to as the useful life of the asset).
Per	Required. This is the period and it must be in the same units as life.

Example

In the example below, we use the SYD function to calculate the depreciation of some office equipment over 10 years.

Function arguments:
- Cost = $40,000
- Life = 10 (years)
- Salvage = $1,000

| B9 | | ▼ ⋮ | ✕ ✓ | f_x | =SYD($C$3,$C$5,$C$4,A9) |

◢	A	B	C	D	E	F
1	**Depreciation of office equipment**					
2						
3		Initial Cost	$40,000.00			
4		Life (years)	10			
5		Salvage value	$1,000.00			
6						
7	Year	SYD	Asset value			
8	0	$0.00	$40,000.00			
9	1	$7,090.91	$32,909.09			
10	2	$6,381.82	$26,527.27			
11	3	$5,672.73	$20,854.55			
12	4	$4,963.64	$15,890.91		Cumulative	
13	5	$4,254.55	$11,636.36		depreciation	
14	6	$3,545.45	$8,090.91			
15	7	$2,836.36	$5,254.55			
16	8	$2,127.27	$3,127.27			
17	9	$1,418.18	$1,709.09			
18	10	$709.09	$1,000.00			
19						

Formula explanation

=SYD($C$3,$C$5,$C$4,A9)

The formula in cell B9 uses absolute references ($C$3, $C$5, and $C$4) for the cost, salvage, and life arguments as these remain the same over the 10-year depreciation period. The *per* argument is a relative reference, cell A9, which changes in relation to the year being calculated.

As you can see from the image above, with the SYD function, the depreciation amount gets progressively smaller, compared to the SLN which is constant over the period.

=C8-SYD($C$3,$C$5,$C$4,A9)

The formulas in the **Asset value** column (C9:C18), subtracts each year's depreciation from the previous year's calculated value of the asset. Hence, this column shows a progressive decrease in the value of the asset over the 10-year period until it gets to the salvage value.

DB Function

The DB function is a depreciation function that uses the fixed-declining balance method to return the depreciation of an asset over a specified period. The fixed-declining balance method calculates the depreciation at a fixed rate.

Syntax

DB(cost, salvage, life, period, [month])

Arguments

Arguments	Descriptions
Cost	Required. This is the initial cost of the asset you're depreciating.
Salvage	Required. This is the value at the end of the depreciation (also referred to as the salvage value of the asset).
Life	Required. This is the number of periods over which the asset is depreciating (also referred to as the useful life of the asset).
Period	Required. This is the period and it must be in the same units as life.
Month	Optional. This is the number of months in the first year of the depreciation if not 12. If this argument is omitted, it is assumed to be 12.

Remarks

- The following formulas are used to calculate depreciation for a period:

  *(cost - total depreciation from prior periods) * rate*

  Where: *rate = 1 - ((salvage / cost) ^ (1 / life))*

- DB uses different formulas to calculate the depreciation for the first and last periods.

First period:

*cost * rate * month / 12*

Last period:

*((cost - total depreciation from prior periods) * rate * (12 - month)) / 12*

Example 1

In the following example, we're calculating the depreciation of an asset over 5 years using the following data:

- Costs = $10,000
- Salvage value = $2,000
- Life = 5 years.

The first year has 12 months so we can omit the month argument.

The formula for the first month will be thus:

=DB(10000, 2000, 5, 1)

Result: $2,750.00

Example 2

In this example, the depreciation is being calculated for an asset that costs $10,000, a salvage value of $2,000, and the useful life is 5 years.

The depreciation is being calculated for the fifth year, and there are 8 months in the first year. The formula for the first month will be thus:

=DB(10000, 2000, 5, 5, 8)

Result: $855.84

Example 3

In this example, we use the SYD function to calculate the depreciation of office equipment with a useful life of 10 years. The initial cost is $40,000 and the salvage value is $1,000.

The first year has only 7 months, so we need to specify that in the *month* argument.

| B9 | ▼ | ⋮ | ⤫ | ✓ | *fx* | =DB($C$3,$C$5,$C$4,A9,$C$6) |

◢	A	B	C	D	E
1	**Depreciation of office equipment**				
2					
3		Initial Cost	$40,000.00		
4		Life (years)	10		
5		Salvage value	$1,000.00		
6		First year (# of months)	7		
7					
8	Year	DB	Asset value		
9		1	$7,186.67	$32,813.33	
10		2	$10,106.51	$22,706.83	
11		3	$6,993.70	$15,713.12	
12		4	$4,839.64	$10,873.48	
13		5	$3,349.03	$7,524.45	
14		6	$2,317.53	$5,206.92	
15		7	$1,603.73	$3,603.19	
16		8	$1,109.78	$2,493.41	
17		9	$767.97	$1,725.44	
18		10	$531.43	$1,194.00	
19					

Formula explanation

=DB($C$3,$C$5,$C$4,A9,$C$6)

The formula in cell B9 uses absolute references ($C$3, $C$5, and $C$4) for the *cost*, *salvage*, and *life* arguments as these remain the same over the 10-year depreciation period.

The *per* argument is a relative reference, cell A9, which changes in relation to the year being calculated.

The *month* argument is an absolute reference, $C$6, which holds a value of 7. This specifies that the first year of the depreciation is 7 months rather than 12. If the first year was 12 months, then this argument could have been omitted.

As you can see from the image above, with the DB function, apart from the first year, the depreciation result is reduced progressively as the value of the asset is reduced.

DDB Function

This DDB function returns the depreciation of an asset for a specified period using the double-declining balance method. The double-declining balance method calculates depreciation at an accelerated rate with the depreciation highest in the first period and decreasing in successive periods.

This function is flexible in that you can change the *factor* argument if you do not want to use the double-declining balance method.

Syntax

DDB(cost, salvage, life, period, [factor])

Arguments

Argument	Description
Cost	Required. This is the initial cost of the asset you're depreciating.
Salvage	Required. This is the value at the end of the depreciation (also referred to as the salvage value of the asset).
Life	Required. This is the number of periods over which the asset is depreciating (also referred to as the useful life of the asset).
Period	Required. This is the period and it must be in the same units as life.
Factor	Optional. This is the rate at which the balance declines. If omitted, the factor is assumed to be 2, which is the double-declining balance method.

 Note The five arguments must be positive numbers.

Remarks

The DDB function uses the formula below to calculate depreciation for a period:

Min((cost - total depreciation from prior periods) * (factor/life), (cost - salvage - total depreciation from prior periods))

Example

In the following example, we use different DDB formulas to return results for the depreciation of a car.

Data:
- Initial Cost: $25,000.00
- Salvage value: $2,500.00
- Life (in years): 10

B8						f_x	=DDB($B$3,$B$4,$B$5*365,1)	

	A	B	C	[
1	**Depreciation of car**			
2				
3	Initial Cost	$25,000.00		
4	Salvage value	$2,500.00		
5	Life (in years)	10		
6				
7	Formula	Result	Explanation	
8	=DDB($B$3,$B$4,$B$5*365,1)	$13.70	First day's depreciation. Defaults to factor 2	
9	=DDB($B$3,$B$4,$B$5*12,1,2)	$416.67	First month's depreciation	
10	=DDB($B$3,$B$4,$B$5,1,2)	$5,000.00	First year's depreciation	
11	=DDB($B$3,$B$4,$B$5,1,1.5)	$3,750.00	First year's depreciation using a factor of 1.5	
12	=DDB($B$3,$B$4,$B$5,10)	$671.09	Tenth year's depreciation	
13				
14				

Explanation of formulas

=DDB($B$3,$B$4,$B$5*365,1)

The formula in cell B8 uses absolute references ($B$3,$B$4, and $B$5*365) for the *cost*, *salvage* and *life*. Life is (10 * 365) because we want to calculate the depreciation in daily units rather than months or years. The period is 1, representing the first day of the life. The factor argument has been omitted so it defaults to 2, hence using the double-declining balance method.

=DDB($B$3,$B$4,$B$5*12,1,2)

First month's depreciation. In this case, the factor argument has been included to specify the double-declining balance method.

=DDB($B$3,$B$4,$B$5,1,2)

The first year's depreciation. Notice that the *life* argument $B$5 has not been multiplied by 12 so the formula will return a result for year 1 as specified in the period argument.

=DDB($B$3,$B$4,$B$5,1,1.5)

This is the first year's depreciation using a factor of 1.5 instead of the double-declining balance method.

=DDB($B$3,$B$4,$B$5,10)

For the final formula, we return the tenth year's depreciation result. Factor has been omitted so it defaults to 2.

Afterword: Next Steps

Thank you for buying and reading this book. I hope it will be a great Excel resource for you in the months and years to come. If you have any questions or comments, please feel free to contact me at: **support@excelbytes.com**.

More Help with Excel

For more help with Excel, you can visit my website for free tips and links to Excel resources.

https://www.excelbytes.com

Leave a Review!

If you found this book helpful, I would be very grateful if you can spend just 5 minutes leaving a customer review. You can go to the link below to leave a customer review.

https://www.excelbytes.com/mxlreview/

Thank you very much!

Appendix

Keyboard Shortcuts (Excel for Windows)

The Excel Ribbon comes with new shortcuts called Key Tips. To see Key Tips, press the **Alt** key when Excel is the active window.

The following table lists the most frequently used shortcuts in Excel 2019.

Keystroke	Action
F1	Opens Excel's Help window
Ctrl+O	Open a workbook
Ctrl+W	Close a workbook
Ctrl+C	Copy
Ctrl+V	Paste
Ctrl+X	Cut
Ctrl+Z	Undo
Ctrl+B	Bold
Ctrl+S	Save a workbook
Ctrl+F1	Displays or hides the Ribbon
Delete key	Remove cell contents
Alt+H	Go to the Home tab
Alt+H, H	Choose a fill color

Alt+N	Go to Insert tab
Alt+A	Go to Data tab
Alt+P	Go to Page Layout tab
Alt+H, A, then C	Center align cell contents
Alt+W	Go to View tab
Shift+F10, or Context key	Open context menu
Alt+H, B	Add borders
Alt+H,D, then C	Delete column
Alt+M	Go to Formula tab
Ctrl+9	Hide the selected rows
Ctrl+0	Hide the selected columns

Shortcut Keys for Working with Data, Functions, and the Formula Bar

The table below covers some of the most useful Excel for Windows shortcut keys when working with functions, formulas, and the formula bar.

Keystroke	Action
F2	Moves the insertion point to the end of the contents of the active cell.
Ctrl+Shift+U	Expands or reduces the size of the formula bar.
Esc	Cancels an entry in the formula bar or a cell.
Enter	Confirms an entry in the formula bar and moves to the cell below.
Ctrl+End	Moves the cursor to the end of the contents in the formula bar.
Ctrl+Shift+End	Selects everything in the formula bar from the current position of the cursor to the end.
F9	Calculates all worksheets in all open workbooks.
Shift+F9	Calculates the active worksheet.
Ctrl+Alt+F9	Calculates all worksheets in all open workbooks, even if they have not changed since the last calculation.
Ctrl+Alt+Shift+F9	Checks all dependent formulas and then calculates all cells in all open workbooks.
Ctrl+A	Opens the Function Arguments dialog box, when the insertion point is to the right of a function name in a formula bar.
Ctrl+Shift+A	Inserts the argument names and parentheses for a function when the insertion point is to the right of a function name in the formula bar.
Ctrl+E	Executes the Flash Fill command to fill-down the current column, if Excel recognizes patterns in the values in adjacent columns.
F4	Changes the selected cell reference or range in the formula bar to absolute references. Further presses will cycle through all

	combinations of absolute and relative references for the selected cell reference or range.
Shift+F3	Opens the Insert Function dialog box.
Ctrl+Shift+Quotation mark (")	Copies the value from the cell directly above the active cell into the active cell or formula bar.
Alt+F1	Automatically inserts an embedded chart of the data in the selected range.
F11	Automatically inserts a chart of the data in the selected range in a different worksheet.
Alt+M, M, D	Opens the New Name dialog box for creating a named range.
F3	Opens the Paste Name dialog box if a range name has been defined in the workbook.
Alt+F8	Opens the Macro dialog box where you can run, edit, or delete a macro.
Alt+F11	Opens the Visual Basic for Applications editor.

Access Keys for Ribbon Tabs

To go directly to a tab on the Excel Ribbon, press one of the following access keys.

Action	Keystroke
Open the Tell me box on the Ribbon.	Alt+Q
Open the File page i.e. the Backstage view.	Alt+F
Open the Home tab.	Alt+H
Open the Insert tab.	Alt+N
Open the Page Layout tab.	Alt+P
Open the Formulas tab.	Alt+M
Open the Data.	Alt+A
Open the Review.	Alt+R
Open the View.	Alt+W

To get a more comprehensive list of Excel for Windows Shortcut, press **F1** to open Excel Help and type in "Keyboard shortcuts" in the search bar.

Glossary

Absolute reference
This is a cell reference that doesn't change when you copy a formula containing the reference to another cell. For example, $A$3 means the row and column have been set to absolute.

Add-in
A different application that can be added to extend the functionality of Excel. It could be from Microsoft or a third-party vendor.

Active cell
The cell that is currently selected and open for editing.

Alignment
The way a cell's contents are arranged within that cell. This could be left, centred or right.

Argument
The input values a function requires to carry out a calculation.

AutoCalculate

This is an Excel feature that automatically calculates and displays the summary of a selected range of figures on the status bar.

AutoComplete
This is an Excel feature that completes data entry for a range of cells based on values in other cells in the same column or row.

Backstage view
This is the screen you see when you click the File tab on the ribbon. It has a series of menu options to do with managing your workbook and configuring global settings in Excel.

Cell reference
The letter and number combination that represents the intersection of a column and row. For example, B10 means column B, row 10.

Chart
A visual representation of summarised worksheet data.

Conditional format
This is a format that applies only when certain criteria are met by the cell content.

Conditional formula
A conditional formula calculates a value from one of two expressions based on whether a third expression evaluates to true or false.

Delimiter
A character in a text file that is used to separate the values into columns.

Dependent
A cell with a formula that references other cells, so its value is dependent on other cells.

Dialog box launcher
In the lower-right corner of some groups on the Excel ribbon, you'll see a diagonal down-pointing arrow. When you click on the arrow it opens a dialog box containing several additional options for that group.

Digital certificate
A file with a unique string of characters that can be combined with an Excel workbook to create a verifiable signature.

Digital signature
A mathematical construct which combines a file and a digital certificate to verify the authorship of the file.

Excel table

This is a cell range that has been defined as a table in Excel. Excel adds certain attributes to the range to make it easier to sort, filter, and manipulate the data in other ways as a table.

Fill handle

This is a small square on the lower-right of the cell pointer. You can drag this handle to AutoFill values for other cells.

Fill Series

This is the Excel functionality that allows you to create a series of values based on a starting value including any rules or intervals.

Formula

An expression used to calculate a value.

Formula bar

This is the area just above the worksheet grid that displays the value of the active cell. This is where you enter a formula in Excel.

Function

A function is a predefined formula in Excel that just requires input values (arguments) to calculate and return a value.

Goal Seek

An analysis tool that can be used to create projections by setting the goal and the tool calculates the input values required to meet the goals from a set number of variables.

Graph

A representation of summarised worksheet data, also known as a chart.

Live Preview

A preview of whatever task you want to perform based on your actual data. So, you get to see how your data will look if you carry out the command.

Locked cell

A locked cell cannot be modified if the worksheet is protected.

Macro

A series of instructions created from recording Excel tasks that automate Excel when replayed.

Named range

A group of cells in your worksheet given one name that can then be used as a reference.

OneDrive

This is a cloud storage service provided by Microsoft which automatically syncs your files to a remote drive, hence providing instant backups.

PivotChart

A specific kind of Excel chart related to a pivot table. A PivotChart can be dynamically reorganized to show different views of your data just like a pivot table.

PivotTable

This is an Excel summary table that allows you to dynamically analyze data from different perspectives. PivotTables are highly flexible, and you can quickly adjust them, depending on how you need to display your results.

Precedent

A cell that is used as a cell reference in a formula in another cell. Also, see Dependent.

Quick Access Toolbar

This is a customisable toolbar with a set of commands independent of the tab and ribbon commands currently on display.

Relative reference

Excel cell references are relative references by default. This means, when copied across multiple cells, they change based on the relative position of rows and columns.

Ribbon

This is the top part of the Excel screen that contains the tabs and commands.

Scenario

An alternative set of data which you can use to compare the impact of changes in your data. This is useful when creating projections and forecasts.

Solver

An Excel add-in that enables you to create scenarios for more complex data models.

Sort

To reorder the data in a list in ascending or descending order using one or more columns.

Tracer arrows

Graphical arrows used to indicate dependent or precedent cells.

Watch

The watch window can be used to display the contents of a cell in a separate window even when the cell is not visible on the screen.

What-If Analysis
A series of methods that can be used to determine the impact of changes on your data. This could include projections and forecasts.

Workbook
This is the Excel document itself and it can contain one or more worksheets.

Worksheet
A worksheet is like a page in an Excel workbook.

x-axis
The horizontal axis of a chart where you could have time intervals etc.

y-axis
This is the vertical axis of a chart, which usually depicts value data.

Index

About the Author

Nathan George is a computer science graduate with several years' experience in the IT services industry in different roles which included Excel VBA programming, Excel training, and providing end-user support to Excel power users. One of his main interests is using computers to automate tasks and increase productivity. As an author, he has written several technical and non-technical books.

Other Books by Author

Excel 2019 Macros and VBA

An Introduction to Excel Programming

Do you often perform repetitive tasks in Excel that can be time-consuming?

You can automate pretty much any task in Excel with a macro.

If you want to automate Excel, *Excel 2019 Macros and VBA* will be a great resource for you.

We start from the very basics of Excel automation, so you do not need any prior experience of Excel programming.

You will learn how to automate Excel using recorded macros as well as Visual Basic for Applications (VBA) code. You will learn all the programming essentials to start creating your own VBA code from scratch.

Excel 2019 Macros and VBA will enable you to create solutions that will save you time and effort, create consistency in your work, and help to minimize errors in your Excel projects.

For more, go to:
https://www.excelbytes.com/excel-books

Excel XLOOKUP and Other Lookup Functions

Create Easier and More Versatile Lookup Formulas with New Powerful Excel Functions

Do you want to create easier and faster lookup formulas?

XLOOKUP is a newly introduced function in Excel that will supersede both the VLOOKUP and HLOOKUP functions. XLOOKUP is easier to use, has more features, and provides greater flexibility in performing lookups in Excel.

This book covers XLOOKUP and other new dynamic array formulas in more depth and with more examples than is practical in a general-purpose Excel book.

After reading this book, you will know how to use XLOOKUP to perform a variety of lookup tasks, from basic to advanced; you will know how to use the new XMATCH function in combination with INDEX to perform complex lookups; you will know how to use the new FILTER and SORT functions to fetch and transform data.

This book also covers the good old VLOOKUP in some depth, if you still need it, depending on the version of Excel you have.

For more, go to:
https://www.excelbytes.com/excel-books

Made in the USA
Las Vegas, NV
10 June 2021